Adolescents
and Their Families

Adolescents
and Their Families

Paths of Ego Development

STUART T. HAUSER

with

Sally I. Powers and Gil G. Noam

THE FREE PRESS
A Division of Macmillan, Inc.
NEW YORK

Maxwell Macmillan Canada
TORONTO

Maxwell Macmillan International
NEW YORK   OXFORD   SINGAPORE   SYDNEY

The Free Press
A Division of Macmillan, Inc.
866 Third Avenue, New York, N.Y. 10022

Maxwell Macmillan Canada, Inc.
1200 Eglinton Avenue East
Suite 200
Don Mills, Ontario M3C 3N1

Macmillan, Inc. is part of the Maxwell Communication Group of
Companies.

Printed in the United States of America

printing number
    2   3   4   5   6   7   8   9   10

Library of Congress Cataloging-in-Publication Data

Hauser, Stuart T.
  Adolescents and their families: paths of ego
  development/Stuart T. Hauser with Sally I.
  Powers and Gil G. Noam.
    p. cm.
  Includes bibliographical references and index.
  ISBN 0-02-914260-1
  1. Adolescence. 2. Parent and child–United
States. 3. Ego (Psychology). 4. Teenagers–
United States–Family relationships.
I. Powers, Sally Isbell. II. Noam, Gil G.
III. Title.
HQ796.H3585   1991
305.23'5–dc20   90-25215
                                  CIP

To Our Families

Contents

Preface

In this book we describe ways adolescents develop during years that can be filled with excitement, surprise, and opportunity, alongside confusion and upsetting mood swings. These kaleidoscopic changes do not occur in a vacuum. As most readers must recognize only too well from their experience, the highs and lows of those years deeply touch families as well as teenagers themselves. For several years we have been meeting with more than 130 adolescents—high school students and psychiatric patients—and their parents, and watching them in family discussions. Our central focus has been what many researchers and clinicians refer to as ego development, explained more fully in Chapter Two. Through many interviews, psychological tests, and family observations, we identified various paths ego development follows, and their intersections with family life. After first acquainting the reader with our thinking about adolescents and family life, we describe twelve boys and girls as they move along those paths of development.

Stuart Hauser began the Adolescent and Family Development Study, from which the data for this book is drawn, and has served as its director from its inception. Alan Jacobson, Gil Noam, and Sally Powers were Associate Directors of the project from the beginning and were involved in designing and supervising the study and instrument development. While working as a team, each of us has also taken an interest in and responsibility for different aspects of the overall study. Dr. Powers was director of the nonpatient, high school student sample. She is currently on the faculty of the Department of Psychology (Clinical Division) at the University of Massachusetts at Amherst and continues to investigate family processes associated with adolescent development, coping, and psychopathology. Within the Adolescent and Family Development Project, Dr. Noam directed the psychiatric site.

His efforts have focused on finding links between adolescent development and psychopathology. His developmental framework of the self and social cognition has led to a line of investigation on symptom formation and recovery from a developmental point of view. This work has fostered the establishment of his research and training center, the Hall-Mercer Laboratory of Developmental Psychology and Developmental Psychopathology at Harvard Medical School.

Dr. Jacobson originally worked intensively with a sample of adolescents with diabetes in the early phases of this project, focusing in particular on assessing ego defenses and other adaptive processes. He continues to contribute significantly to understandings of adolescent development and family life through our extended parallel studies of adolescents with diabetes and their families.

Dr. Hauser has taken primary responsibility for *Adolescents and Their Families: Paths of Ego Development.* Drs. Powers and Noam collaborated on many of the analyses and interpretations that form the core of this book and reviewed numerous earlier versions of the chapters.

The most important contributors to this book are people whom we cannot, of course, thank by name: the adolescents and parents, who gave so much of their time, energy, and good will over the years. In the interest of protecting each person's privacy, we have scrupulously maintained confidentiality through using pseudonyms and disguising other identifying data (such as occupation and location). Our appreciation of their devotion is profound. Without their cooperation and honesty these studies could never have been undertaken.

Stuart T. Hauser
Sally I. Powers
Gil G. Noam

Boston
November 1990

Acknowledgements

Ten years ago a high school guidance counselor, troubled about several especially detached students that he and others were unable to reach, asked me, "What kind of families do they come from?" I realized that I had no ready answer for him. From my clinical experience, I knew something about families of hospitalized psychiatric patients. But his concern was broader. Although I had my suspicions and intuitions, I did not know exactly what bearing family life might have on students' alienation from school, nor how it might promote their engagement with studies, activities and teachers. The literature offered few clues. I continued to ponder that counselor's serious question and soon began to plan, with Sally Powers, Gil Noam and Alan Jacobson, the studies that eventually led to new understandings of adolescents and families, and then to *Adolescents and Their Families: Paths of Ego Development*.

Many colleagues, students, and friends contributed generously in a variety of ways to these studies. Two colleagues have been vital intellectual beacons. Elliot Mishler, a most generative mentor and friend for many years, first introduced me—as a psychiatric resident—to the idea of sensitively studying families. He remains a valued senior colleague and friend at the Laboratory of Social Psychiatry at the Massachusetts Mental Health Center. Jane Loevinger has deeply influenced these studies through her outstanding theoretical and measurement accomplishments (Loevinger & Wessler, 1970; Loevinger, 1976). Our ideas about ego development paths clearly build on her noteworthy work.

A number of other colleagues and teachers played vital roles in developing our approaches and understandings. David Reiss, from the very start, has been a superb colleague and friend, with his dual involvements and competences in the worlds of social science and psychoanalysis. Our many informal conversations and professional exchanges have been major influences. Even further back in time, it was Ernst Prelinger, my thesis adviser at Yale University School of Medicine, from whom I first learned about studying adolescents over time (Hauser, 1971). While I was at the National Institutes of Mental Health, Lyman Wynne, Helm Stierlin, Roger Shapiro, and John Zinner set superb examples of how one studies adolescents within their families.

A host of friends and colleagues from the psychoanalytic and psychiatric community have been supportive of this project through their thoughtful comments and questions at formal presentations, clinical discussions, and informal gatherings. I am especially grateful to Avery Weisman, George Vaillant, Peter Knapp, James Sabin, Lewis Kirshner, William Kates, Edward Shapiro, Silvio Onesti, and Henry Smith. All have been responsive to the quest for ways that research about adolescence could draw from psychoanalytic observations, and be strengthened further by theory and method from the fields of developmental psychology and family studies. Along these same lines, many stimulating insights have come from my adolescent and young adult patients, who, like the participants in this study, must also be thanked as a group for sharing the intricacies of their growing-up and family experiences.

Colleagues in developmental psychology, who devote their work to the study of adolescents within their families, have been valuable commentators and critics over the years. The late John Hill shared many interests and visions in this area. All of us regret his premature loss. Fortunately, Catherine Cooper, Laurence Steinberg, Harold Grotevant, Larry Fisher, E. Mavis Hetherington, Anne Petersen, Judy Smetana, and W. Andrew Collins continue to share their work with us as well as respond to and apply our approaches. Other wonderful assets are the outstanding younger colleagues who have joined me in recent years as post-doctoral fellows, graduate students, and undergraduates. Valuable discussions have taken place over these years as we worked together on their projects and they responded to this project in our various seminars and meetings. These students include Joseph Allen, Campbell Leaper, Patricia Waters, Judi Stein, Roberta Isberg, and Deborah Rogell.

There are important daily requirements for maintaining a long-term study of adolescents and families. First, there must be a stable and congenial workplace for many meetings, interviews, discussions, analyses, and writing. Miles F. Shore, Bullard Professor of Psychiatry and Superintendent of the Massachusetts Mental Health Center, has been a truly exemplary department head, ever available with respect to our concrete space and funding needs, as well as being a highly imaginative administrator. I and my colleagues appreciate his provision of a secure base for this long term project. We have had generous and continued funding from private and federal sources since 1975. The Spencer Foundation, in 1975, provided the grant that first launched this project. I am indebted to H. Thomas James, then president of the Spencer Foundation, for his recognition and, at that time, his gamble as he invested in a new investigator and new study. Subsequent helpful funding was furnished by the MacArthur Foundation, the Psychoanalytic Research Fund of the American Psychoanalytic Association, and grants from the William T. Grant Foundation and National Science Foundation. The latter funds were awarded to Sally Powers for more extended longitudinal analyses of our observations of ego development and family processes.

Additional substantial support came from the National Institutes of Mental Health, through successive Career Development and Research Scientist Awards. It is difficult to overestimate the extraordinary value of those awards, as they provided the significant protection of time needed to carry out these studies. I appreciate the help of Leonard Lash for his able administering of this special program for many years. In the later phases of the project, to support final data collection and analyses, we were helped by grants from the Maternal and Child Health and Crippled Children's Services Research Grants Program, the National Institute of Child and Human Development (NICHD), and the Milton Fund of Harvard University.

During many stages of data collection, instrument development, and data analyses we were fortunate to have the skilled services and devotion of very talented staff members, who were a pleasure to work with, including Eydie Kasendorf, Dena Grossier, Merill Mead, Stephanie Beukema, John Houlihan, Jennifer Johnson, William Beardslee, Judy Wolch, Eileen Schwartz, Christine Huber, and Ornea Medeas. The Constraining and Enabling Coding System was diligently developed, applied, and refined with the valuable efforts of Bedonna Weiss, Donna Follansbee, Daranee Raja-Park, Wendy Greene, and Patricia Waters. Most recently, Barbara Book, Wendy Greene, Mary Kay Bowlds, Emily Borman, and Hilary Levine, as successive research coordinators of the project, have maintained our data archives, assisted in new analyses, and arduously closed final gaps in our data. Many of the statistical analyses for this book were ably carried out by Richard Rassulis, Robin Bliss, and William McMullen. Julie McCarter provided superb index assistance.

In the last stretch of writing I greatly benefited from the excellent skills of our "in-house" editor, Victoria Alexander. I have no question about how much the flow and substance of this book have improved through her keen eye. These contributions were added to by two very helpful editors at The Free Press, first Laura Wolff and then Susan Milmoe, our current editor who has shepherded this book, and its authors, skillfully through the last steps. Both have been heroically patient and thoughtful in their intelligent suggestions along the way. Our first connection to The Free Press was through Kitty Moore, whom we also thank for this linkage.

Finally, at the most personal level, I want to thank Elizabeth Hathaway for so often generously sharing her beautiful home at Wings Neck, where much of the writing and thinking for this book took place. Barbara, Ethan, and Joshua Hauser once more patiently endured my many psychological and physical absences as I was immersed in aspects of this long project. In their younger years, my sons curiously asked why I was spending so much time doing "those [family] score sheets." In later years they grasped the nature of the project and were wonderfully responsive to some of my strange questions about their experiences growing up. They offered me first-hand glimpses of adolescents growing up in a family. Those observations and conversations have surely enriched this work. I am, yet again, most deeply indebted to Barbara Hauser. She deserves the highest praise for her intelligent substantive and editorial criticism of my work in general, and this book in particular. I suspect that without her encouragement and wise support, this book would never have been completed.

Stuart T. Hauser

Boston
November 1990

ONE

Adolescents and Parents
The Developmental Tasks

Introduction
The Challenge and Paradox
of Adolescence

Of all the stages of life, adolescence is the most difficult to describe. Any generalization about teenagers immediately calls forth an opposite one. Teenagers are maddeningly self-centered, yet capable of impressive feats of altruism. Their attention wanders like a butterfly, yet they can spend hours concentrating on seemingly pointless involvements. They are often lazy and rude, yet, when you least expect it, they can be loving and helpful.[1]

Dramatic transitions characterize and define many phases of the life cycle. In adolescence an especially poignant and compelling drama unfolds. Growing teenagers are bidding farewell to childhood and discovering paths to adulthood.[2] Their goodbyes and hellos are conditioned not simply by new social demands—"Grow up!" "Why don't you get a job!"—although the demands on occasion can be overbearing. Sometimes in harmony, but often in conflict, with the new social pressures (high school curriculum and class schedule, part-time work, competition for college and full-time jobs, dating) are biological changes. Powerful forces are fired by the significant hormonal shifts associated with adolescence, which in turn are responsive to the stresses inherent in this transition.[3] The previous child-body is changing shape, assuming new functions, enlarging. A major growth spurt is occurring, and the voice is changing; intensifying sexual appetites, bring confusion and occasional satisfaction.

This daunting combination of social and biological forces generates the deep challenge and paradox of adolescent development: to separate from the family while connecting with it in new ways. Adolescents follow different paths from childhood to adulthood, and their paths frame and are framed by the family landscape. In this book we trace the passages to adult life as they lead through transformations in separation and connection.

Hosts of observers have described the vicissitudes of adolescent development. Scholars from numerous disciplines have reached for coherent views of this complex era in the life cycle, when individual development so strikingly intersects with social and historical currents.[4] We add to this burgeoning literature by looking closely at adolescent development *and* the adolescent within his or her family. We are not the first to observe and write about adolescents and their families. Others have described values, socialization practices, and the dynamics of power in families of adolescents.[5] Their analyses set the stage for our own work on the connections of family relationships and family processes to adolescent development. We pose two critical questions: What are the varying paths to adulthood through the teenage years—smooth, twisting, or arrested? In what ways do family processes affect which variation is followed?[6]

CLINICAL AND THEORETICAL PERSPECTIVES

Adolescence can be disturbing for both youths and their families as various tensions and dilemmas surface in new and sometimes unexpected ways. Established family patterns may shift under the influence of cognitive, biological, and social changes. Cognitive transformations are especially salient, as many adolescents are beginning to think more abstractly and to delight in logical analyses, which open the way to intricate reflections and challenging questions regarding family relationships and traditions. Biological changes are often associated with body and self-image conflicts,[7] leading to new or intensified demands for parental assistance. Parents' responses to these bodily and intellectual changes may reflect their own ambivalence or conflicts.[8] Finally, adolescents' confusions over new social opportunities and competing or inconsistent sexual norms and behaviors frequently emerge in struggles over family rules and limits.

When teenagers handle these changes successfully, they become clearer about themselves, their goals, and their directions. New kinds of family relationships evolve, which support greater independence and closeness with others outside the family.[9]

We know that adolescents vary dramatically in their coping ability. The psychiatric literature abounds with examples of difficult passages from child to adult status.[10] But there is evidence of *diversity* beyond labeled psychiatric patients. For many years, students of normal adolescents, like Jack Block and Daniel Offer, have called our attention to the striking variations in development during the teenage years. They describe a rich landscape of patterns, a landscape defined by important variations in impulse control, autonomy, and relationships with family and peers.[11]

Studies of psychopathology and normal adolescent development point to the importance of adolescent–family dynamics in healthy functioning and in psychopathology during this developmental era.[12] How do daily family experience and the overall fabric of family relationships determine which of the various paths through adolescence is taken? What family strengths *promote* new patterns of individual autonomy and connectedness with others? In what ways do families, often inadvertently, *obstruct* progressive development and the evolution of family ties that are compatible with the demands and opportunities of adolescence?

These questions guided our observations of 133 fourteen- and fifteen-year-old adolescents and their parents over a period of three years. We spoke at length with high school students and with adolescents of the same age who were hospitalized for psychiatric treatment. The teenagers who were interviewed also completed questionnaires specially designed to assess their current levels of ego development and self-esteem. We assessed the development of their parents (using the same questionnaires) *and* watched how those parents and their adolescents spoke with one another during family discussions. The stories of adolescents and their families that we present in the second part of this book are drawn from these many observations. They convey the diversity of adolescent passages to adulthood and of the family settings in which these journeys take place. Chapters 2 through 4 provide a backdrop for the portraits in Part II. In Chapters 2 and 3 we present our perspectives on individual development (that of parents as well as adolescents) and on the family processes that affect it. Chapter 4 describes the study from which our portraits are drawn.

CHAPTER
2

Ego Development

Some hallmarks of adolescence are visible to almost all observers: pubertal changes, often accompanied by painful increases in self-consciousness; sexual, cognitive, and moral struggles; and surprisingly sudden mood changes. Others are less visible, but nonetheless powerfully influence the quality of adolescent development: for example, the effects of delayed or precocious sexual changes upon self-esteem, self-image, and relationships with friends.

Even less visible to the casual observer of adolescents is *ego development*, the evolution of meanings that the teenager imposes upon inner experience and perceptions of people and events.[1] Ego development refers to a sequence of increasingly mature stages of functioning across the domains of personal relationships, impulse control, moral development, and cognitive style.[2] Linked theoretically and empirically with adaptation, coping, and many social behaviors, ego development is especially relevant to understanding reciprocal relations between adolescent growth and the family setting, as previous studies by our own group and others have shown.[3]

The first studies of ego development relevant to our work focused on normal children and adults. Understandably, a major concern of early researchers was to determine the viability of the ego development construct, and the approach—a specially designed sentence completion test—to measuring this development.[4] These issues satisfactorily addressed, in recent years investigators have begun analyzing clinical problems in terms of ego development.[5] This new direction is not surprising, since ego development refers to behaviors and attitudes involved in impulse control, anticipation, responsibility taking, social judgment, and cognitive complexity, dimensions most compromised in impaired individual functioning.[6]

Ego development has several key dimensions—internal versus external locus of control, selflessness versus egocentrism, and narcissism versus healthy connections with others. Early stages are marked by a sense of external control, an egocentric view of the environment, and limited abilities to relate to others. Later stages mark a progression toward internal control, an appreciation of subtle differences among people, objects, and events; and strengths that can lead to intimate, collaborative relationships.[7] These developmental themes are germane to the transformations of autonomy and relatedness experienced directly by adolescents and indirectly by their parents.

ADOLESCENT AND ADULT EGO DEVELOPMENT

Although the stages of ego development are often associated with chronological age, they are deliberately defined *independent* of age and are seen as forming an invariant hierarchical order[8] Table 1 lists all the stages and their distinguishing features. Each stage is more complex than the last, and theoretically at least, none can be skipped in the course of development. Some teenagers and adults may not develop beyond a particular stage. Among adolescents and adults are representatives of each stage, who can then be characterized in terms of the features specific to the stage at which they have remained. Consequently, this view of development depicts not only an evolving sequence of stages but a typology of individual differences in the form of character styles or key patterns of adolescent and adult inner experience and behavior.

The first ego development stage that includes any form of verbal expression that can be measured through a verbally based ego development measure is the impulsive stage.[9] As the name suggests, impulses predominate at this point in development. Control over them is undependable, and the exercise of self-control is perceived as undesirable or unattainable. Rules are not recognized. Actions are seen as "bad" or "good" according to whether they are punished or rewarded:

Raising a family "is a horror."

My main problem is "I like boys, and they won't leave me alone, and I like it."

When they talked about sex, I "could kick them in the pants."[10]

The teenager's or adult's conscious feelings and thoughts focus on satisfying physical needs, especially those sparked by sexual and aggressive drives. His or her view of the world is self-centered and concrete.

Table 1 Loevinger's Stages of Ego Development

Stage	Impulse Control "Moral" Style	Interpersonal Style	Conscious Preoccupations	Cognitive Style
Preconformist				
Presocial (I-1)*	. . .	Autistic	Self vs nonself	. . .
Symbiotic (I-1)	. . .	Symbiotic	Self vs nonself	. . .
Impulsive (I-2)	Impulsive, fear	Receiving dependent, exploitive	Bodily feelings, especially sexual and aggressive	Stereotypy, conceptual confusion
Self-protective Δ	Fear of being caught, externalizing blame, opportunistic	Wary, manipulative, exploitive	Self-protection, wishes, things, advantages, control	. . .
Transition from self-protective to conformist (Δ/3)	Obedience and conformity to social norms are simple and absolute rules	Manipulative, obedient	Concrete aspects of traditional sex roles, physical causation as opposed to psychological causation	Conceptual simplicity, stereotypes
Conformist				
Conformist (I-3)	Conformity to external rules, shame, guilt for breaking rules	Belonging, helping, superficial niceness	Appearance, social acceptability, banal feelings, behavior	Conceptual simplicity, stereotypes, cliches
Transition from conformist to conscientious: self-consciousness (I-3/4)	Dawning realization of standards, contingencies, self-criticism	Being helpful, deepened interest in interpersonal relations	Consciousness of the self as separate from the group, recognition of psychological causation	Awareness of individual differences in attitudes, interests and abilities: mentioned in global and broad terms

	Impulse Control, Character Development	Interpersonal Style	Conscious Preoccupations	Cognitive Style
Postconformist Conscientious (I-4)	Self-evaluated standards, self-criticism	Intensive, responsible, mutual, concern for communication	Differentiated feelings, motives for behavior, self-respect, achievements, traits, expression	Conceptual complexity, idea of patterning
Transition from conscientious to autonomous	Individuality, coping with inner conflict	Cherishing of interpersonal relations	Communicating, expressing ideas and feelings, process and change	Toleration for paradox and contradiction
Autonomous (I-5)	Add: Coping with conflicting inner needs†	Add: Respect for autonomy	Vividly conveyed feelings, integration of physiological and psychological causation of behavior, development, role conception, self-fulfillment, self in social context	Increased conceptual complexity; complex patterns, toleration for ambiguity, broad scope, objectivity
Integrated (I-6)	Add: Reconciling inner conflicts, renunciation of unattainable	Add: Cherishing of individuality	Add: Identity	

SOURCE: From Loevinger, J., and R. Wessler (1970), as adapted by Hauser et al. (1983). Reprinted by permission of Jossey-Bass, Inc.

*The symbols for the stages I–2, I–3, I–4, I–5 are borrowed from the Sullivan, Grant and Grant (1957) description of interpersonal maturity, although these levels do not correspond to exactly the same meanings as in the previous work (Loevinger & Wessler, 1970; p. 16). The delta (Δ) designator for the self-protective stage is derived from Isaacs (1956), who refers to a similar stage as "opportunistic." The transitional stages (e.g. Δ/3, I–3/4) were conceptualized and designated with these symbols by Loevinger and her colleagues (Loevinger & Wessler, 1970).

†"Add" means in addition to description applying to previous level.

Directly following this preoccupation with immediate satisfaction is the self-protective stage. The individual at this stage understands that there are rules, but obedience is motivated only by self-interest. Morality is purely pragmatic: Avoid what is bad, or you will be caught. Relationships with others are manipulative and exploitative:

Most men think that women "are helpless. They can do whatever they want to them."

At times she worried about "her husband dating other women when he came in at 2:00 in the morning."

Nonetheless, independence develops during this stage: Children and adolescents do things for themselves; adolescents and adults feel they don't need the "older generation."

There is an important transition between the self-protective stage, where conscious concerns are so prominently focused on control and domination, and the next, the conformist stage. More conventional responses now occur, mixed with continued reference to exploitation, self-interest, and domination. The individual's perceptions and thoughts fall between those of the simpler self-protective stage and the more complex ones that characterize conformity, in which social norms and the needs of others must be recognized. Taken together, the first stages and this transition make up the "preconformist" level of development.

Most people reach the conformist stage during childhood or adolescence.[11] Rules are now obeyed because they are rules. Morality is only partly internalized. Shame about transgressions against rules now becomes meaningful. Interpersonal reciprocity begins to emerge, although relationships are viewed more in terms of concrete events and actions than in terms of feelings or motives. Where inner states are expressed, they tend to be stereotyped, clichéd, and moralistic:

A wife should "care for her husband."

I am "happy and in a good mood so please forgive my foolishness."

At times she worried about "what she was going to wear."

At this stage the individual is most concerned with material things, appearance, conventional behavior, reputation, and status.

Following the conformist stage is another important transition, marked by a growing realization that the "right ways" of living are relative to situations. Although many stereotypes still prevail, there is now less absolute conviction, less dogmatism, than in previous stages. As self-awareness grows, so does the capacity for self-criticism, introspection, and an understanding of psychological causation. With greater self-awareness comes freedom from dependence on the social group for strict behavioral guidelines.[12] This transition and the conformist stage itself form the "conformist" level of ego development.

In the next, the conscientious, stage there is a consolidation of the changes begun during this last transition. Rigid stereotypes vanish, replaced by an abiding interest in differences among people. Relationships are understood along the lines of feelings, rather than only actions and events. Inner standards now guide behavior, surpassing external rules as the primary motivator:

> When people are helpless "they need to be offered help in a positive manner and one they are able to accept."

> My father "is a happy-go-lucky sort of man, but is stubborn when it comes to certain things."

Adolescents and adults who reach this stage can engage in meaningful self-criticism. Conscious thoughts involve ideals, achievements, obligations, and questions about how people differ from one another.

After this stage there is another important transition, marked by even more complex responses. Individuals at this juncture are able to tolerate paradoxical relationships, no longer reducing them to polar opposites.[13] Distinguishing this transition, and especially pertinent to our analyses, is the greater value placed on interpersonal concerns. A growing recognition of emotional interdependence accompanies a decreasing emphasis on striving for independence:

> When I am nervous, I "tend to become self-centered and overlook the needs and desires of others."

This change contrasts noticeably with the emphasis on achievement expressed by adolescents and adults at the earlier conformist levels.

Pivotal for those at the next stage, called autonomous, is the ability to cope with inner conflicts in more complex ways, such as those between obligations and needs, and between conflicting ideals. The same conflicts may have been vaguely experienced at earlier stages, but not as part of an inner struggle, central in the individual's awareness. Along with facing and tolerating the complexities of one's own inner conflicts comes tolerance of the conflicts that others experience, and how they resolve them:

Sometimes she felt that "she did not see life at a depth she does because it would mean less responsibility."

When a child won't join "he shouldn't be forced; but one should seek out the reason and give help if necessary. It is not unhealthy to want to do things individually."

The moral condemnation characteristic of earlier stages is gone. Interpersonal concerns are a pervasive conscious interest. The adolescent or adult at this stage understands the need for others to be independent, to learn from their own mistakes, rather than feel obligated to prevent others from erring. Conscious concerns address self-fulfillment, individuality, role differentiation, and complexity of options.

The integrated stage reflects a progression from "coping with conflicts to reconciliation of conflicting demands, and, where necessary, renunciation of the unattainable".[14] This is the highest developmental level, and it is more theoretical than empirical. No more than 1 percent of adults in the United States have been found to be at this stage.[15] Individuals at this stage understand questions or dilemmas from several different vantage points, often blending ideas about personal relationships, rules, ideals, and conflicts:

A good mother "lets go, loves without demanding conformity to her own ideals and standards—and helps guide if possible."

I feel sorry "for people imprisoned in their worlds of ignorance and prejudice and for those who do not attempt to know themselves."

It is difficult to combat the tendency to idealize this stage as the utopian height of development. Yet with respect to this developmental model, it is important to have explicit ideas about the endpoint that defines ego development from its beginning through the stages just described. This most advanced set of stages and transition are referred to as the "postconformist" level of ego development.

Before discussing ego development paths, ideas crucial to our understandings of adolescents and their families, we sound a critical cautionary note: It is ever tempting, and mistaken, to categorize an adolescent or adult as being at one of these stages, and thereby to imply that this "explains" him or her. Descriptions of stages do not capture all of the individual's thoughts, feelings, or behaviors. Stages represent predominant features of the person, "core" perspectives and styles. Moreover, the stages are not concrete structures, they are concepts that meaningfully characterize how the person thinks, perceives, and feels. To assume that these stages, or the paths we shall soon describe, fully explain what the individual experiences and how he or she behaves in the world violates the meaning of this view of development and grossly underestimates individual complexity, as it dismisses the person by placing him or her into a stage category.

In Part Two, as we trace differing paths of ego development, our portrayals of adolescents and parents will enhance the reader's picture of this aspect of development and the ways it may shape interactions between parents and teenagers who are trying to resolve conflicts.

ADOLESCENT EGO DEVELOPMENT PATHS

A range of ego development trajectories, of adolescent "growth curves," that can be found during adolescence is presented schematically in Figure 1. Some boys and girls begin their adolescent years in the early (preconformist) stages of ego development, continuing to be highly dependent on their parents, almost unaware of differences between themselves and others, and relating to peers and adults through largely exploitative styles. Such adolescents use relatively

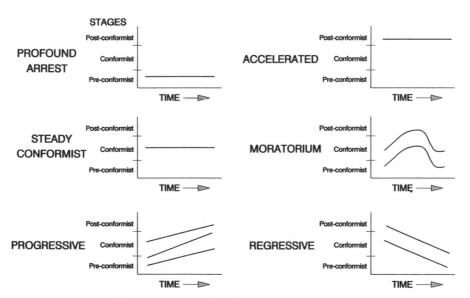

Figure 1.   Ego development trajectories.

simple cognitive constructions, responding to situations and questions with few options (either/or, "black-and-white" thinking). These adolescents are operating at the earliest stages, ones marked by impulsiveness and self-protection. If they remain at those stages for two or more years, they exemplify profoundly *arrested* ego development.

Other adolescents are preoccupied with being accepted by friends and complying with prevailing social rules. In their awareness of individual differences and complex views they are certainly more advanced than those who are arrested. Yet that awareness is still limited. Such teenagers, functioning at the conformist level, tenaciously accept and rarely question socially prized traditions and slogans. If they persist at this level during the adolescent years, they are called *steady conformists* and exemplify attenuated arrests in ego development.[16]

A third group of adolescents gradually move from preconformist to conformist, or from conformist to postconformist stages, over several years. These are the adolescents who clearly shift from simple concrete thoughts and observations to conventional behaviors or, more dramatically, from socially conventional perceptions to original insights and behaviors. Occasionally, an adolescent may move from the earliest stages to the most advanced over one or two years. These adolescents exemplify *progressive* ego development trajectories.

A fourth group of teenagers exhibit, from the very start of adolescence, features of the most advanced stages of ego development. They adhere to norms based on inner standards, express increased autonomy from their parents' views, and show an abiding interest in mutuality with others as well as in the complexity of experience. If they remain at this postconformist level of ego development, they exemplify an *accelerated* ego development trajectory, a path that contrasts most strikingly with that of the early arrest. While small in number, those representing the accelerated trajectories are clearly a special group of teenagers, astute and perceptive from an unexpectedly early age.

There is also the *regressive ego development* path, where an adolescent shifts downward in his or her level of development (e.g. from conformist to pre-conformist) over the years. These individuals change from recognizing complex thoughts and feelings within themselves and others to having simpler perceptions, giving greater emphasis, usually through their projections, to the disquieting and threatening feelings that they see as residing in the other person. Finally, there is a trajectory that we term (after Erikson, 1959) *psychosocial moratorium*, where the individual at first decreases and then increases levels of ego development. Accompanying these swings are stunning changes in the adolescent's understandings of others' views and affective states and striking vacillations in ways he or she responds to others. Such oscillations are sometimes considered to reflect "experimentation" by an adolescent, as he or she tries out new roles and/or enacts conflicting yet personally prized ideals and wishes (Erikson, 1959).

PARENTS' EGO DEVELOPMENT

Distinguishing these developmental trajectories helps us understand passages through adolescence.[17] We can consider parents in analogous ways, whether they remain at one stage throughout their child's adolescent years, or also change as their adolescent does. While adults do not show the kind of rapid or sudden developmental change that we associate with children and adolescents, we do know they develop in the years following late adolescence and throughout their adult years.[17] Interesting and relevant questions can be posed about their ego development in relation to that of their families. How does a father's ego development influence his interactions with his wife and son? Are a mother's changes in ego development responsive to or coordinated with those of her son? By observing parents over the same years of development as their adolescent sons and daughters, we can identify profiles of parent ego development, together with their connections to both adolescent trajectories and family processes.

We know from our observations that parents at lower stages of ego development engage less actively in family discussions, often concentrating on a single overriding thought or feeling as they speak with their sons and daughters. They do not offer examples of how a parent might form and express complex perceptions, thoughts, and feelings. In contrast, those parents who have reached higher stages of ego development actively participate in family discussions, expressing acceptance and empathy, thereby providing vivid illustrations of parents who hold many perspectives, who are open to varied aspects of problems and new ideas.[18]

Mothers and fathers represent several ego development profiles: early arrest, predominantly conformist, consistent conformist, predominantly advanced, and consistently advanced. These adult development profiles are linked with both adolescent trajectories and family processes. As we explore each of the adolescent trajectories, we also look at how specific parents think and feel about development, especially with respect to the generations: parents' perceptions of their relationships with their own parents *and* with their son or daughter.

Our stories of adolescents and their families are presented from the vantage point of these developmental paths. Yet individual adolescent development is embedded within the overall family system and is touched most intimately by specific family relationships. The family of the adolescent engages our interest in the next chapter, as we consider how individual development and family processes intersect.

The Family Setting

Adolescents live their daily lives and develop within several social settings: family, peer, and school. While each of these contexts contributes to adolescent development and adaptation, in this book we focus on the family setting—the relationships and daily interactions that frame adolescent development. The family plays a special role in child and adolescent development.[1] It is the arena in which young people forge their earliest attachments, first experience separation and loss, discover the world of siblings, and begin their lifelong learning of social and physical skills.

Research on relations between family processes and adolescent development has flourished in recent years and is characterized by increasing conceptual clarity and empirical rigor.[2] There is a growing consensus regarding the significance of family ties, parental models, and reciprocal influences. Not only do families affect adolescent development, but aspects of adolescent development (for example, puberty, cognitive changes) affect the life of the family. Current studies tend to focus on family diversity, the contributions of families to adolescent development, and the impacts of adolescent development upon families.[3]

FAMILY RELATIONSHIPS:
THE DIALECTIC OF SEPARATION AND CONNECTION

Families vary enormously in their tolerance for the differentiation and autonomy of their members, and that diversity is especially salient during adolescence. At one extreme are those families who applaud the new steps (physical and psychological) of their adolescent members. At the opposite extreme, the one receiving most attention in clinical work, are the families who are profoundly and continuously disturbed by the changes in their adolescent members as they prepare to depart from the family group. The changes may challenge a specific parent or rock the entire family. Close emotional bonds may be jeopardized, a rigid power structure may no longer be enforceable, or the family's stringent moral beliefs may falter when challenged by a shrewd and skeptical adolescent.

An important component of adolescent development, one we alluded to when we examined ego development in the preceding chapter, is advancing individuality, encompassing the experience of separateness and self-assertion.[4] In adolescence, when differentiation is so important and at times problematic, separateness and self-assertion can be overriding issues in family relationships, enhancing or deterring adolescent ego development. When it recognizes the increasing independence of an adolescent son or daughter, a family can accept and encourage continued differentiation, supporting new opinions and insights even if they are at odds with ones previously shared by all family members. On the other hand, family members may be surprised or alarmed by unexpected disagreements and challenges from the previously agreeable adolescent. The family that feels threatened by such challenges tends to respond by devaluing the new opinions or—perhaps more devastatingly—by withdrawing from the excited, "impossible" teenager. These dramatically varied family responses to adolescent separation and differentiation represent an underlying motif throughout this book. In the final chapter, we consider these reactions with respect to challenges and crises inherent in the parenting of adolescents.

Sustaining either gradual shifts or sudden spurts in adolescent autonomy requires more than the family's acknowledgment of separateness and encouragement of self-assertion. Continuing bonds between adolescent and parent, although now transformed, provide a crucial backdrop for growth through adolescence and into adulthood. Such connectedness can be expressed through mutuality (respect for the views and feelings of others) and permeability (openness and responsiveness to others).[5]

These key features of relationships are reflected in verbal and nonverbal exchanges within the family. A family's stance regarding respect and openness is ordinarily taken for granted, not questioned or made explicit until challenged by the addition of a new member; by a major change, such as adolescence, in an old member; or by therapy. In families where the adolescent member is advancing in ego development or unusually advanced at an early age, the adolescent, and often his or her parents, express their separateness by expressing their distinct perceptions and their awareness of how they differ from one another. Self-assertion may be recognized in the clear account by a teenager of how she has arrived at a particular point of view.

Connectedness in families of progressive or accelerated adolescents appears as respect for and responsiveness to others' views. In some families, encouragement of members' thoughtful self-expression is conveyed through discriminating self-disclosures, as when a father tells his daughter about his own adolescent struggles and provides touching details of his early history and conflicts. His openness implicitly offers her permission to disclose her intimate and painful inner complexities.

On the other hand, family relationships can inhibit or interfere with adolescent ego development. Adolescents and parents may fail to see themselves as distinct or unique, and may respond as though they were "two (or three) peas in a pod." This way of perceiving oneself in relation to others can seriously blur an adolescent's understanding of how, though an integral part of the family, he or she is distinct from other members. In these families there are especially strong countervailing pressures against the adolescent's ambivalent movements toward new autonomy, an autonomy that is at first tentative and is often combined with almost transparent yearnings to be closely held. Parents and adolescent may avoid recognizing how they now increasingly differ from one another in their ideas, feelings, and behavior. Yet the differences surface in charged conflicts over mundane matters—the car, dating, curfews, and the like. Reluctance to acknowledge and appreciate new differences is especially prominent in families of *steady conformist* adolescents, as we shall see vividly illustrated by Lou and his parents in Chapter 6.

Family relationships can also obstruct adolescent development through restraints on self-assertion and disruptions in connectedness. Adolescent or parent, for example, may remain vague when expressing an idea or may quickly abandon it when challenged. Disruptions in connectedness between parent and teen are painfully familiar and on occasion dramatic. Instead of mutuality, conversations demonstrate self-centeredness and asynchrony, with parent and adolescent remaining on "different wavelengths" as they talk about either completely different subjects or vastly different versions of the same one. Disengagement or nonparticipation—by parent or adolescent— also reflects ruptured connections.

Similarly, impaired listening and diminished openness characterize families in which the adolescent's development has been slowed or arrested. Pressure to find a rapid solution to a family conflict can lead to premature resolution or closure, as a mother, for instance, imposes the "right" answer instead of remaining open to unexpected solutions or new ideas from other family members. The family of Charlie, one of the adolescents with *arrested* ego development, portrayed in Chapter 5, richly illustrates these dynamics. Impatience and anxiety over sharp differences can also erupt as disrespect, ridicule, and abuse. The result is a family characterized by virtually impenetrable walls, barriers between members built upon misunderstandings, vagueness, and fear of being hurt. New thoughts or perceptions are unwelcome in such families. Other barriers to openness are relatively immutable coalitions or alliances within the family, ones that do not change in response to new insights, new perceptions, or other signs of a family member's growth. In those circumstances, the family system is entrenched: Lacking elasticity, it does not change in response to an individual member's changing awareness, needs, and insights.

Here, then, are the essential dimensions of family life surrounding paths of adolescent development. We have highlighted the importance of specific kinds of family relationships, involving individuality and connectedness. These relationships, representing deeply held commitments and feelings between family members, unfold and are revealed in hundreds of day-to-day conversations, at special family events, and during long stretches of time when parents and adolescents are together—on vacations and other trips. Important clues about these bonds appear in many facets of family members' talk, in both word and gesture.

FAMILY DISCOURSE:
THE MICROSTRUCTURE OF RELATIONSHIPS

The fine-grained texture of family relationships is apparent when we look closely at the specific moment-to-moment exchanges between family members, which reflect such basic themes as respect, empathy, curiosity, abuse, and indifference. At the microscopic level of analysis of conversations between parents and children, and between parents, we see specific features of family relationships. These *family interactions* are markers of relationships, not fully representing them, yet providing traces of their presence, valuable clues to how they influence family members and the family system. A mother's reluctance to part from her child, to allow him to be separate, may be signaled through her indiscriminate repeated praise of his every thought. Her son may respond by avoiding the expression of any unusual "new" thoughts or feelings, thereby pleasing her by remaining close and adopting her thoughts and feelings. By tracking such interactions, observing the convergence and divergence of these streams of behavior within a family's discussions, we gain a more detailed view of how family relationships unfold over time. While mapping discrete interactions, or even sequences of them, cannot possibly capture the full richness of family relationships, it does provide insight into how specific styles of interaction may emerge in the daily life of a family and how those styles may enhance or undermine adolescent development.

Certain questions are especially amenable for study at this close range. For instance, in the course of a family conversation, how does parental self-assertion influence expressions of an adolescent's individuality or connectedness within the family? How might this influence lead to variations in the adolescent's ego development? How does the adolescent's level of maturation influence his or her responsiveness to those parental interactions? A teenager functioning at a high level of development will find her own place in the family discussion, explaining her ideas or maintaining curiosity in the face of parental discouragement or ridicule of new ideas. Discovering adolescent strengths, such as advanced levels of ego development and high self-esteem, together with their contributions to continued growth—in some cases despite adverse family conditions—will ultimately advance our understanding of the diverse passages from adolescence to adulthood.[6]

CONSTRAINING AND ENABLING FAMILY INTERACTIONS

Our approach to identifying developmentally significant family interactions is based on ideas originally drawn from observations of families with psychiatrically disturbed adolescents. Inspired by Helm Stierlin's analysis of how disturbed families oppose the separation of their adolescent members, we delineate specific ways that members may *constrain* (restrict, limit) or *enable* (facilitate, enhance) one another as they speak together.[7] These constraining and enabling interactions reflect the specifics of individuated family relationships, the mechanisms through which they promote or inhibit adolescent ego development.[8] The ways in which parents and children talk with each other may enhance individuality in relationships by explaining, expressing curiosity, and engaging in joint problem-solving. Talk that promotes connectedness includes expressions of acceptance and empathy. On the other hand, talk that constrains relationships between family members diminishes experiences of individuality and connectedness through expressions that devalue, seduce, distract, or withhold.

One way to think about the two styles of talking is in terms of their overall frequency: how often they occur in the family, and between which members. Another way is to think about the flow of talk within the family. Are parents and adolescents linked through reciprocal talk, such as mutual explaining? Do they "miss" each other, as when, for example, a mother introduces an irrelevant topic whenever her son speaks of a new idea that he is thinking about?

Parental constraining may be couched in talk that expresses detachment, lack of curiosity, or other forms of subtle discouragement. As role models for their children, parents who characteristically engage in this type of communication make it difficult for their children to progress to higher levels of ego development, where curiosity, initiative, and engagement are valued. More direct parental opposition in the form of devaluing, mockery, or withdrawal may daunt or even shut down an adolescent's first forays into new ways of thinking about feelings, relationships, and conflicts.

Yet we must be cautious about attaching blame. Parental behaviors do not necessarily *cause* an adolescent to remain at a low stage of development. The direction of influence is rarely, if ever, so simple. An adolescent's provocative comments may evoke uncharacteristically authoritarian, and sometimes harsh, responses from one or both parents. Similarly, a teenager's repeated rejection of advice from his parents can lead to their anger and eventual withdrawal. After many offers of help with completing college applications, Jim's parents no longer offered suggestions or even asked about his progress in dealing with that worrisome task. Besides discouraging offers of concrete assistance, adolescents can undermine other forms of parental support and initiative, including curiosity and explanations. Throughout her later high school and college years, Joan persistently refused to discuss her nascent career plans with her mother. When her budding career then called for a major dislocation, she no longer found her mother curious or poised to offer information about her experiences in moving to new places.

It is extremely difficult to determine the degree to which an adolescent's developmental status and behavior respond to rather than shape the family's interactions. One approach to this knotty direction-of-effects problem is through the study of adolescents and their families over time. An unexpected arrest or regression in a teenager's development after repeated exposure to constraining parental inter-actions would be strong evidence that these processes do indeed have a causal role in adolescent ego development. A second approach to this problem is to observe conversational sequences, seeing whether, for instance, an adolescent son withdraws his opinion following a particular constraining comment by his parent. Such a response would also argue for the developmental impact of parental communi-cation styles, since we know that restricted participation in family discussions is typically associated with arrests in adolescent ego development.

Through one of the most visible constraining interactions, distrac-tion, family members interfere with the expressed perceptions, thoughts, or feelings of one another by making tangential points, changing the subject entirely, or making self-contradictory responses. A parent may insert seemingly irrelevant or vaguely formed ideas whenever the adolescent offers a new perception or thought. Distrac-tion may take the form of confusion and oversimplification, reflecting a failure to acknowledge the distinctions and complexities in another person's speech. A father may interfere with his son's self-awareness or poise, so that his train of thought or concentration is unsettled or, at the extreme, undermined.[9] Each time Lou began to spell out a new idea, his father interrupted to tease Lou about his "off-the-wall" ideas.

Frequent distraction by parents can undermine a key aspect of adolescent ego development, cognitive complexity, which thrives on openness and responsiveness. In discussing one of the moral di-lemmas we used in our family interaction task, Mrs. Jones presents a clear example of this disabling communication style:

JOHNNY: It's not morally wrong to steal a drug, because it's, you know—

MOTHER: (*interrupting*) It's not the same story, you're on a different story. Dr. Smith [the interviewer] didn't leave no card [giving the story to be discussed].

JOHNNY: You could not say it's morally wrong. It's only morally wrong if you feel it's morally wrong.

(*Mother expresses loud sighs while playing with microphone*)

Mrs. Jones's speeches and actions are confusing and distracting, inter-rupting his train of thought, introducing a tangential idea, and making other demands on his attention (playing with the microphone).

Adolescents may also distract their parents. Judy, for example, pointedly interrupts her father during a heated dialogue. In the midst of explaining why he took a different position from hers, Judy cuts him off, insisting, "That's because you're a lawyer!" Judy's talk diverts attention away from the substance of her father's argument by disrupting the flow of his reasoning and dismissing his ideas as simply the consequence of his professional work. Through her interruption, then, Judy both changes the subject and discounts her father's explanation. Whether the parent or adolescent initiates the distraction, it is easy to see how this kind of behavior, if consistent, will deter the expression of new or different views, lest they be summarily dismissed.

In some constraining interactions, the parent or adolescent is quick to pass judgment on the other's thoughts and feelings. Consistent parental judging may impair adolescent ego development.[10] Such interactions represent relatively immutable, nonmutual relationships between family members. These severe, often dogmatic and critical responses[11] are characteristic of lower stages of ego development, where the emphasis is upon the good and badness, the rightness and wrongness, of thoughts and actions:

JUDY: I see dad's point of view [answer to the dilemma the family had been discussing for some time]. I, I—

MOTHER: (interrupting) But you don't see *mine*, of course!

Her mother's remark expresses an inflexible opinion about the significance of her opinion, underscored by her certainty that Judy does not appreciate it, as underscored by her exclamatory "of course!"

When Jim's father begins to explore possible answers to a particular dilemma, Jim cuts him off, saying, "It has to be yes or no, that's all!" Jim's insistence on the "right" way of responding to the dilemma is highly judgmental. The intensity of his stance is marked by the phrase, "that's all!"

Four other constraining interactions that we trace are withholding, indifference, excessive gratifying (seductiveness), and devaluing. In these interactions parents and adolescents undermine, discourage, and obstruct exchanges with one another. We illustrate these processes and their links with family relationships through our six case studies of adolescents who have not progressed beyond the conformist level.

In striking contrast to these constraining interactions are the enabling ones: explaining, problem-solving, expressing curiosity, focusing, accepting, and empathizing. Through this style of expression parents may enhance or catalyze an adolescent's opportunities for continued growth.[12] Moreover, through their own enabling adolescents may elicit parental contributions that promote more complex and thoughtful exchanges. For instance, a son's reflective explanations may elicit helpful paraphrasing (focusing) and continued curiosity from his parents. These interactions, most often engaged in by adolescents who are accelerated or continuing to progress in their ego development, encourage reciprocal explaining or empathizing from parents.

Through focusing interactions, the speaker attempts to make the other person's ideas more coherent and closer to the point at hand. Focusing may involve dramatization of another's point, emphasizing its meaning through paraphrasing in more direct language, or illustrating the implications by introducing hypothetical cases. For example, in response to Laurie's idea that it is wrong to prolong life artificially, her father remarks, "Say you've got an appendicitis, you've got an appendicitis, and your side was hurting like hell, do you want to, do you think it's wrong for the doctor to prolong your life?" Her father's question, citing a hypothetical instance, is intended both to point out the implications of Laurie's position and to encourage her to consider specific consequences of her ideas.[13]

A parent's focusing, conveying the message that the son or daughter has been carefully listened to, demonstrates and encourages respect for individuality (self-assertion and separateness). This is important, since increasing self-definition and self-control are basic aspects of advancing ego development.[14] In addition, focusing can express a parent's connectedness, through such interactions as "limit-setting," wherein parents teach attention control and impulse control to their adolescents.[15] Consider those moments when a teenage son is expressing a confusing mix of disconnected and tangential thoughts, seemingly driven by his moody reaction to his father's last remark. Through a well-timed blend of focusing, explaining, and problem-solving, his father or mother may guide him back to the discussion at hand. Even more to the point, such guidance illustrates both the parent's awareness of how their son has veered from the discussion *and* their interest in his returning, reconnecting.

The parents of adolescents whose development shows accelerated or steady progression will, for different reasons, engage in these kinds of focusing interactions and others—curiosity, empathy—that promote and encourage individuality. In earlier years these parents probably responded to attentional lapses by focusing on the matter at hand. By adolescence, their children have successfully internalized the behaviors expressed so regularly by their parents.[16] Besides benefiting from parental behavior that encourages individuality in relationships, adolescents with accelerated and progressive ego development draw thoughtful, focused, or questioning responses *from* parents responding to their son's and daughter's attentiveness and curiosity about their thoughts and feelings.

A second noteworthy form of enabling conveys acceptance of another family member by expressing agreement, warmth, and encouragement. Simple mechanical agreement is not necessarily a sign of acceptance and may even reflect "pseudomutuality."[17] For instance, by feigning agreement and full acceptance with his son's objections, a father tries to cajole his teenage son into going along with his views. Or a daughter may manuever to mollify her mother, who is objecting to new curfew times, by agreeing—in the abstract—with her mother's worries about "school nights" and, of course, school performance.

Two family excerpts show how accepting can flow from parent or adolescent: In the first, Jane is describing her memory of a story being discussed by her family:

JANE: Yeah, but they didn't say anything about the court system in the story.

MOTHER: Right!

Although brief, her mother's speech shows more than mere agreement, conveying strong support for Jane's point.

A dialogue in another family shows how Bob accepts his mother's speech:

MOTHER: My reasoning is different now, because the story's different now.

BOB: Yeah, I see, it's different now.

Bob endorses his mother's position about the importance of a new context as he reiterates her idea. Yet Bob's remark is not an echo of his mother's speech, which could be a sign of minimal acceptance or even nonacceptance, depending on the circumstances.

Our own analyses and those of several other researchers highlight the close ties between ego development and expressions of acceptance. We find that parental acceptance is associated with higher levels of adolescent and parent ego development, paralleling observations that adolescent girls functioning at higher levels of ego development are more accepting of (warmer toward) interviewers than girls at lower stages.[18] There is evidence as well that accepting and supportive family transactions promote ego development. Bell and Bell[19] report that families of adolescent girls who had higher ego development scores described their families as much more concerned, helpful, and supportive than did girls functioning at lower ego development levels.[20]

These and related studies emphasize the strong positive influence of a parent who is perceived as warm or nurturant.[21] A comprehensive review of parenting practices cites parental support as having a consistently positive relationship with all aspects of social competence (e.g. cognitive development, moral behavior, self-esteem, creativity) in children and adolescents.[22] We know that higher levels of ego development are characterized by greater tolerance and acceptance of deviance, conflict, and individual differences. Several lines of work, then, point to the importance of parental acceptance in promoting higher levels of adolescent ego development. Interactions conveying acceptance probably enhance ego development by making the family environment safe for the adolescent to risk "trying out" new ideas and perspectives, or expressing new feelings (such as confusing yet sharply felt conflicts of love and hate) toward parents and other intimates.

Four other types of enabling speeches are explaining, expressing curiosity, problem-solving, and empathizing. Through these interactions, parents may promote a son or daughter's thinking about a specific issue the family is trying to define or resolve. A mother's curiosity about her son's new idea might invite him to continue exploring it and eventually to articulate deeper meanings. Similarly, a father's encouragement of his daughter's active problem-solving may intensify her thoughtful cooperation with him and with other family members. These interactions are elements of highly individuated relationships, ones distinguished by their respect for the uniqueness of each family member and for the connections among members. It is also important to recall that adolescent enabling can contribute to the tone of family conversation and thereby elicit or sustain helpful parental behaviors, such as further explaining, greater curiosity, or acceptance of the child's new contributions.

CONSISTENCY, PERSISTENCE, AND INDIVIDUAL CHANGE WITHIN FAMILY DISCOURSE

Another developmentally salient aspect of family interaction has to do with change: How adolescents and their parents modify their thoughts and feelings, or tenaciously resist such change, during conversations. The extent to which an adolescent builds upon or continues the ideas of another family member is strongly related to his or her level of ego development.[23] Similarly, the examples set by parents, whether cherishing their son's or daughter's new ideas or insights or dismissing them, are connected to parental development.

Besides direct interactions with their son or daughter, parents exemplify change indirectly, through parent-to-parent interactions. There is an extensive, largely clinical, literature stressing the importance of internalization or identification in child and adolescent ego development.[24] Adolescents are strongly influenced by observations of their parents' behavior toward themselves, their siblings, and each other.

One kind of behavior especially relevant to adolescent ego development is the change or consistency in parents' thoughts, and feelings (e.g. acceptance) as expressed with their children. We distinguish four ways in which parents and adolescents change over the course of a conversation (or argument) with one another. The individual may develop his or her position further and contribute in new ways to the discussion (progressive discourse). In contrast, the family member may move to a simpler or less coherent statement and diminish his or her contribution to the discussion (regressive discourse). Third, the parent or adolescent may be repetitious, neither elaborating his point nor nor reducing his complexity (foreclosure). Finally, there may be an unmistakable shift to a new focus of interest (topic change).

In turning to individual change and how it reflects and influences adolescent development, we have shifted our own focus to how the *individual member* behaves in family relationships as they unfold over time. Parents and adolescents who actively build upon their previous ideas, drawing from other family members, are likely to participate in individuated relationships within a family context that fosters progressive and accelerated trajectories. On the other hand, parents who become less coherent, repeat themselves, and frequently change the topic will shape a family atmosphere that represents a pattern more along the lines of disengagement. In such families, instances of keenly focused listening or warmly accepting interactions will be few and far between. Adolescents with severe or moderate (steady conformist) arrests will be found in such families, where redundancy and slippage are commonplace features of their parents' contributions to family discourse.

To this point we have reviewed aspects of family life that are intimately linked with adolescent ego development. Our interest is in determining how the family contributes to the adolescent's growth, and how this growth (or disruptions in it) affects the family. In the first section of the chapter we described relationships within the family that promote adolescent ego development, relationships distinguished by their emphases on individuality and connectedness. When these significant features are compromised or absent, the family cannot support optimal development. Under such circumstances, there is a greater risk of an arrest—severe or attenuated—in adolescent ego development.

In the second part of the chapter we looked more closely at family discourse as a way of gaining insight about specific links between family bonds and variations in adolescent ego development. Enabling interactions, such as explaining, focusing, accepting, reflect relationships that are highly individuated. These interactions between parents and adolescent, as well as between parent and parent, both enhance and reflect the adolescent's ego development. On the other hand, constraining interactions, where devaluing, distracting, and excessive gratification are apparent, signal relationships in which individuation is resisted or ardently discouraged. When these interactions prevail, the adolescent may well encounter developmental difficulties.

In our thinking about individual development and family life two themes are central. The first is the importance of individual differences (for which there is much evidence). Not *all* adolescents will respond uniformly to specific enabling or constraining interactions with their parents, which is why we earlier said adolescents in families where constraining interactions are predominate "may" experience developmental difficulties. We do not know whether certain balances or constellations of constraining and enabling interactions are more optimal for development. The best combination may depend upon the individual characteristics of the adolescent, with those who are more vulnerable for instance, requiring more enabling and less constraining.

The second theme is the active role played by the adolescent in family relationships and discourse. We identify the ways in which adolescents with different developmental trajectories encourage or discourage crucial interactions with their parents; and thereby recognize the "two-way street" of family dynamics, the fact that the individual adolescent is an active, not a passive, player in the life of the family.

These several levels of analysis—relationship, discourse style, individual—are required to understand the interplay between the family and adolescent ego development. Our ideas about the family and its connection with adolescent development are most richly conveyed to the reader in Chapters 5 through 8, where we describe twelve boys and girls who are following four different paths through adolescence.

Assessing Ego Development and Family Interactions

The portraits of adolescents and their families that we present in coming chapters are drawn from a large ongoing longitudinal project in which we follow boys and girls from their early adolescence through later adolescent years and into young adulthood. We examine the development of the adolescents and their parents, and relationships within their families. But before going into what we have learned about these adolescents and their families, we must first provide an overview of how we studied them. Without burdening the reader with technical detail about our methods (which can be found in the four Appendixes), this chapter describes the groups we studied, how we observed them, and how we explored various aspects of individual development and family life.

In order to study a wide range of developmental patterns we deliberately followed two groups: psychiatrically hospitalized adolescents likely to be at risk for later problems in their psychological development, and high school freshmen with no foreseeable problems in their development. Our clinical experience suggested that many of the hospitalized adolescents would show early developmental arrests and be functioning at low levels of ego development. Although the hospitalized adolescents were not psychotic, there were strong reasons to expect that most of them would be developmentally impaired with respect to their perceptions of others, interpersonal styles, understanding of their surroundings, and impulse control.[1] In contrast, we expected that our group of high school freshmen with no apparent psychiatric problems would include many teenagers with progressive or accelerated ego development.

In other words, we assumed that the high school group would

include adolescents whose development was either proceeding without major difficulty or unusually advanced. But our interest in these students goes beyond their contrast with the more disturbed adolescents. They are members of a low-risk group, and by intensively studying these adolescents and their families, we have the opportunity to discover how family relationships and interactions may contribute to "healthy" development during the teenage years.[2]

The psychiatric patients consisted of successive adolescents admitted to the Children's Unit of a private university-affiliated hospital between autumn 1978 and winter 1980, who agreed to participate in the study. Almost all of these patients carried diagnoses of adjustment or personality disorders. The average age was 14.3 for the patient group and 14.6 for the high school group.

The high school students were drawn from 230 freshman volunteers attending a suburban high school in order to match these students as closely as possible with the psychiatric sample. All of the adolescents and their families were paid $30.00 annually for participating in the family discussion.

Members of both adolescent groups were predominantly from upper-middle-class and middle-class families.[3] Despite the demands of our procedures, all of the adolescents and their families completed the various tests, interviews, and family discussion tasks after joining the project. The total number of adolescents and families that entered the first year of the study was 146, comprising 76 high school students and 70 psychiatric patients, with equal numbers of boys and girls. In Appendix A we describe in greater detail our recruitment of the adolescents and their families, as well as other relevant demographic features.

Our contrasting samples, then, provide the opportunity to study teenagers who vary dramatically in their developmental trajectories. Based on extensive observations of these adolescents and their families, we analyze how such diverse courses of development are influenced by family forces and, in turn, impact upon the family.

Shortly after agreeing to participate, the ego development of each of the adolescents was assessed, using a measure directly linked with the theory presented in Chapter two.[4] On a second visit, within one month of the first, each adolescent met with one of our clinical interviewers for his or her first annual interview.[5] The interviewers were always, deliberately, kept unaware of each adolescent's ego development. This was an exploratory, semistructured interview in which several topics were always covered, in whatever order seemed most natural. These topics included school experience, peer relationships, family life (current and past), illness experience, and wishes or fantasies about the future. Within two months after the first interview, the adolescent and his or her parents assembled for the family discussion task, described below. This same sequence of ego development assessment, clinical interview, family discussion, was repeated in each of the next two years.

STUDYING ADOLESCENT AND PARENTAL DEVELOPMENT

Our overarching questions are how the psychosocial development of an adolescent is influenced by parental development and family forces, and how the adolescent's development, in turn, influences the family group. In order to trace the developmental level of the adolescent and his or or parents, we rely on a specific measure of ego development. There are two reasons for this. First, theoretical and empirical evidence suggests that individual ego development—which encompasses interpersonal style, conscious concerns, and impulse control—is intimately connected with family processes. Second, and perhaps even more important, we can measure ego development with a sentence completion test that has been used in numerous studies of adolescents, with results that attest to its reliability and validity.[6]

We used the Washington University Sentence Completion Test[7] to assess ego development, testing adolescents and parents separately. Each year, subjects were asked to respond to thirty-six incomplete sentences, or stems, such as "When they talked about sex, I _____," or "A mother is _____." Each response was removed from the subject's whole test and rated by a trained coder, along with other subjects' responses to the same stem. All of the subject's responses were then reassembled in order to derive his or her ego development stage. The purpose of first removing the answers from the individual test (a standard procedure for scoring these materials) was to minimize the risk that the scorer could be influenced by a given subject's other answers.[8] We measured the ego development of all adolescents within two months before observing their family interactions. Parents' ego development was assessed prior to their participating in family discussions—at the beginning of our meeting with the family, as described below. All our references to "ego development" are an expression of status at a point in time and are based on perceptions and attitudes reflected in the responses of adolescents and parents to this test. Our formulations of adolescent ego development "paths" and "trajectories" are based on these annual assessments, which were then used to classify adolescents into one of the paths (e.g. arrest, progression) discussed in Chapter two. Besides helping us gauge each individual's ego development stage, the individual sets of sentence completions provide the equivalent of a rich written interview, offering many insights into adolescent and parental experiences of relationships with one another, as well as their views of themselves, others, and their surroundings.

STUDYING FAMILIES

There are many possible approaches to an understanding of how adolescents develop within their families. Given the complexity of teenager–family interactions and influences, it is not surprising that a broad array of methods have appeared over the years, each with special strengths and limitations. Broadly speaking, the methods fall into three categories: self-report questionnaires clinical interview, and direct observation.[9]

Asking people about their experiences within their families is perhaps the most direct way to learn about family life. Traditional socialization studies use this technique, querying parents and children about disciplinary and other childrearing practices.[10] Other studies that rely on individual questionnaires tap features of the family rather than specific parent–child characteristics. Prominent examples are Moos's "family environment" investigations,[11] Olson's studies of cohesion and adaptation,[12] and the work of McCubbin and his associates in the area of family stress and coping.[13] Although the conceptual foci of these investigations clearly differ, all share the same method: asking individual family members about their family life.

The obvious strengths of questionnaire investigations include their directness, relative simplicity of execution, and disclosure of how various members experience the family. Of primary importance is the fact that this technique draws information about a family member's perceptions and constructions of family life; we discover the meanings that individuals attach to their family experiences. Yet there are also significant limitations associated with the self-report in this form. First, although it offers glimpses of individual experiences of the family, such a method cannot alone provide an understanding of the actual relationships within the family. Second, knowledge of the family as a "unit" with multilayered patterns of relationships is difficult to derive from separate reports by family members.[14]

The second approach to studying families is the more traditional clinical interview designed to elicit narrative reports of family experience. Using a relatively unstructured interview format, a clinically skilled interviewer inquires about the person's previous and current family relationships. These interviews often involve troubled patients describing problematic relationships, but this way of proceeding is not restricted to patient groups. In recent years several studies, including our own, have used semistructured clinical interviews with samples of "average" and talented adolescents and young adults.[15]

Clinical interviews can also be used with families. In fact, such interviews are at the core of family therapy. Through exploratory sessions with several family members, relationship issues, family values, and family "myths" are identified and addressed. There are many versions of family therapy, ranging from the more associative, psychodynamically based approaches[16] to those that are more structured and focus on family systems.[17] Within this clinical genre, the works most relevant to our explorations of adolescents within families are the family therapy studies of Roger Shapiro and his colleagues,[18] who describe the themes of individuation, differentiation, and separation within the families of psychiatrically disturbed adolescents.[19]

Fewer studies of normal adolescents have included unstructured clinical interviews. In the 1960s Murphey and associates[20] followed a group of adolescents through "transitions" to college. Open-ended interviews with the teenagers and their parents suggested several types of passage from high school to college, based on variations in autonomy and relatedness with the family.

Our own research approach is *direct observation* of the interactions between adolescents and their parents as they attempt to resolve or sustain differences of opinion in the family. This method is quite different from those that rely on individual reports of what a parent or child *was* or *is* like in the family. We focus on the *actual* ways that the teenagers and their parents deal with one another. Families gather within many contexts, ranging from the daily routine of meals to those special occasions marking key transitions, such as graduations, weddings, and funerals. Rather than observe such moments within the normal flow of family life, our technique is to bring the family together to discuss differences among members.[21]

In light of the richness and frequency of adolescent–parent situations occurring in the real world, the reader might wonder why we decided to stage these interactions. Since we were specifically interested in how adolescent–parent relationships might shape and be shaped by individual development, we wanted to observe theoretically relevant interactions (such as explaining, showing curiosity, or undermining) in many families, in which the children's ego development would present a variety of levels. Knowing the circumstances surrounding their interactions and making sure those circumstances were approximately the same for all the families, we could be more assured that what appeared to be important differences among families were not the result of unanticipated factors, such as the number of siblings present or the context in which a particular exchange took place (e.g. a protracted argument at dinner). By bringing families together to discuss a problem that we presented to them, we could, to a large extent, control or at least monitor these potential confounding factors.

In our study, parents and adolescents first met individually with trained interviewers to consider two difficult, perhaps disquieting, moral dilemmas. Each parent and adolescent responded to questions from Lawrence Kohlberg's Moral Judgment Interview,[22] which asks the subject how best to solve several moral dilemmas embedded within specific stories. One, for example, involves "Heinz," whose wife is dying of cancer. He cannot afford the steep price ($2,000) that the druggist is charging for the radium that might cure his wife. But the druggist will not sell it to him for the amount ($1,000) that he can afford, despite the fact that this greatly exceeded the druggist's cost. Heinz decides to break into the store to steal the drug, so as to save his wife's life. After reading this story to the parent or adolescent, the interviewer asked a series of linked questions: Should Heinz have disobeyed the law? What if he doesn't love his wife? Should one should steal to save a pet's life? Are there extenuating circumstances that override legal considerations? Should Heinz's friend, who happens to be a police officer, report the incident? What verdict should the jury render?

A second story is about Joe, whose parents have promised him he could go to summer camp if he saved enough money to pay for it. After working as a newspaper boy, Joe now has the money for camp. But Joe's father suddenly gets the chance to go on a fishing trip with his friends and immediately needs Joe's savings to finance the trip. The interviewer's questions now focus on rights, obligations, and parental relationships: Does Joe's father have the right to take his son's hard-earned money? Should one always keep a promise? What are the most important elements of relationships between fathers and sons, between parents and their children? (The interested reader can find entire interview protocol Appendix C.)

Following this thirty- to forty-minute interview, family members were brought together, and the differences in their solutions were brought out.[23] The interviewer always presented these differences in the same order (first, mother and child versus father; followed by father and child versus mother; and then mother and father versus child).[24] Family members were asked to explain and defend their individual positions and to reach a consensus that would represent the whole family. The interviewer then left the room, after announcing each set of differences. The ensuing discussions of all these differences usually lasted from forty to forty-five minutes. The discussions were audio-taped in order to preserve exact speeches, interruptions, simul-taneous speeches, and nonverbal clues, such as laughter, hesitation, and stuttering. The tapes were then transcribed. Our family analyses are based on these carefully recorded and transcribed discussions that took place in the first year of the study. We also used the audio-tapes, where necessary, to clarify wording or to permit fuller apprecia-tion of the feelings behind and between words.

We chose moral dilemmas to generate family discussions because theory, clinical insights, and intuition suggested that value conflicts, moral concerns, and "fidelity" issues would be among the most salient for many adolescents.[25] Our expectations regarding their significance for adolescents and their families were amply fulfilled, easing our anxieties over how much we might be limiting the generality of our observations by using an artificial "laboratory" task, as opposed to a spontaneous exchange in a natural setting. We were impressed, and delighted, with the intensity expressed by the adolescents and their parents as they defended their own positions and challenged oppos-ing views, at times searching for agreement while at other times attacking, confusing, and fragmenting their discussions. Often families spontaneously remarked (to our relief), "This is like our dinnertime arguments." These observations of family members' involvement sug-gest that the moral dilemma discussions were touching deep-seated issues within the family, reflecting numerous dimensions of the fam-ily's relationships and interactions.[26]

The final step in studying the families involved detailed examination and analysis of these discussions. Since qualities of family relation-ships (e.g. connectedness) and family interactions (e.g. acceptance) were our primary interest, these analyses had two purposes: to eluci-date the pertinent aspects of family relationships and to assess the relevant moment-to-moment family interactions and their sequences. We analyzed *relationships* by carefully reading the transcripts and listening to the audiotapes to draw out key themes within each family illustrating aspects of individuated relationships (autonomy, mutu-ality, openness). Additional clues to these relationships were gleaned from the adolescents' and parents' sentence completion tests and from the adolescents' clinical interviews. Intensive case study analyses were performed for twelve adolescents and their families, representing four paths through adolescence: early arrest, steady conformist, accelerated advancement, and progressive development.

Family interactions were identified and measured using the Constraining and Enabling Coding System, based on the interaction concepts discussed in Chapter 2. The technical rules followed by our coders, procedures for training them, coding reliabilities, and examples of several interaction codes (distracting, judgmental, focusing, accepting, progression) are given in Appendix D. The readers interested in applying this approach to their own social interaction materials (clinical interviews, observed family discussions, family and individual psychotherapy interviews) can obtain the entire coding manual from Dr. Hauser, as described in Appendix D.

Application of these empirically defined codes to our entire set of transcripts permitted extensive comparison of the four adolescent trajectories in terms of the occurrence of certain types of family interactions and special sequences of interest, for instance, mutual enabling. In addition, through the twelve case analyses we can explore family experience in terms of both relationship patterns and interactions.

As we examine the individual cases and larger groupings of subjects for evidence of connections between adolescent development and family context, we consider ways in which development may be promoted or slowed, if not halted, by family dynamics. At the same time we watch for those ways in which families are changed—temporarily or permanently—by the developing adolescent. In addition to clarifying particular associations, such as that between enabling interactions and high levels of ego development, we address two intriguing questions:

What family dimensions promote and sustain high levels of adolescent ego development under adverse conditions (such as psychiatric hospitalization during adolescence)?

What family dimensions may lead to and sustain arrests ego development under favorable conditions (such as seemingly positive high school experience)?

In the next chapters, using ego development observations from three years of the study, we describe four paths through adolescence, first summarizing what we have discovered about each path from our entire sample of teenagers and their families. We then take a more intensive look at specific teenagers who have followed each path: profound arrest; steady conformist; progressive development; and accelerated development. In each case study we explore linkages among the adolescent, parent, and family relationships. These portraits illuminate the intricacies of the varied paths through adolescence, their intersection with adolescent and parental perceptions and feelings, and their embeddedness in the family's interactions. By intensively studying teenagers with high levels of development we learn about individual and family strengths. The teenagers with arrested ego development teach us about vulnerabilities.

Preceding the intensive case studies, we review selected quantitative findings, based on analyses of all subjects fulfilling the criteria for a given trajectory. Through these analyses we examine basic aspects of each trajectory, such as consistent family profiles, adolescent coping patterns, and influences of gender and psychopathology on the developmental path. In addition, these other analyses permit comparisons of interaction patterns and parental ego development among the trajectories.[27]

CHAPTER
5

Paths Through Adolescence

In the next chapters we introduce the reader to six ego development paths through adolescence.[1] First we take a wide-angle view. We survey the boys and girls with whom we spoke and whom we observed in their families to look for general characteristics of each developmental type: the number of teenagers who followed each path, links to psychiatric conditions, gender differences, and family structures. Adolescents following these paths cannot simply be characterized in terms of variations in "health" or "illness." They differ along many other, less global dimensions: how they experience their inner and outer worlds; the range of their emotions, wishes, and ambitions; their interpersonal styles; and their family dynamics.

We then shift gears to look in depth at twelve adolescents and their parents. Through closer scrutiny of these thirty-six family members we illuminate intricacies of adolescent development within the family and the dynamics of separation and connection.

The six paths we identify represent a spectrum of possibilities. At one extreme are those adolescents whose development appears to be profoundly interrupted. Year after year they experience the world, and other people, in conflicted and restricted ways. At the other extreme are those boys and girls who began our study with unusually complex perceptions and thoughts about themselves, and about their relationships with others. These remarkable adolescents continue to see and understand themselves and their surroundings in subtle and complex ways over the several years of the study. Between these extremes are less profound arrests in development and less clear-cut progressions.[2]

PROFOUND ARRESTS IN DEVELOPMENT

Teenagers following this path have a limited range of emotional responses to other people and key events. They are restricted in their perceptions and expectations, often framing their experience of themselves and the world in either/or terms. They rely on stereotypes and have interpersonal styles that emphasize giving *or* taking, one-up *or* one-down. An understanding of events or people as complex and multifaceted is not within their repertoire. With respect to morality, the uppermost concern is "getting away with it." Abstract principles, concerns about ethics or values, are simply not relevant.

Among the 133 adolescents who participated in our study for two or more years, forty-one remained arrested at an early point in their ego development, twenty-five boys and sixteen girls. Their average age was 14.1, which is similar to the average ages of adolescents following the other paths. Unlike the other groups, adolescents with arrested development were almost equally divided between those living in two-parent families and those living in families headed by a separated or divorced parent. They could not be distinguished from the other groups by birth order or number of siblings. Their parents showed much variation in ego development. Fathers spanned the earliest self-protective to the highest autonomous stages. Mothers represented a narrower developmental range, from the transition-to-conformist to the transition-to-autonomous stage. Despite this interesting difference in ranges, mothers and fathers did not differ in their average levels of (conformist) ego development.

Thirty-four of these profoundly arrested adolescents were hospitalized psychiatric patients; seven were high school students. Thus, 26 percent of our patient group "arrested" in their development, continuing over the years to function at the earliest stages, in contrast to only 5 percent of the high school students. This finding does not necessarily suggest that a psychiatric illness—or hospitalization—"causes" developmental arrest. The picture is probably much more complex. Consider, for instance, the possibility that John's troubles in school, resulting from his impaired impulse control, began a chain of events that eventually led to his hospitalization. The experience of being hospitalized, in turn, exacerbated his already low self-esteem and his frightened avoidance of new people. His experience in the hospital may also, inadvertently, have heightened John's frightened, combative way of relating to legal and school authorities. Did a developmental arrest lead to his hospitalization, or did his hospitalization cause his subsequent developmental arrest? The answer is most likely to be both. A vicious cycle of disturbing experiences and outright failures led to more distress and failures. Since the adolescents with developmental arrests had strikingly low levels of self-esteem, many may have enacted that kind of scenario. Besides their deflated views of themselves, these teenagers used coping strategies that relied heavily on constriction and detachment, narrowing their perceptions of themselves and others, increasing their distance from potentially supportive friends and adults.[3] Within their families they did not focus well, contribute to problem-solving, or show signs of being empathic with either parent. Instead, they persistently obstructed and discouraged coherent conversations with their parents by making distracting or angry remarks, being demeaning, and openly expressing disdain or indifference. Not surprisingly, the profoundly arrested adolescents did not often continue a train of thought begun in an earlier comment. More often, successive contributions to an ongoing discussion were diffuse and minimally connected to the ongoing discussion.

As if to compensate for their teenagers' restricted and problematic engagement—indifference or outright insults—their parents expressed much curiosity and made repeated efforts to guide the discussion toward resolving different family opinions. These parents seemed surprisingly accepting of their actively rebuffing sons and daughters; in this respect they were no different from the parents of any of the other adolescents in our sample. This observation certainly suggests that the parents of profoundly arrested adolescents are not—at least currently—acting in ways that might be interfering with their adolescents' development.

Yet on closer examination, we see that parents *and* teenagers within these families were less responsive to one another than first appeared to be the case. When we looked at exchanges of enabling (e.g. accepting, explaining, empathizing) between adolescents and parents, we found that, when compared with the families of all the other adolescents, these families—both parents and adolescents—showed the least reciprocation of such speeches. Clearly, with these teenagers offering such minimal efforts at problem-solving, so little empathy, and so much indifference and withholding, the chances for positive engagement between family members are indeed limited. Missed connections are apparent also in yet another context. In the one-parent families mothers were considerably less empathic than in the two-parent families. In other words, there were signs of even less responsiveness between parent and adolescent in the single-parent families. In such family situations, one parent's resources for actively understanding a distant and distancing adolescent may be especially taxed.

The teenagers with profoundly arrested development revealed their impoverished connectedness in many ways: They were unempathic, withholding, indifferent, and devaluing. Moreover, there were few indications that these teenagers achieved noticeable differentiation from their parents: They rarely tried to solve problems, guide the discussion in relation to the task at hand, or paraphrase a parent's point. Nonetheless, their parents for the most part remained involved, asking many questions, gently prodding and directing the discussion when possible.

STEADY CONFORMISTS

Teenagers who reach, and remain at, the conformist level are the most familiar and least worrisome for adults as well as their peers. They participate in group activities, have friends, are usually not puzzling to others, and, by and large, are "team players." Group norms and other regulations do not pose a problem for these adolescents. For the most part, they see the importance of cooperating, of going along with standards set within the school, within their families, and within the larger social setting. Steady conformist adolescents are aware of inner feelings, but they usually express them in generalized terms or as clichés. Yet these cooperative and seemingly adjusted teenagers do not advance beyond their preoccupations with acceptance and the achievement of group-defined goals, and thus represent a milder— socially acceptable—form of developmental arrest. What are the more specific characteristics of these most commonly encountered teenagers? In what ways does family experience sustain their lack of movement to more differentiated ways of perceiving and responding to inner and outer events?

Twenty-four of the adolescents entered the study at the conformist level and did not move beyond it. An impressive preponderance, twenty-two, were high school students. Almost one-third of our high school sample were following this path, as against 3 percent of our patients. Because they were functioning in line with community and school standards, behaving in socially acceptable ways, and offending hardly anyone, these teenagers would be unlikely to generate the kind of disturbance that often leads to psychiatric hospitalization. More puzzling is the rare steady conformist who *is* hospitalized. We look in depth at one of these teenagers, Amy, in Chapter 6.

The steady conformists were equally divided between boys and girls. Seventeen of them were from two-parent families. In comparison with the profoundly arrested adolescents, the steady conformist adolescents used coping strategies that were less constricting and less detaching from other people.[4] The ego development of parents of steady conformists also differed from that of the severely arrested group. Instead of a wide range, we now see a narrow one, with mothers ranging from the conformist to the transition-to-autonomous stage, and fathers from the self-aware to the transition-to-autonomous stage.

These teenagers made many connections with their family members. In conversations and arguments with their parents they were accepting and empathic. Consistent with their conformist functioning, they were often concerned with keeping the family's discussion on track, reminding their parents to follow the interviewer's instructions about how to resolve their different opinions. More generally, these adolescents stood out from those who were severely arrested along the lines of their enabling interactions: They explained more and were more focusing, curious, and accepting. These cooperative teenagers were also more available as they spoke with their parents. In contrast with the severely arrested adolescents, they rarely withheld answers to parents' questions, nor were they angrily indifferent. Their enthusiastic participation in the task was also apparent as they elaborated previous points and continued lines of argument that they or their parents had begun earlier. Through this continuing and cumulative participation in discourse with their parents—what we term "progressive discourse change"—the steady conformists differed strikingly from the severely arrested adolescents, who tended to lose the thread of an argument, participating in increasingly fragmented ways as the discussion unfolded.

Like their sons and daughters, the parents of the steady conformist teenagers offered many explanations in the family sessions. But they were also less curious than parents of adolescents following the other ego development paths, and more indifferent and withholding than the parents of the severely arrested adolescents. Perhaps because their children were so responsive, there was less need for these parents to ask many questions or be consistently acknowledging.

Yet when we turn to examine actual *sequences* of exchanges between family members, we discover that this positive cooperative ambience within the family is less pervasive than it appears at first blush. Rather than respond in kind to an enabling (e.g. accepting, explaining, focusing) speech, parents or adolescents in the families of steady conformists were more likely to be undermining—indifferent, withholding, distracting, or devaluing—after a family member had explained a point or was accepting. This imbalance between mutual enabling and undermining was present for both one- and two- parent families. Higher levels of indifference and distraction, together with this preponderance of undermining, certainly implies that there may be more conflict and missed signals in these families than might be expected if the steady conformists were simply the products of cooperative, conforming families. Such conflict—undermining and provocation—is amply illustrated in Chapter 6 by Lou and his parents.

Teenagers following the steady conformist path both connected with their parents and maintained a modicum of separateness. But these adolescents and their parents spoke with one another in more conflicted ways (undermining) and the parents were *less* acknowledging than those of the severely arrested adolescents. This degree of conflict, diminished parental curiosity, and restrained parental acknowledgment may not provide the emotional and cognitive nutriment necessary for the adolescent to advance beyond the conformist stage, where the teenager is seeking *not only* connection but also independence and greater differentiation.

THREE PATHS OF PROGRESSION

Those subjects who showed progressions in their ego development began at levels of either very low (preconformist) or intermediate (conformist) stages, and within the next years began to function at unmistakably higher stages. There is a "family" of progressions. In what we call early progression, a teenager shifts from a strikingly low level of development, functioning at a self-protective stage, to a conformist stage. Such shifts occurred for both high school students and patients. A second type, advanced progression, occurs when the adolescent moves from conformist to more advanced postconformist stages. Finally, there is dramatic progression, in which an adolescent shifts from one of the earliest stages to one of the most advanced. Characteristic of adolescents following these paths is noteworthy *change*—transformations in understandings of self, friends, and parents. Teenagers following early progression paths advance from concrete, often one-dimensional ("either/or") views to socially acceptable yet more complex perspectives. Those following later progression paths move from conventional views to ones based on inner principles and show a greater appreciation of individual differences.

Progressive ego development was the most prevalent developmental path in our sample, accounting for close to one-third of the high school students and patients. Since there are such clear qualitative differences between the three kinds of progression, we consider them separately here and in Chapter Eight.

EARLY PROGRESSION

The teenager following this path changes from viewing the world and himself or herself in concrete and simple terms, guided by immediate satisfaction, to recognizing many group standards, the importance of meeting others' expectations, and belonging to various groups. He or she is no longer purely preoccupied with self-interest and self-protection. The world is now experienced as more complex than black or white, your fault, not mine.

One-quarter of the teenagers (fifteen boys and nineteen girls), equally divided between the psychiatric patients and the high school students, traversed this first path of progression. This is of obvious interest, since so many (fifty-four) of the psychiatric patients entered the study at very low levels of development. Almost one-third of this group of initially more disabled patients advanced to conformist stages subsequent to their discharge. The fact that two-thirds remained arrested following discharge indicates that the situational change, from a restricted and probably regressive environment to a family environment with new (often more specialized) schools and neighborhoods, cannot alone explain the change in development. In earlier sections we considered those factors that might keep teenagers "stuck" in these earliest stages. Now we can turn to those factors that might facilitate a progression to later developmental stages. Although an equal number of our high school students also shifted from early to intermediate stages, the more important statistic involves what *proportion* of those initially functioning at the preconformist stages advanced to the conformist ones. In the first year, twenty-four of the students were described as functioning at the early impulsive or self-protective stages. By the second and third years, seventeen of these students, or 71 percent (as against 33 percent of the patients), were expressing conformist perceptions and understandings.

The early progression group came from predominantly two-parent families, with 40 percent living in one-parent families. Their parents' ego development varied widely. Mothers ranged from the conformist to the autonomous stage, with most functioning at the conscientious stage; fathers, from the self-protective to the transition-to-autonomous stage, with most, like mothers, functioning at the conscientious stage. This comparison already reveals a difference between the profoundly arrested teenagers and those who followed the early progression path. Mothers and fathers of the arrested adolescents were predominantly at the conformist stages.

In their first-year family discussions we see yet more ways that teenagers following the early progression path differed from those who remained profoundly arrested in their development. These teenagers were more engaged with their parents, as they would paraphrase a parent's remarks, sometimes voice dogmatic opinions in response to a parent's opinion, and occasionally criticize a parent's view. In addition, adolescents of this group were less distracting than those who were profoundly arrested. Like their children, the parents of the early progression adolescents showed many signs of engagement with their sons and daughters and with one another, connecting through empathic interactions and minimizing distracting ones. The parents of adolescents following the early progression path also were highly reciprocal of their sons' and daughters' enabling (explaining, accepting, focusing) contributions, a difference especially striking in the two-parent families, where there was three times more mutual enabling than in the comparable group of severe arrests. The conversations of the parents of the early arrest adolescents were marked by almost four times more undermining (enabling followed by constraining) than mutual enabling sequences, in comparison to an approximate balance between these processes for the early progressions.

We have some clues, then, about how the families of the early progressions may have been different at the very start of our observations. Their parents were at higher levels of ego development. The teenagers appear to be somewhat more engaged with their parents, both positively (focusing) and negatively (devaluing, judging). And— perhaps most importantly—within their families many of the adolescents who advanced from the early stages of ego development (impulsive, self-protective) experienced higher levels of mutual enabling, as well as a greater balance between mutual enabling and undermining processes.

ADVANCED PROGRESSION

Along this path, the adolescent moves from a concern with group norms and acceptance to an interest in inner standards, complexity, and individual differences. Conscience and integrity are now the watchwords, rather than acceptance and belonging. A small number, six, of the teenagers followed this path. All six were high school students. Two-thirds of them were girls, and two-thirds were from two-parent families. With respect to parental ego development, four of the mothers functioned at postconformist levels, and two of the four were at the transition between the conscientious and the autonomous stages. Similarly, only one of the fathers was at a conformist stage; the rest functioned at either the conscientious or the autonomous stage.

These teenagers differed from those following the other paths. Compared to the group of steady conformists, they made more efforts at problem-solving and showed more empathy; they were less devaluing and withholding. Compared to the severe arrest and early progression groups, the differences in empathy, withholding, and devaluing are especially pronounced. These six teenagers showed more progressive discourse change than the severe arrest and early progression groups. Finally, they spoke more often in the family sessions. (Since all the family scores are adjusted for number of speeches, this increased rate does not inflate or deflate the other values.)

Family influences on this second type of progression may be mediated through the higher parental ego development levels, with parents serving as models for the adolescents in daily conversation, as they respond—in words and in actions—to significant problems with one another and with their children. In terms of the interactions that we identified and counted, other than diminished focusing and considerably less distracting, there is scarcely any difference between parents of the advanced progression group and those of the steady conformist or early progression groups. On the other hand, the parents of the teenagers following the advanced progression path show more empathy than the parents of the profound arrests.

Since this group and the ones to follow include much smaller numbers of adolescents, any conclusions about them and their families must be made with caution. Nonetheless, it is interesting to note that these adolescents talked more and related to their parents in more connected (empathic) and differentiated (problem-solving) ways than their counterparts who remained at the conformist stage. The parents of these teenagers were at higher levels of ego development than the parents of steady conformists or of those following other ego development paths. In addition, these parents interfered less with their adolescent children during family discussions, in that they engaged in fewer distracting *and* fewer paraphrasing speeches.

DRAMATIC PROGRESSION

The change from experiencing the world as dichotomous to recognizing multiple groups and social norms and cherishing individual differences among people constitutes a dramatic personal transformation. Three teenagers, all patients, underwent this stunning change within one or two years of entering the study.[5] In addition to being patients, these two girls and one boy were all members of two-parent families. Two of their mothers functioned at conformist stages, while two fathers were at the conscientious stage.

The way these teenagers, then at the earliest stages of ego development, spoke in their families during the first-year discussions clearly distinguished them from those who remained profoundly arrested over the next years. The dramatic progression adolescents were markedly more accepting and empathic in responding to their parents; they often tried to move a derailed discussion back on track. Rarely were they indifferent, judgmental, or seductive toward their parents. A second illuminating comparison is between the first-year family conversations of the dramatic progression and the early progression groups. The teenagers following the dramatic progression path were more involved in guiding discussions and were more accepting and empathic. At the same time, these unusual adolescents were less dogmatic, indifferent, and withholding.

The mothers of these teenagers more often guided the discussions and were more accepting and empathic than those of the severely arrested adolescents. In addition, they distracted more—often interrupting others' speeches—and spoke more than mothers of the adolescents following any of the other paths. Comparisons between mothers of the dramatic and early progression groups showed parallel differences.

ACCELERATED DEVELOPMENT

Unusually mature adolescents frequently evoke delighted and, at times, perplexed reactions from adults, as they express unexpectedly insightful perceptions about themselves and their surroundings. Far earlier than most of their peers (and many adults), they comprehend complex personal relationships and can articulate subtle aspects of their inner lives. These children may be considered "gifted," but not in the ordinary sense of academically gifted children. Rather, their strengths lie in their ability to see and convey shades of gray, contradictory ideas, paradoxes, and novel perspectives. They are aware of many, often inconsistent, feelings. Differences among friends are welcomed, not simply tolerated or rejected in favor of more palatable stereotypes.

Only six teenagers began at these advanced stages and remained at them over the next years. While an admittedly small proportion of our sample, 4 percent, these precocious teenagers are important exceptions. These two boys and four girls were all from the high school group and from two-parent families. Their parents were also functioning at high levels of ego development, with all but one at postconformist stages. One patient began at an advanced stage, and then functioned at a slightly lower stage over the next two years, before returning to the same high, post-conformist, stage in her final year. While not technically "accelerated" because of this dip she is considered at length in chapter 9, because of her unusually advanced development.

Like those in the advanced progression group, these teenagers made many efforts to guide family discussions and to clarify their parents' ideas. They rarely withdrew from active interactions or were demeaning or excessively gratifying (responding to curry favor or continued attention from the other speaker). In comparison with the other extreme type, the severe arrests, the teenagers in the accelerated development group were more focused, more active in guiding discussions, and more empathic, as they spoke with their parents. Consistently, these teenagers were also less rebuffing toward their parents: Rarely did they turn away from them or mock their ideas.

Other than distracting more, their parents were very similar to those of teenagers following the advanced progression paths. But contrasting them with those of the severe arrests, we see that the parents of the accelerated development group explained less and were less curious and focusing. Again, there is the suggestion that parents are being *responsive* to the adolescents. There is less reason for parents of these accelerated adolescents to explain, ask questions, or focus discussions with children who are forthcoming and already deeply engaged. At the same time, the parents of the advanced group were more accepting than those of the severe arrest group.

In broad strokes, these are the group portraits, the salient family and individual characteristics of adolescents who followed six paths of ego development. While these composite pictures provide us with clearer ideas about each of the paths, we do not yet have a detailed understanding of how adolescents following the various paths experience the world and relate in their families. Certain questions can be pursued only with this second kind of information. For instance, do parents of Steady Conformist adolescents speak and behave in certain ways that restrain their sons' and daughters' separation from the family? Do profoundly arrested teenagers provoke parents to be less encouraging of their differentiation from other family members? These questions, touching on complex interactions flowing between parents and adolescents, require a closer look *inside* the families of teenagers following these paths of arrest and advance.[6]

In Part II we listen closely to the voices of twelve adolescents and their parents. To be sure, while these twelve teenagers bring color and flesh to our more abstract ideas of ego development paths and linked family dynamics, they do not represent a complete picture of the entire group following each path. Other teenagers and families will be heard from along the way, as we pursue our two core questions: How does the developing teenager shape his or her parents' and family life? And how does this special and intimate society—the family—contribute to the course of adolescent development? These narratives convey the message that paths of individual development are embedded within the intricate matrix of family relationships. The twelve teenagers and their families illustrate, often poignantly, the ways that adolescents and parents handle the central dilemma posed during this phase of the life cycle: how to separate from the family and reaffirm one's place within it.

TWO

Adolescents and Parents
Individual Portraits

Profoundly Arrested Ego Development: Charlie Brown, Ellen Foster, Mike Wary

Each of the intensive studies of adolescents and their families in this chapter and the next three is presented in three parts. In the first part we draw on our interviews with the teenager and his or her sentence completions, covering what he or she was thinking, feeling, and doing at the time. In the second part we introduce other members of the immediate family, as seen through the adolescent's eyes. Our understanding of the adolescent's parents is then expanded by considering their responses to the ego development sentence completion test, which convey the parents' perceptions of themselves, their families, and their surroundings. In a sense, these responses serve as "written interviews."

In the third part, the centerpiece of each case study, we listen to how the teenager and parents speak with one another as they try to resolve their different views and to reach family solutions to difficult moral dilemmas. In the aim of extracting most fully the abundant information in these rich family discussions, we perform two "passes." To begin with, we identify family *relationship* features exemplifying individuality and connectedness, characteristics connected with paths of adolescent ego development. These family features are based on careful readings of the discussions. At the next level of analysis we examine how the *interactions*—constraining and enabling—among family members are linked with those relationship qualities and with paths of adolescent ego development.

The individual interview excerpts and family conversations that follow are all real. We have disguised each person's and each family's

identity to protect privacy. The voices, however, are unchanged. All of
the dialogues and sentence completions are as originally spoken or
written.

CHARACTERISTICS OF PROFOUND ARREST

Teenagers whose ego development is arrested are noticeably restricted in their perceptions and feelings regarding other people and
events. They are preoccupied with satisfying their own impulses.
Friends and parents are valued for their role in overcoming immediate
frustrations, and the world is perceived in relatively simple either/or
and for-or-against terms. Stereotypes predominate, and interpersonal
styles emphasize giving *or* taking, one-up *or* one-down. Understanding events or people as complex and multifaceted is not in their
repertoire. With respect to morality, the uppermost concern is "getting away with it." Abstract principles and concerns about ethics or
values are not relevant.

Rarely is there a single cause for such arrests in ego development. As
in the following cases, most often one can find numerous reasons.
What we do know from the cases with which we have intensive
experience is that family relationships and interactions probably contribute to and reverberate with these serious arrests in adolescent ego
development.

Perhaps the most tenable general conclusion is that arrested ego
development in adolescence may arise from major vulnerabilities in
the developmental history of the child (at times appearing as formally
diagnosed psychopathology), limited parental resources, or chronic
stress within the family environment (as a result, for example, of
economic hardship or divorce). There may be powerful incompatibilities between the arrested adolescent and his or her peers, as
the teenager's physical development, academic achievements, or social skills are somehow "off" from those of his or her friends or
schoolmates. Charlie, the first of the arrested adolescents, illustrates
several of these individual and family features.

CHARLIE BROWN

Charlie is one of the least happy of the unhospitalized adolescents.
Feeling oppressed and unsuccessful at school, virtually ignored at
home, and isolated from his friends, he has few positive experiences or

hopes to speak of in his first year of high school. Because of his academic difficulties, Charlie has been placed in a special school program offering individualized scheduling and paid jobs within the school. Although he appreciates those efforts, school is nonetheless a burden for him. Throughout his first interview he describes his feelings of oppression and repeated humiliation by teachers and friends. Before the fifth grade, Charlie had been pleased with school. Then, coinciding with a change to many new teachers and classrooms, school became harder. Around that time life with his friends also changed. They began to smoke cigarettes and marijuana:

> . . . like in the early grades, I had a lotta friends, right? Then it suddenly getting really stupid. They started, uh, smokin' pot and cigarettes and stuff like that. They started getting really stupid. So I said, "forget it."

The interviewer asked Charlie why he didn't join his friends. Charlie rejoined, "'Cause it's stupid, I don't know." Charlie's only clue about why he has rejected cigarettes, drugs, and ultimately his friends, is his memory of being forced to smoke a cigarette when he was six years old, illustrating his experience of oppression while growing up:

> . . . I was playing in the park with this other kid . . . and this kid comes over and goes, "Take a puff." I go, "No!" and he puts it in my mouth. . . . Tasted terrible . . . didn't like it at all.

Rejecting his friends' new habits led to counterrejections and fights, and right into one of the organizing strands of Charlie's life, the Oppression Cycle:

CHARLIE: Well, like I started, I'd hang around with [friends] for a while, but then they go, "You're not smoking cigarettes. Get outta here. I don't know you." You know, stuff like that.

INTERVIEWER: How did you feel when they did that?

CHARLIE: Umm, little, you know, little umm scared and mad. I don't know because they were my friends and had—like I knew 'em three or four years. Now they're all bums . . . like in class when they look at me. They just look at me, they're staring at me. Like mean faces and stuff like that, that, like, I'm gonna go out of the class and they're going to beat me up or something.

Charlie's fear of being pushed around is pervasive. In the early years of elementary school, for instance, Charlie remembers a time when the principal wrongly accused him of stealing a book and another when he was pushed against a hot radiator by an impatient teacher. In none of those instances does Charlie suspect that he may have incited these adult bullies. He does have a fleeting awareness of strong feelings about the episodes, and—in contrast to the other arrested adolescents—controls his reactions, not resorting to violent actions or threats. Charlie *imagines* violence, and quickly retracts when he senses that he may lose control. When the principal, whom he heartily disliked, subjected Charlie to a prolonged interrogation for a supposed theft and detained him after school, Charlie was vividly aware of his feelings:

INTERVIEWER: What went through your mind when [the principal] was accusing you? You say your face got red. Did anything go on in your head?

CHARLIE: I got mad, I felt like punching him, yeah.

INTERVIEWER: What did you imagine?

CHARLIE: Imagined that I punched his head in, heh. And his head would fall off. (*giggling*)

When the teacher pushed him against a hot radiator, Charlie was outraged and momentarily lost his cool:

[That] got me really angry and I went like, that (*motions as if pushing her away*) I got away and . . . then I walked to the office. . . . I walked right out the door, 'cause . . . you shouldn't do that! It's not right, you're not supposed to do that. I mean supposed to touch any, any kid in school.

Charlie has little to say about his friends, other than telling of visits to their houses, "playing pinball or fun to eat over or somethin'. Stuff like that." He has no girlfriends and adamantly denies any interest in "going out" with girls: "Waste of, waste of time. . . . I gotta do other things. . . . It's not that important." During the entire interview, Charlie is unhappy and restless. Rarely does he spontaneously speak of any thoughts or feelings. Describing his daily experiences, Charlie points to the oppressive demands of school:

INTERVIEWER: What do you think about mostly?

CHARLIE: What do I think about? Homework, heh . . . we have to do homework . . . all the time.

INTERVIEWER: What do you think about when you think about homework?

CHARLIE: When I do the homework, I do it right when I get home. I get it over with. Stop thinking about it. I can't stand thinking about it.

Foremost in Charlie's thoughts about the future is work:

I wanna be a radio broadcaster. Or a veterinarian, or an auto mechanic or somethin' like that. You know (*laughing*) auto mechanic.

His first choice is "a vet," because they earn the most money. Paralleling his concrete reason for choosing this work are Charlie's images of working as a vet:

INTERVIEWER: What do you imagine you'd do if you were a vet?

CHARLIE: Open 'em up and, you know, like if he swallows a comb . . . or somethin' to take it out . . . 'n everything.

INTERVIEWER: Would that be difficult at all?

CHARLIE: Not if he's sleeping. If he's alive I wouldn't wanna do it . . . Like if he was awake, I mean.

Charlie's sentence completions illustrate his concrete views and their striking lack of complexity. He describes rules as "rules," and says "I sat down" when completing the stem "When they talked about sex." In addition:

Men are lucky because "their men."

Being with other people "Feels good."

Education "is to learn things."

Related to his impoverished perceptions are Charlie's intense judgments and stereotypes. At the end of the interview, Charlie proclaims his scorn for kids who deviate from "normal":

INTERVIEWER: Are there any things you hope you won't be like, maybe you want to be sure you won't be like?

CHARLIE: Yeah. . . . One of those kids . . . hippies. They're slobs and stuff. They're like sloppy, weird. They dress weird, they act weird. They have a mind of their own or . . . something.

These unwavering opinions are fueled by Charlie's doubts about his own adequacy, attractiveness, and acceptability to others. During the interview Charlie speaks about his unhappiness and isolation. His concerns with normality and his harsh criticism of adults and teenagers who are different reflect his own self-loathing, laid bare in his sentence completions:

When I am with a woman "I feel normal."

Usually he felt that sex "was normal."

My main problem is "that I'm ugly."

Sometimes he wished that he was "big."

Charlie's fixed ideas are unmistakable when it comes to sex roles:

A man's job is "to do the dirty work."

Women are lucky because "they do nothing."

A wife should "clean the dishes."

When his wife asked him to help with the housework "he said later."

A man should always "Be the leader."

The worst thing about being a man is "going with your wife shopping."

Like the other teenagers who are arrested in their development, Charlie is explicitly and pervasively aware of aggression, loss of control, and punishment. He experiences harsh and chaotic feelings, and violent images. While he does not express these feelings directly in his behavior, he gives them clear voice in his sentence completions:

If my mother "was crazy."

When a child will not join in group activities "He is punished."

Crime and delinquency could be halted if "guns were taken away."

A good father "is the kind that hits."

My conscience bothers me if "someone killed my friend."

CHARLIE'S FAMILY

Charlie is the younger of two children. He portrays his older sister, about to graduate from high school, as inconsiderate, one more oppressor:

She's pushy. Like she teaches ballet, dancing and stuff. And I got some records, she takes 'em without permission. (*giggles*) And then she brought it back one day. It was all scratched up. One side. I got mad and I was screaming. I was screaming, "Why'd you take it without my permission?" She goes, "Tough" (*nervous giggle*) and I go, "I'll take your record. I'll scratch it and I'll play it on my old record player. I'll scratch it." (*giggles*)

Charlie did not carry out his threatened retribution. Even more offensive are his sister's ways of excluding him from her current life or future plans: "She always talks to my mother about everything." Most salient in Charlie's joint description of his parents is that "they scream at each other." His mother often confronts and screams at him about his messy room. But Charlie's overriding perception is of how she excludes him in favor of his sister:

Yeah, we [Charlie and his mother] get along okay, but she, she usually talks to my sister all the time, like if, if I want something, she'll just keep talking to my sister. She'll ignore me in a way, just keep talking and talking. I get mad and go, "Get out." I don't talk to her . . . to hell with her, and I throw something.

It is when Charlie receives low grades in school that his mother becomes more attentive and "pushy." She then punished him: "Like if I get a bad report, they get mad and I have to stay in the room. Have to go to bed earlier. I can't go out. I can't put TV on or anything."

Mrs. Brown, thirty-nine years old, is a secretary who left college after the first two years. In contrast to Charlie, her development is at the conformist level. Yet her sentence completions are extremely uneven, varying widely in their thoughtfulness and complexity. Some responses, simple and terse, are reminiscent of Charlie's:

Raising a family "takes a lot of work."

When they avoided me "I felt badly."

If my mother "were here we would go out for a drive."

When people are helpless "they need a helping hand."

At times she worried about "her health."

But Mrs. Brown also expresses more subtle and articulate views:

My father "was a very successful, fair, and generous man."

Rules are "an important part of life and the order of things."

When a child will not join in group activities "he should not be pushed, he must take his own time."

I am a "woman, mother, executive secretary, and friend to many."

Mrs. Brown has clear views about right, wrong, and correct behavior:

What gets me in trouble is "sometimes being too truthful."

A pregnant woman "should take care of herself."

A wife should "try her best to care for her husband and family."

A good mother "should always be there when the children need her."

My conscience bothers me if "I don't call my mother at least once a day."

A woman should always "be proud to be a woman."

One source of Charlie's experience of his mother as "pushy" may be related to her strong moral convictions and her unease about anyone who does not meet her standards. She is also a likely source of Charlie's harsh judgments and stereotypes.

Charlie describes a more relaxed and positive relationship with his father, who is less "pushy." They rarely argue. Various outings, such as fishing and boating trips, characterize his experience with Mr. Brown. His father is also concerned about Charlie's school difficulties, but "he don't like push it as much." Mr. Brown is a forty-five-year-old carpenter who completed high school and then attended technical school in the evenings. Although he functions at the same level of ego development (conformist) as his wife, Mr. Brown's responses reveal different, more complex themes. What is most apparent is his devotion to and seeming joy in family life, consistent with Charlie's descriptions of his relationship with his father. The importance of the family for Mr. Brown is evident in his sentence completions:

Raising a family "can be lots of joy as long as there is love."

A man's job "is to work, care, and help his family and enjoy it."

Women are lucky because "they can be home with their children, and this is great."

A good father "is one who participates in all family matters."

A wife should "be a good person to her family and friends."

My father and I "were good friends."

If I had more money "I'd take my in-laws on vacations."

Enhancing the pleasure he experiences with his family is Mr. Brown's interest in understanding others, his flexibility, and his openness to new experiences:

When a child will not join in group activities "it can mean he is left alone during home life."

When they avoided me "I just turned and found another group."

The thing I like about myself is "that I laugh most things off and try to do most joyous things."

Being with other people "is always an education."

When people are helpless "they should look for the easiest way to do things."

Rules are "meant to be discussed."

When they talked about sex "I dive right in."

Men are lucky because "they can try all types of work."

When I am criticized "I listen, that's all."

Such flexibility and openness stand in stark contrast to Mrs. Brown's rigid convictions about right and wrong, good and bad. Along with his willingness to take in new experiences, Mr. Brown reveals self-doubts, vulnerabilities, and yearnings:

My conscience bothers me if "I leave my work knowing there's an error."

What gets me in trouble "is that I may say the wrong thing at the wrong time."

A man should "always be ready for anything."

Sometimes he wished that "he could give me much more."

I feel sorry "that I couldn't get a complete education."

I can't stand people who "are over-educated."

The sharp differences between Charlie's parents parallel those between parents of other arrested adolescents. Through the teenager's descriptions, and through the parent's own sentence completions, one parent consistently emerges as harsher, more inclined toward fixed judgments, and less endowed with empathy. In the Brown family, it is Mr. Brown who is more relaxed and relates more easily to Charlie, while Mrs. Brown is the harsher parent.

CHARLIE WITHIN HIS FAMILY

Mrs. Brown dominates family discussions, ever poised to cut them off abruptly the moment she concludes that Charlie and her husband agree with her. Her voice of certainty is always audible. In the very first discussion, for instance, Mrs. Brown leads the group with her aggressive questioning, dismissing any answers that differ from hers. She and Charlie have decided that if Heinz doesn't love his wife, he should not steal the drug for her. Mr. Brown thinks he should:

MOTHER: First of all, is it right to steal?

FATHER: No. No, it's not right to steal. No but does it make a difference if . . . he doesn't love his wife? That's the question.

MOTHER: Should he steal if he does love his wife?

FATHER: The particular story with the drugs. (*Charlie laughs in embarrassment; and then Mother laughs*) That's what I'm talking about. I'm not talking about stealing a fountain pen. (*Charlie laughs*) I'm talking about stealing a drug to cure a person. Never mind his wife, it's just a human being.

MOTHER: (*interrupting, with vehemence*) So you should steal, so you should steal?

FATHER: If no one is gonna help you . . . (*Charlie laughs*)

MOTHER: He went to everybody he knew.

FATHER: They're gonna let her die—

MOTHER: (*interrupting*) Which, which.

FATHER: Well, he went to the wrong people. (*laughing*)

MOTHER: (*laughing*) There were agencies. The drug wasn't proven—

FATHER: (*interrupting*) Yes.

MOTHER: Wasn't on the market. How did they know this would even help the person?

FATHER: Well, (*mumbles*) 'cause he's gonna take (*Charlie laughs*)

MOTHER: (*interrupts*) Did other, did other doctors (*laughs*) say that it would? What would happen if he stole the drug and the wife died anyway? (*Charlie laughs boisterously*)

FATHER: (*to Charlie*) What are you laughing for?

CHARLIE: You.

Mrs. Brown attacks her husband, who is opposing her. By undermining and embarrassing her husband, behavior not at all apparent in Charlie's description of her, she probably discourages Charlie from taking such risks as being self-assertive or defying her ideas or wishes. If, through such actions, his relationship with her will be jeopardized or he'll be humiliated, the safer course is to remain submissive and not to experiment with new thoughts or actions. Charlie participates at moments when he is unmistakably allied with his mother, a no-risk situation. His clearest communications are bursts of laughter, signals usually directed toward his father and in concert with Mrs. Brown's disdain for her husband's thinking. That disdain is clearly heard in their discussion of Joey, the newspaper boy, and breaking promises to strangers:

MOTHER: (*to father*) Well, you just said you wouldn't [keep a promise]. The question was would you keep . . . a promise to someone you might never see again. . . . If you make a promise you should keep it, shouldn't you?

FATHER: If I made the promise, yeah.

MOTHER: All right, well you made—

FATHER: (*interrupting*) I'm sayin', I wouldn't promise someone. I wouldn't make any promises. (*Charlie laughs*)

MOTHER: (*laughs*) No, no, no, no, no! But this question said you *did* make the promise.

FATHER: Oh . . . okay.

MOTHER: You weren't listening.

FATHER: Okay, that's what it was. (*laughs*)

MOTHER: I'd hate to have you on a jury. (*laughs*)

FATHER: (*laughing*) They'd never finish the case, that's for sure. You'd probably throw it out of court.

Having made her point and told her husband how inept he would be on a jury, Mrs. Brown now turns to him and Charlie for their revised answers about whether they would break a promise to a stranger:

MOTHER: (*to Charlie*) All right. What do you say, should you keep the promise?

CHARLIE: Yeah.

MOTHER: (*to father*) And would you say the same?

FATHER: Same. (*mother laughs*)

Mr. Brown is aware of his wife's forceful positions and her drive to get the family to support her conclusions:

INTERVIEWER: [*to family, following the discussion*] You worked it out?
FATHER: She worked me out. (*whole family laughs*)

Mrs. Brown acknowledges her control of the evening's discussions and justifies her role in terms of what she sees as her careful consideration of the issues being discussed. Even in this self-reflective moment, she levels more criticism at both Charlie and Mr. Brown:

MOTHER: So I seem to be the domineering, overpowering factor in all this because mainly, I think, it's basically that I am thinking more about it [the dilemmas]. They [her husband and Charlie] they're just (*snaps fingers*) quickly whipping off something in their mind and . . . I'm . . . weighing things a little more so, and I don't really mean to change their opinions. I give my opinions and they say, "Oh wow, gee, I guess you're right."
FATHER: Right, her opinion does sound a little better. (*Charlie laughs*)

Mr. Brown's reply to his wife's critical observation of his "whipping off" answers, and the need for her therefore to exert forceful, thoughtful influence upon the family, serves as an important reminder that both he and Charlie may *invite* her dominant voice to shape their more amorphous ideas and perceptions. If Mrs. Brown comes forward with her clear opinions, how can Charlie or Mr. Brown be "wrong"? Mr. Brown voices misgivings about the extent of his education and the nature of his work; Charlie feels inferior at school. Neither would like to expose himself still further. When Mrs. Brown fearlessly dives into the fray, they are spared exposing themselves as any more inadequate or wanting than they already feel.

Charlie is the most passive member of these family discussions. When he does participate, it is usually in the form of one- or two-word answers, or laughter at his father. He is undoubtedly reluctant to express his ideas in this public setting and wants his mother to take over, probably fearful of her sharp words should he say something "stupid." While we cannot simply assume that her dominant style has "caused" Charlie's developmental arrest, we can more plausibly suspect that her overpowering responses are triggered by his relative silence and seeming inadequacy.[1] Moreover, her responses and his father's self-effacing expressions may sustain Charlie's arrested development. Charlie has limited space to explore, to experiment. Witnessing his father's fate when expressing a new idea or sharing a casual observation or notion may give Charlie pause before venturing forward with a new idea. A telling moment occurs when, in a rare episode, Charlie opposes his parents. Like many of the teenagers in our study, Charlie does not think that Officer Brown should "tell" on his friend Heinz. But, in contrast to most of the other families, the Brown family rushes through discussion of this disagreement:

MOTHER: All right, Charlie, now even though [Officer Brown] didn't know for sure this was the person who did that—

FATHER: (*interrupting*) No, he knew.

MOTHER: No, he didn't. At that point, he didn't know for sure.

FATHER: He saw Mr. Heinz leaving the drugstore.

MOTHER: (*mumbles*) Okay, but he didn't know why he was leaving the drugstore. That was circumstantial evidence.

FATHER: But when he read the paper the next day—[*Charlie mumbles.*]

MOTHER: (*interrupting father*) When he read the paper the next day . . . So it was his duty and as a citizen to just let the police know what he saw. And that—

FATHER: (*interrupting*) As a police officer, it's his duty, more so than as a citizen.

MOTHER: Right . . . and, yeah, he hadda let them know what he saw. And . . . then when they question they could find out from others if he was the one that broke in, or if he wasn't the one who broke in.

FATHER: Right.

MOTHER: (*to Charlie*) So do you agree that he shouldn't have reported it? Because he was, seeing, the same—

CHARLIE: (*interrupting*) Yeah, yeah.

MOTHER: I guess it wasn't that terrible. It was a robbery, but what if it had been a murder, someone who was killed and you saw someone in the area. Shouldn't you report even if the person might not have done it? You should always report whoever you see in the area—

CHARLIE: (*interrupts*) Mmmm, mmm

MOTHER: —because the person might have been the one who did it, right?

CHARLIE: Yup.

MOTHER: Then (*laughs*) knock on the door [to indicate that the family has reached agreement].

FATHER: Man, that's a hell of a ten minutes [time family was told they had to discuss the disagreement]. We're breakin' the records.

Mr. Brown recognizes the speed with which the family has resolved this difference. Charlie rapidly changes his position after his mother's barrage. Charlie's rare expression of thoughts or feelings is precisely the opposite of his mother's style. It is likely that Charlie welcomes her strong participation here, quickly settling the issues for him. We cannot be sure about this, since he says little about his thoughts or feelings. But Mr. Brown does acknowledge that his wife's opinions "sound a little better." Mr. Brown and possibly Charlie may believe that their reflections, interpretations, and conclusions are inferior to Mrs. Brown's. Rather than expose their inferior ideas, the best solution is for them to give free rein to her, especially since this is exactly what she wants anyway. Separateness and self-assertion, aspects of individuated relationships, are not discernible in these exchanges among the Browns. Mrs. Brown asserts *herself* through repeated monologues, as she powerfully speaks out her beliefs, overriding or perhaps taking over for her son and husband.

With respect to more specific family interactions, Charlie makes few enabling speeches. Rarely does he focus, encourage the family to stay with the point of the discussion, or empathize with one of his parents. On the few occasions that he does speak in these ways, explaining or showing curiosity, it is toward his mother. Knowing as we do of her greater involvement in the family discussions and in the general life of the family, we can understand his enabling efforts vis-à-vis his mother as a response to her strong, sometimes overwhelming, presence in his ongoing discourse with her. In contrast, Charlie is more constraining toward his father, often speaking in distracting and devaluing ways to him. This pattern is consistent with our observations of Charlie's mocking laughter toward his father during the rare moments when Charlie even communicates with him. The idea that Charlie may "welcome" his mother's opinionated loquacity receives additional support through our observations of his constraining and enabling interactions. Charlie does little to distract or in any other way obstruct her. Rather, as if to encourage her, he frequently silences his father, mocking, interrupting, laughing, and being generally intolerant of him. We see here the strong effect of his mother. Charlie's negative stance toward his father in these discussions is surprising, given the warm quality of their outings together.

As we might expect, Mrs. Brown is more enabling toward Charlie than toward her husband. When speaking to Charlie she explains, attempts to focus, expresses curiosity, and tries to return him to the point of the discussion if he has strayed. Yet neither she nor her husband is accepting and empathic in responding to Charlie. There are at least two possible reasons for this. Charlie is a boy of few words. Consequently, he offers few opportunities for either parent to be accepting or empathic toward his positions or feelings. And when Charlie does express himself, it is often through tangential comments that are annoying or bewildering—hardly remarks that would elicit empathic responses from either parent.

ELLEN FOSTER

Ellen, a fourteen-year-old girl, had been in the hospital for close to one year when we first met her. Before being admitted to the children's unit, she had spent several months in a juvenile home. In her interview she poignantly swings from describing feelings of having no control over events in her life to insisting that she is in charge. Accompanying her swings is her pervasive anger, directed at both the interviewer and surrounding adults. Ellen's history is replete with episodic impulsiveness and confusion about it, a confusion barely disguised by bravado about being in control. Besides control, a second major theme for Ellen is her yearning for certainty. Intolerance of uncertainty is a salient characteristic of adolescents and adults who have arrested at the earliest levels of ego development, and Ellen is no exception. Her amazingly positive stance toward the hospital is closely tied to the structure that the hospital program provides:

> [The time in the hospital] just went by so fast, y'know, it does. Times goes by fast here, 'cause you do the same things, day after day, really. . . . Y'know, you get to go to the caf [cafeteria], whatever, you know. Go to school, use your privileges. . . . You have, like, all your time scheduled up, when you're free . . . it just goes by so fast, I don't even look at my day when it's over, you know.

And at the end of every day, Ellen thinks, "What have I got to do tomorrow?" Ellen does not directly acknowledge any appreciation of the benefits of this scheduling. Rarely does she offer positive statements about the hospital or anything else. Yet she devotes more time and energy to her description of the hospital and all its activities than to any other topic discussed during her interview.

Within the highly scheduled time slots are objectionable activities. Being in school with considerably younger kids, even "six-year-olds," is offensive to Ellen. She will do her best to avoid school. Even more distressing are cognitive therapy activities that involve "shapes." Ellen feels that doing "shapes" is absurd and irrelevant to her school work. She resists mightily:

> Now I'm not going to do shapes, and then go back into regular school. It's not going to help me any, 'cause they don't do shapes. [It's] like a memory thing or something. . . . I think they could do something else to make it useful, instead of just . . . that kind of stuff.

Ellen's reaction to the "shapes" accurately reflects how she handles most distress in her life. Blending denial and action, Ellen moves to wipe out the offending agent:

ELLEN: The point is, I *don't* have to do them [shapes], so I just dropped it out of my mind. . . .

INTERVIEWER: When it first came up, do you remember how you felt about doing shapes?

ELLEN: I used to tip over the table, and walk out of the room.

INTERVIEWER: How did you feel?

ELLEN: That I wasn't going to do them. . . . Pissed.

Her tenuous control over feelings and impulses is visible in many contexts. In written form it appears in her completion of the sentence, When I get mad: "I walk out of the house." More dramatically, months before her admission Ellen became upset with the judge who had ordered her back to the juvenile home. She first verbally abused him and then tipped over his table. Her memories of her mother's being "unable to handle me" may also be colored by her awareness of an inability to control herself, as well as a wish for her mother to take charge and provide structure.

Ellen's confusion over who's "in charge" illuminates the centrality of self-control in her life. On the one hand, she firmly believes that she will control her own destiny after leaving the hospital: "It's not how I would *like* things to be; it's how things are *gonna* be" (her emphasis). Joined with this view is her opposing idea that there is no choice on her part. The court and the hospital dictate her actions, set the course of her life, and keep her in her place.

Not surprisingly, school is an arena for these conflicts. Ellen consistently stays away from the hospital school, as she did from her old neighborhood school. When asked about "regular school," she first tells the interviewer, "I never went." Then she qualifies her answer: "It wasn't that I never went; I never *lasted* too long." She would skip classes and then be suspended for skipping them, which would lead to more days away from school. Ellen was selective, skipping only particular classes. The principle behind her selectivity had to do with "feeling good" and "doing good." She showed up at certain classes "'cause I liked those [classes] and I could do good in them. . . . It's not that I felt good, it's like, I like the teachers, and I, um . . . got along with them good."

When asked about the classes that she skipped, Ellen describes both her deficits and her dislike of the work:

> I could *never* do it. I just didn't like them or anything. . . . It was just never . . . I just never got interested in English or social studies.

As the interviewer persists in questioning her about school, Ellen becomes visibly impatient, insisting on the irrelevance of these courses for her. Her protest is reminiscent of her feelings about "shapes":

> I don't think those subjects are important to me. . . . Social Studies—what is—*social studies?* I don't want to learn about the past . . . you know? I don't wanna . . . Indians or whatever— whatever. I don't want to learn about it.

Leaving classes, and then schools, began long before social studies. Starting in the first grade, Ellen was "kicked out" of or left four different schools, attending special education classes for part of that time.

Ellen ran away from her family several times over the same number of years:

> . . . 'cause I didn't like it at home, so I just left. . . . I went to a halfway house for thirty days. I left my house when I was eight years old, and went to a foster home, till I was nine and a half.

In Ellen's eyes, the cause of these difficulties is her mother:

> My mother couldn't handle me . . . she didn't know how to deal with me. She just couldn't handle me. . . . I never stayed in school. You know, my mother [wouldn't think] "What's this eight-year-old kid doing?" You know . . . I don't get along with my mother.

Ellen sees her departures from school and home as part of her life-style. While she may at times wish her mother had intervened, she rarely acknowledges any conflicts or turmoil about those experiences.

It is through an indirect route, Ellen's sentence completions, that we see some awareness of inner conflicts—her own and others':

At times she worried about "Me, and where I was."

My main problem is "School, and staying at home."

Sometimes she wished that "Went to school and stayed home."

Rarely does Ellen speak of having several different feelings at once or of feeling sympathetic to anyone. Within the interview, while Ellen grudgingly acknowledges that she has "a lot of different moods," it is anger that she usually points to:

INTERVIEWER: What do you remember about being in an angry mood?

ELLEN: What do—I mean when . . . hitting someone. . . . I've hit people that said "Hi, Ellen," 'cause it was early in the morning, and I ain't one of them kind of people that react to other people in the morning pleasantly. . . . It was just that I didn't feel like listening to them.

While describing this mood and her behaviors, Ellen becomes increasingly testy toward the interviewer, eventually tuning him out and not responding to his questions ("I dunno").

Asked about her friends in the hospital, Ellen worries about being critical and refuses to talk about them:

There're so many, I don't want to even name them all. . . .
Friends are friends. I don't judge them good or bad. . . . Friends are friends. I know a lot of people in here [the hospital], and I know a lot of people out there, and they're just friends.

As the interview continues, Ellen's irritation and impatience with the interviewer mount. She says less and less, while showing growing sarcasm and direct annoyance toward him, at the same time denying that she is at all upset. Visible within the interview, then, is one of Ellen's basic mood swings: from irritation to feelings of inadequacy and helplessness, followed by withdrawal. In the past, similar situations have led to her lashing out or walking out. In the interview her withdrawal and irritation are sporadic. On occasion Ellen "returns" when telling of her juvenile home experiences and legal entanglements. These descriptions are factual, and she generates them, in contrast to her not answering those meaningless, abstract questions asking her to "describe a friend, a close friend." Because that subject is not as ambiguous or threatening to her, she is able to remain engaged with the interviewer while portraying her life in these homes or her skirmishes with the law. It is as if there are certain "classes" within the interview that she is willing to attend and others from which she bolts, unwilling or unable to tolerate the painful feelings that they trigger.

Ellen's view of her future is also constricted. She describes a "plan" to leave the hospital in the summer to "get myself back together, and then try school again." But she bridles at the suggestion that this was planned with her doctor: "It's been planned by me! I'm the one who said it." Ellen goes on to portray her vision of the future, expecting to attend nursing school in order to become a pediatric or intensive care nurse. But the vision is flat, without details or texture. Her daydream is of *one* career path—no deviations or questions, period. And its origins, she argues, are "uh, that I was in a hospital once."

While much of the way Ellen views herself, her relationships with others, and her future is consistent with her early stage of ego development, this arrested development cannot "explain" her behavioral lability, runaway episodes, and the disturbing cycles of anger and anxiety. Turning now to her parents and her experience within her family, we look at the role that these other forces, family relationships and interactions, may play in Ellen's feelings and behaviors.

ELLEN'S FAMILY

Ellen's descriptions of her parents and brother are terse. She is clear about one possibly very important fact, that she was adopted. Telling the interviewer that her mother "couldn't handle me," she quickly adds, "She's not my real mother . . . she adopted me." Possibly, behind her view that her adoptive mother "couldn't handle" her is the belief that her "real mother" could not handle her, thus leading to her adoption.

Ellen remembers her adoptive parents as far back as when she was one and one-half years old. And she adds that she was in numerous foster homes before then. Her description of her mother is harsh and one-dimensional: "She's a bitch . . . she bitches all the time; I'm sick of her, too." When the interviewer asks what she bitches about, Ellen is evasive: "I dunno . . . 'cause I don't even listen to her when she does." Ellen alternates between describing her mother's character and her mother's complaints: "It's not that she bitches; she's just a bitch, and I hate her." In the year before coming to the hospital, Ellen had run away from home, had lived in many foster homes, and finally had been detained at a youth detention center. At the time of the interview she was seeing her mother every few months and becoming aware of changes in her feelings: "I—I'm getting to like her now . . . she's giving in to me."

Her sentence completions both parallel these perceptions and add others that she has not articulated or consciously experienced:

If my mother "would understand me more."

My mother and I "fight all the time."

When she thought about her mother "She tried to clear it out of her mind."

A good mother "Is a lucky one."

Mrs. Foster, fifty-two years old, is a high school graduate who works as a secretary. Her ego development is at the self-aware transition, clearly higher than Ellen's. Through her sentence completions, Mrs. Foster portrays a picture of burden, possibly in reaction to the difficult course that Ellen's life has taken:

Raising a family "A rewarding, but difficult task."

A good mother "Loves her family and sacrifices for them."

Sometimes she wished that "Life was easier."

At the same time, Mrs. Foster conveys her intense involvement with family members and dedication to family roles.

If my mother "Was happy, I was happy."

My mother and I "Understand and support each other."

When she thought of her mother, she "Saw inner beauty."

My father "Was always home and dependable."

A woman feels good "When members of family compromise, etc."

A wife should "Share all phases of family raising."

Mrs. Foster is at a loss when responding to stems that require more direct self-description. For instance, she completely omits answers to two stems: "The thing I like about myself" and "The worst thing about being a woman."

Through her other responses, we gain glimpses of her concerns over being hurt and hurting others:

When they avoided me "I was hurt."

My conscience bothers me "If I hurt other people or am dishonest."

I feel sorry "for less fortunate people."

Control, a theme so central to Ellen, is also problematic for Mrs. Foster. She feels that rules are "important and necessary," and that her strong will is what gets her in trouble. She asserts that her main problem is an "inability to be consistent," and when she is mad "I talk loud, and repeat or recall past experiences."

Other facets of Mrs. Foster's self-portrait touch on the importance of depending on other people, her inhibitions, and self-resignation. It is possible that these motifs underlie the importance she ascribes to being with and pleasing others. We already know how much significance she attaches to family members. She extends this attitude to the larger social world:

Being with other people "is important to me."

When I am with a man "I depend on him."

For a woman, a career is "Important, but not essential."

If I can't get what I want "I assume it wasn't meant for me."

Ellen's feelings about her father are less intense and less severely critical. Although she characterizes him as "okay" in her sentence completions, she is more enthusiastic as she speaks about him, emphasizing his capacity to bypass struggles with her:

My father's excellent. . . . He just—doesn't really care what goes on. I never get in a struggle with him, so, I mean, there's not reason for him to give in.

Mr. Foster is fifty-one years old, a high school graduate, and a technical artist. His ego development level is postconformist, higher than that of either Ellen or her mother. His sentence completion responses, which are more differentiated than those of his daughter or wife, depict a man with many uncertainties about himself and fragile self-esteem. In contrast to Ellen and her mother, whose self-doubts are more implicit and have to be inferred, Mr. Foster clearly voices nagging doubts about himself:

When they avoided me "I wondered what was wrong with me."

When I am with a woman "I usually feel nervous, shy, and unsure."

I feel sorry "About not being able to really communicate our feelings towards our daughter."

At times he worried about "not being intelligent, and worthy of his responsibilities towards his family."

What gets me in trouble is "Not being knowledgeable about the things that are essential in my life."

My main problem is "I can't express myself adequately to be understood or convincing."

When I am criticized "I feel insulted and inadequate."

Sometimes he wished that "He could live his life over."

Mr. Foster's responses are colored by sadness and regret, which he traces to the loss of his own parents:

If my mother "had lived, I expect my life would today be considerably different."

When he thought of his mother "He was sad and depressed because he lost her."

My father and I "Did not have a significant relationship, because of his early departure from the family."

In addition to his self-doubts and sadness, Mr. Foster is preoccupied with control and rules, matters so dear to Ellen and her mother. Mr. Foster stresses the virtues of rules and structure:

A man's job "is usually a difficult endeavor, requiring discipline and fortitude."

The thing I like about myself is "An ability to discipline and control the activities of my life."

Crime and delinquency could be halted if "Parents were more aware of children's activities, and more disciplinary."

A good father "is one who tempers his love and concern with discipline."

Rules are "intended for a specific purpose."

In contrast to his ample reflections about these benefits, Mr. Foster provides only a fleeting picture of the difficulties brought on by rules:

Women are lucky because "usually, she isn't required to do the physical tasks of males."

Men are lucky because "their freedom is a little less boundaried than women."

The worst thing about being a man is "for the man to work every day."

More indirectly, Mr. Foster also expresses discomfort and unease around control of sexual and self-centered feelings. He feels "embarrassed" when there is talk of sex and cannot "stand" people who "are selfish, and concerned only for themselves."

It is curious, in light of Mr. Foster's strong comments about the importance of rules and structure, that Ellen and he have not had—in her eyes—the pitched battles that she portrays with her mother. Possibly his commitment to rules and structure has led to a thoughtful and consistent stance with her, which Ellen may welcome. Moreover, his differentiated view of himself and others probably allows him to respond with more flexibility and empathy to her challenges. There is an openness in his thinking and, perhaps even more significantly, a tolerance of ambiguity that he conveys in several sentence completions:

Raising a family "is a responsibility of unknown success."

When a child will not join in group activities "there is the indication of psychological difficulties."

Being with other people is "social and usually a learning experience."

Drawing upon their own self-descriptions (their sentence completions) and Ellen's observations, we see that Mr. and Mrs. Foster differ dramatically. Ellen's mother is inhibited, with highly conventional ways of perceiving herself and others. She expresses many self-doubts, especially concerning her own sense of inner control. Ellen's father is sad and regretful. At the same time he holds complex perceptions of himself and others, together with a belief in growth and openness. It is Mr. Foster who is highly responsive to feelings and thoughts within the family. From what we have seen and heard, it is unlikely that his wife or Ellen expresses such qualities in their relationships. Distance and obliviousness to others' worlds are more likely to characterize their experiences with each other and with him.

The fourth family member is Ellen's older brother, sixteen years old at the time of the interview. She gives little information about him: "I don't even consider him—he's, yeah, get along good (*said list-*

lessly). . . . Got his own stuff to worry about." She does not answer when asked whether her brother has also had legal difficulties. After telling the interviewer that her visits with him "go good," she refuses to go any further in describing him or the visits: "There's nothing to talk about!" Both parents are also silent about Ellen's brother in their sentence completions, possibly reflecting the centrality of Ellen in their lives.

ELLEN WITHIN HER FAMILY

The troubled, brittle relationships so often pointed to by Ellen and her parents are immediately apparent in the family's discussions, in which Ellen participates grudgingly and irritably. The most heated exchanges are with her mother, whom she frequently criticizes and harangues, attempting to change her opinions. Early in the discussion Ellen points out her mother's flaws, as her mother offers an example to elaborate a particular point or expresses an idea. For instance, after Mrs. Foster describes "feeling compassion, feeling sorry . . . a feeling that sometimes overpowers me . . . ," and then hesitates about her reasoning, Ellen ridicules her: "Well, I think . . . you—it's just that you have a soft heart . . . you're soft." And then Ellen goes on to compare her mother with a teacher whom she does not respect, "down in school." The barrage of criticism that Ellen unleashes later in the family discussion is predictable from her earlier descriptions of her mother.

Turning to Mrs. Foster, we expect to find little, if any, openness to considering Ellen's feelings and thoughts. The family observations are certainly consistent with this prediction. In her responses to Ellen's confrontations, Mrs. Foster repeatedly sidesteps her daughter. She accepts Ellen's point and then completes her already begun example, or almost instantly deflects the discussion, introducing a totally new topic that takes the family off in a new direction. A striking dance between Ellen and her mother takes place over and over again: Ellen criticizes and her mother withdraws. After the first of these "disengagement cycles," Ellen presses to close the discussion, announcing that the family has reached "the conclusion." In a later occurrence of this cycle, Ellen is more direct with her mother, reminding her that she has dropped Ellen's point. She then presses Mrs. Foster to consider the critical remark that she is in the midst of evading. Ellen's attempt to refocus her mother only partially succeeds, as Mrs. Foster introduces yet another deflecting story. As we see in the following excerpt, Ellen copes with this repeated deflection by wanting to "conclude" or leave the discussion.

Mrs. Foster tells of how she once promised a stranger that she would bake for a charity bake sale. Every two weeks since then, to her dismay, the stranger has requested her continued involvement. Mrs. Foster still accedes to these requests, resulting in the delay or cancellation of other priorities, such as cleaning Ellen's room. Ellen is irritated by her mother's priorities:

ELLEN: You *do* too much for people.

MOTHER: But I thought, if you promised somebody, that you really should—it's important to me, a commitment.

ELLEN: Yeah, but you *promise* people too much. Not promise. I mean you do things for people too much.

MOTHER: Yeah . . . I just felt that way about it. But, uh, and then about some of the other questions that they [the family interviewers] asked us. What was some—do you remember some of the things . . . you have to [write to] finish the sentence? How do you feel about some of those things? Did you have to?

ELLEN: Yeah, I did that, like a month ago.

Father and mother then begin to give examples of the sentence stems, and in a moment Ellen jokes about their answers. But soon, and impatiently, Ellen returns to her previous point, one that her mother had stayed with only briefly:

ELLEN: I just said, I said if . . .

MOTHER: Yeah.

ELLEN: —that you do too much for people.

MOTHER: Right. I mean, that—or well, like, if you felt—

ELLEN: (*interrupting*) *I'm serious!*

Evading criticism once again, Mrs. Foster urges Ellen to weigh her reasoning carefully when she and Ellen disagree about something, such as "[school] courses that aren't going to lead you anywhere." Ellen becomes agitated and demands the "conclusion of the discussion."

There are several ways that we can interpret Mrs. Foster's episodic disengagement. One is that she is reacting to Ellen's long-standing hostility toward her, not wanting to cause any disruptions in the already fragile bond between her and her daughter, and possibly between Ellen and both parents. An alternative view is that this very pattern of disengagement and desire for surface harmony is what fuels Ellen's anger. She is aware of her mother's inaccessibility and her lack of attunement to many of Ellen's views. Ellen may well experience her mother's diversions as continued rejections or dismissals.

Mrs. Foster's attempts to achieve harmony are certainly consistent with the importance she attaches to tranquility and "good" feelings within the family. Later in the discussion, Mrs. Foster underlines her view about the significance of tolerance, respect and "congeniality":

FATHER: What was most important? You said one thing was to do things together, right?

MOTHER: Um-hum. To be able to, um, uh, discuss differences, I think is important . . . instead of just quietly being made to accept a thing. I think it's important to be able to feel secure enough with one another that—that you can express your opinion without somebody falling completely apart. (*Ellen groans*) I think it's important to have congeniality . . . tolerance of each other. Your opinions are very different from mine, but yours are not necessarily the . . . right or wrong ones. They are your opinions and own beliefs, and they should be respected as such.

Ellen follows her mother's elaborate opinion by announcing that she wants to end the discussion, and "get the lady [interviewer]," whereupon her mother becomes tentative and disappointed.

The asynchrony between Ellen and her mother is the most prominent feature of the family discussion. Mr. Foster usually supports and agrees with Ellen, or summarizes certain more abstract principles underlying her positions. Ellen hears support within these statements and does not, visibly, appreciate her father's more complex summaries of her ideas. She engages minimally with him during the discussion. In his exchanges with Mrs. Foster, the quality of "missing" one another is not evident, and Mr. Foster carefully ponders her points, often summarizing or drawing conclusions from his wife's ideas.

At first blush, we might think that these many episodes of non-engagement between Ellen and her mother reveal one family consequence of Ellen's arrested development. It is possible that Ellen's behavior is so demoralizing to her mother that a more enriched and engaged discussion is virtually impossible. Not so apparent is the answer to the other important question: To what extent has this dynamic—criticism/disengagement—*contributed* to Ellen's arrested development? Without a responsive, available mother, despite her father, have Ellen's vulnerabilities been exacerbated? Since there are several strong contenders for etiological primacy—the many early homes, school failures, temperamental vulnerabilities (irritability)—it would be foolhardy to argue for the family as a certain "cause"

of Ellen's arrested development. Yet we do know that the family pattern we see in this first year of observation was followed by later years of
continued arrest in Ellen's ego development, suggesting at the very
least that this family dynamic may sustain this path of development.

Alongside the obvious disengagement is a markedly higher level of
interaction between Ellen and her mother, in terms of *both* enabling
and constraining behaviors, than between Ellen and her father. Ellen
explains more to her mother and also distracts her more. With respect
to the overall rate of Ellen's speeches, then, her description of her
parents is borne out: intense involvement with her mother and minimal involvement with her more understanding father.

When we consider Ellen's parents, we see more symmetrical participation by mother and father as they explain and clarify ideas for her,
and are so clearly accepting of her contributions to the discussion.
Especially visible is her father in his efforts to guide the discussions
and in his curiosity about Ellen's views. Yet Ellen does not reciprocate.
These observations of Ellen and her family reveal a young adolescent
locked in a disappointing relationship with her mother and connected in a limited yet supportive way with her father.

MIKE WARY

Mike, a fourteen-year-old, had been hospitalized for eight months at
the time of his interview. He was one of the only patients who actually
asked to participate in the study. Such a direct request parallels his
account of how he "chose" to enter the hospital, after hospitalization
was recommended to him and his family by a school guidance counselor. Most of the patients implied or insisted that they had been
"tricked" into coming to the hospital, but Mike described his increasing panic and avoidance of school, climaxed by a violent suicide threat:

MIKE: Yeah, then they [his parents] brang me back [to school], and she
[his mother] told my coordinator and he almost went to the bath-
room in his pants. He was, uh, he said, "Oh, my God, he may be
suicidal. I don't want him in school."

INTERVIEWER: You scared him.

MIKE: Scared the life out of him, so he kicked me out of school. Told my
parents he didn't want me in here. He said, "I want him to have
psychiatric help." And my mother knew I wasn't serious. Before I
came in here [the hospital] my mother said, "Do you want to go
here?" If I would have said "no," I would have went back to school.

INTERVIEWER: So how come you said "yes"?

MIKE: Because I knew I needed the help, knew I did. I said, "I want to go into the hospital."

Besides his more direct requests (to be hospitalized, to join the project), a second distinctive characteristic of Mike is his preoccupation with violent thoughts and actions. At the start of the interview, he tells of the suicide threat that he made to his mother, frightening her and the coordinator. He held "a butcher knife" and announced, "I will kill myself if you force me to go to school." Before the butcher knife episode, Mike had punched a hole in the door at home. He had also imagined "blowing his [father's] head off" with his gun, and Mike had gone after his sister "with a gun one day." The incident with his sister illustrates the close connection that Mike makes between fear and violence. Angry at Mike for splashing her while they were doing the dishes, his sister went down to his room to tell him that she wouldn't continue to do chores with him. Mike knew that she was annoyed, and "after a while she gets on my nerves." He had anticipated her coming to his room and had tied up his large dog before opening the door, because he was worried that the dog might attack her:

MIKE: I don't trust my dog. I aim my gun at her [sister]; my dog might think she's an enemy and my dog went "ARGH." (*laughs*) My dog would go straight at her. . . . She came down to my room to tell me this [her quitting the dishes], flew open the door and I aimed the gun straight at her face.

INTERVIEWER: Wow!

MIKE: And she turned around and ran back.

This description by Mike is reminiscent of Ellen's preoccupation with controlling her impulses. What is different about Mike is his directly expressing these impulses, particularly aggressive ones, and the pleasure he takes in frightening his sister and others. To some extent, the violence is driven by his worries about his own safety:

INTERVIEWER: So what are you doing with a gun now?

MIKE: Me? Run around causin' trouble.

INTERVIEWER: (laughs) Where do you . . . ?

MIKE: (*making shuffling noises*) In my room (*emphatically*). And anyone that goes in there (*laughs in a sinister way*), they don't walk out in one piece.

INTERVIEWER: Oh, you really like to keep your room pretty safe.

MIKE: Yeah, I just put my gun with my dog. Who's gonna go in there?

INTERVIEWER: A lot of protection between your gun and your dog huh?

Mike's few friendships are also colored by violence and fear. With much wariness, he tells the interviewer about his friend who deals drugs. With some pride, Mike describes how the police fruitlessly searched his house for clues to the whereabouts of that friend. Delighted, Mike watched the strain and frustration of his parents and the police.

Mike traces his difficulties back to preadolescent years. School experiences became increasingly disturbing before high school:

MIKE: I was getting sick of it [school]. But I didn't stay out. But in the seventh grade I started skipping . . . it started driving me insane. When I was younger, didn't really mind it. I loved school anyways. . . . But as I got older, I got fed up, and I said, "I'm sick of it." And that was that.

INTERVIEWER: What did you get fed up with?

MIKE: Well, for a while school was . . . just like fun and all that. Sixth grade was like leading to high school . . . fifth grade to sixth grade It's a big change; not like fourth to fifth in elementary . . . when you go to the fifth in one school and the sixth in another school.

The combination of changing schools, changing classes, and taking more demanding classes was more than Mike could tolerate:

MIKE: Like in fifth grade, we just sit in class and we'd have maybe four subjects with one teacher, and one with another, and two with another. But we really didn't have to change classes, but then here we had to.

INTERVIEWER: Was that one of the things that bothered you, changing classes?

MIKE: I wouldn't even know the teacher that well. I tried to know one of them and I'd forget about the other one. It just didn't work out. . . . The main thing was in the seventh grade I had a real—one of those teachers you don't like. I had her for English, math. . . . There are forty-five-minute periods. . . . I had her for three different things each day . . . and after a while I got sick of it.

INTERVIEWER: What didn't you like about her?

MIKE: She kept yelling at me.

Mike became more and more aware of his difficulties at school but found no way to correct them.

MIKE: Like after a while, I figured I got some kind of problem

INTERVIEWER: Yeah

MIKE: She [the teacher] doesn't realize it, but I do. The problem is gettin' to me . . . mixing me up with my work, and she kept giving it to me. She gave all the kids a lot of work, and I couldn't keep up with it. My grades were going down and I started quittin' . . . (pauses) after the winter, and then I quit.

Before quitting, Mike told his parents that he couldn't manage all the work, that he was forgetting work in one class and unable to understand it in another, yet "they [his parents] wouldn't listen to me." Intensifying his feelings of failure and helplessness at school was his experience of not being heard by his parents:

MIKE: Yeah, I tried talking to 'em. While they were nice, they wouldn't really talk to me about it, not really until one time. And I said, "Hey, they don't listen to me, I don't listen to them." They say they would listen to me about my work, and I can't do it, and they won't listen. I'm not going to school. . . . Okay, they'd say, "I'll talk to you," and they never ended up talking to me.

Mike was failing more subjects and having more humiliating confrontations with his teachers. He responded by avoiding school and "hiding out" in his room when his parents thought he had left for school. Through an elaborate scheme of returning home after his father left him at the bus stop, going to a different level of the house where his room was, and disguising any noise he made to sound like his dog, Mike kept his whereabouts secret from his parents for long periods of time. The exhaustive secrecy and the panic that accompanied Mike's school failings highlight his way of handling distress. He "got fed up with school . . . and started skipping it." Mike views himself as disabled at school, victimized by his disability, and unable to receive help from his teachers (who embarrass him in class) or his parents (who do not listen to his concerns). Mike graphically depicts his "overloaded circuits" and confusions:

I knew something was going wrong, up here [points to his head], because there was something going wrong. . . . I have this stupid thing with the sun rays. They bother me. Like, I'm walking. The sun rays go into your eyes, you know, they go into your head . . . usually they don't disturb you. But with me they go and disturb my brain. I'm like, I was reading a story. I really got fed up with school, I couldn't take it, I'd be reading a story.

Right in the middle of the story I couldn't remember what I was going to say; computer, when it's overloaded, you push a button. All the stuff it has in it blanks out, becomes very black too. . . where I am and I don't remember. . . . It's just like it blanks out and I don't remember.

In Mike, we see special characteristics associated with his ego development arrest: his image of his brain as fragile and vulnerable, a not very sturdy computer; his pleasure in threatening and frightening others. Together with these special features are those themes that characterize other adolescents with arrested ego development. Functioning at the lowest measurable level of ego development (impulsive), Mike's sentence completions touch on the basic issues of brittle impulse control, a morality of stark rights and wrongs, and lopsided social relationships based on power and weakness:

Crime and delinquency could be halted if "there is not as many drugs in the world."

When a child will not join in group activities "he will be restricted."

What gets me in trouble is "doing wrong things."

A man should always "have a gun."

Rules are "for the birds."

When they talked about sex "I was mad."

If I can't get what I want "I will yell."

When I am criticized "I walk away."

The worst thing about being a man is "to work so hard for so little."

Men are lucky because "they are strong."

Mike has a limited repertoire of ways to protect himself from outside assaults. He resorts to threats, using knives, guns, and his dog, and to hiding out in his room.

MIKE'S FAMILY

Mike is the oldest of four children. His younger sister, thirteen years old, is a full sister from his mother's first marriage. The two youngest siblings, his seven-year-old and six-year-old sisters, are half siblings, from his mother's second and current marriage. When Mike was between three and four, his mother left his father. At that time he wanted to stay with his father, but that was not allowed. He did not see his father again until he was five or six years old, since his father's car was repossessed and he said he wasn't coming, "'cause he couldn't get the car. Then after that I didn't see him. Then I said, 'Okay'."

When Mike was five years old, his mother remarried. Mike describes his mother as a moody, unhappy person who is currently in psychotherapy. He recalls her being "down on us kids" when she was depressed. He also tells the interviewer how irritated he gets with her:

> Some days I get pissed. She pisses me an awful lot. Not now, she used to. . . . Like at one point [motions as if to punch a hole through the wall], that's when I'm pissed at her. Thinking about it right now pisses me off.

Setting off much of his annoyance with his mother is her extreme irritability. Mike believes that this moodiness led to the break-up of his parents' marriage.

Mrs. Wary is thirty-six years old and works as a housewife. She has completed two years of college. Her ego development is at the self-aware stage, where there is a dawning awareness of inner rules and differences among people. Self-criticism, regrets, and unhappiness pervade her writings:

> I feel sorry "that I am unable to show most of the love and warmth that I have within. It embarrasses me, for some reason, to show these feelings."

> When I get mad "I have a tendency to lose my temper verbally, and if I can't play it out or show my anger, I hold grudges."

> My main problem is "sexual. My husband and I haven't had sex in four or five years."

> The worst thing about being a woman "is menstruating."

> Men are lucky because "they don't have to do housework."

Her "good feelings" are usually expressed separately from the more extensive unhappy and unpleasant feelings. At times she speaks of both sentiments at once:

> Being with other people "That I don't know frightens me. I'm extremely shy with strangers. On the other hand, when I am with friends I am extremely talkative and open."

The thing I like about myself is "that I am honest!!! I can also be very sympathetic towards others, and I'm very good at listening."

A pregnant woman "should be experiencing one of the most wonderful times of her life. i.e. Feeling the fetus more, and anticipating of the new little one."

A woman feels good when "she (married, I assume) is shown love. All women should feel good when praised and/or complimented."

Mrs. Wary's attitudes and feelings toward her family convey sadness and strong yearnings:

My mother and I "disagree about most things and do much arguing."

My father "is dead."

A woman should "be loving, understanding, supportive toward her husband. Also, she should be a good sexmate."

A good mother "is one that will be considered a friend or pal by her children as they are growing up and right through adulthood."

Mrs. Wary writes conspicuously complex, many-sided responses alongside simple ones. Thoughtful and conflicted sentiments are mixed in with concrete and evasive responses:

Raising a family "Can be rewarding, fun, etc. as well as trying, etc. Raising a family encompasses much more room or time to answer, therefore I was 'over brief'."

When they avoided me "who avoided me?"

If my mother is "or was what??"

What gets me in trouble is "nothing."

Education "two years college."

Rules are "to be obeyed and if they seem unreasonable, see if there is some way to change the rules. If there isn't, you're stuck with them."

When a child will not join in group activities, "I will encourage them but never force."

I am "me."

At times she worried about "Who???"

If I can't get what I want "sometimes I pout and sometimes I accept it. (Acception usually rules)."

A woman should always "I don't think there is anything *all* women should always be."

Mike's frustration and irritation with his mother may stem from his experience in hearing such confusion and regret from her. Consider the impact, perhaps the "overload," that Mike must experience when his mother expresses, to him or her husband, such shifting feelings, moods, and behaviors (ranging from abstract thoughtfulness to concrete dismissal).

Mike's stepfather, Mr. Wary, is five years younger than his wife. He attended the first two years of college and works as an electronics salesman. In past years he was more available to Mike, but now he leaves early each morning and returns sleepy, with a headache most evenings. When he is at home, Mike describes him as similar to his mother:

Sometimes he gets me mad. . . . Different things. . . . Threatens me. . . . Like one week he wants me to clean up my room and I say "Okay," and he says, "Hey, if you forget, you're not coming home next weekend."

Mike is more direct in describing the violent feelings he has toward his stepfather, paralleling his image of his stepfather's own violent actions:

INTERVIEWER: Do you get along with him most of the time?

MIKE: Yeah. Yeah, but at some point I feel like getting out my gun and (*mumbles, as though talking through clenched teeth*) . . . but wouldn't be able to blow his head off.

INTERVIEWER: Why?

MIKE: It's not that strong. He—he used to have a hand gun.

INTERVIEWER: Do you have a gun?

MIKE: Yeah, now I do. 'Cause he hadn't gotten that thing [gun]. You could put [it] right into an engine. . . . Over halfway into the engine. . . . By the car. . . . Halfway through the engine, so if you try to shoot there . . . you could see it all blow up.

Mr. Wary functions at the same conformist level ego stage, self-aware, as his wife. Yet his sentence completions indicate more evenness and awareness, as he stresses reasonableness and his perception of his role as "architect" of the events that have occurred in his life. He expresses an acute sense of responsibility. And, in contrast to Mrs. Wary, he is hopeful about "not being defeated":

If I can't get what I want "I sometimes compromise."

When his wife asked him to help with the housework "He complained but acquiesced."

Education "is important but what you accomplish with yours is more important."

What gets me into trouble is "talking without thinking things through."

A good father "loves his children and sets a good example."

I feel sorry "when I hurt someone."

Men are lucky because "they have the opportunity to dominate in a relationship with a woman."

My main problem is "a lack of self-discipline."

When I am criticized "I try to improve."

The worst thing about being a man is "Having responsibility for others."

Considerateness and protection are other themes expressed by Mr. Wary:

Raising a family "requires patience and dedication."

When a child will not join in group activities "Ask him why not."

Crime and delinquency could be halted if "people were generally considerate of others."

I can't stand people who are "inconsiderate."

I feel sorry "when I hurt someone."

A wife should be "Supportive of her husband."

Women are lucky because "society is protective of them."

Nowhere in these writings do we see any signs of the violence that Mike attributes to his stepfather. The "gun" that he places in Mr. Wary's hands my be connected to Mr. Wary's belief in "protection."

While Mike's stepfather offers some hints of unhappiness, particularly about his own parents and his lack of self-discipline, Mr. Wary's self-descriptions primarily emphasize his optimism and striving for improvement. He cites "Success" in several responses.

Mike's difficulties with his stepfather represent a clash between their ways of coping. Mr. Wary attempts to confront difficulties and master them. Mike frightens others and retreats. Perplexed and frustrated by Mike's strategy for resolving problems, Mr. Wary may react with episodic rage over Mike's lack of self-discipline. In fact, Mike's perceptions and attitudes are probably more similar to his mother's, who feels trapped and pessimistic about the future.

Mike feels singled out from his siblings. "I'm the oldest and my parents take more out on me." His full sister, one year younger than he, bothers him the most, because "any little thing will get her pissed off." This was the sister whom Mike decided to frighten with his gun. Of his two younger siblings, he likes the four-year-old, because "she acts like she's about ten." On the other hand, the seven-year-old "is acting like a four-year, which gets me so pissed." Mike's solution is his characteristic one: "Put it this way, if had my wish, I'd probably hang 'er. I don't like 'er at all."

MIKE WITHIN HIS FAMILY

The Wary family discussions are marked by the limited and fragile engagement between Mike and his mother. The fear, distrust, and pessimism they each express individually are enacted in the family arena. Mr. Wary, consistent with his more optimistic perspective, repeatedly reaches out to connect with Mike and with the task at hand. For the most part, however, his efforts are futile.

Mike's presence is clear from the start. His interactions with both parents are succinct, definitive, and usually combative. Early in the discussion, Mike's stepfather asks him why he wants Heinz to receive a sentence rather than probation:

STEPFATHER: Um, you want to give your reason for supporting a sentence to us, Mike?

MIKE: No. I want to hear yours (hmmph), hers.

Mike is then silent for a long time, episodically interrupting his parents' conversation to make tangential points or to proclaim his lack of understanding of what Mr. Wary is talking about. Mr. and Mrs. Wary carry on an extended dialogue over whether Heinz should receive a sentence, and why. Mr. Wary offers "reasonable" analyses of the issues and tries to draw Mike into the discussion. These energetic attempts are but momentarily effective. After reentering the discussion, Mike quickly withdraws, becoming increasingly irritable, confused, detached, and abusive:

STEPFATHER: You know, I think that in reality I could see the point of the druggist in wanting to get his buck for his invention. But I could see Heinz's point. . . . They were not talking just about money. My wife's life is at stake. . . . I think the most reasonable thing would have been . . . if Heinz had convinced the druggist, one-half the money now and finance the rest later, and the druggist would do that. . . . Do you agree, that would have been the reasonable thing overall?

MIKE: Yeah, it sounds reasonable, but—

STEPFATHER: (*interrupts*) No, I understand that he didn't do that. . . . It was, I suppose, within his legal rights, although I think he said it normally was. You know, kinda rotten person.

MIKE: I don't know. What did he have to say?

STEPFATHER: We're trying to agree on a compromise here . . . we've heard all the facts and I guess we've agreed . . .

MIKE: I'll give him ten years.

STEPFATHER: You know, we're all agreed; you—you wanna hard sentence—

MIKE: (*interrupting*) I don't give a hell!

STEPFATHER: —and Mom wants a light sentence.

MIKE: I don't wanna hard one . . .

STEPFATHER: Well . . . sometimes se- sentences work in a couple of ways like—

MIKE: (*interrupting*) I don't know.

STEPFATHER: If you do some kind of maliciousness, let's say break into somebody's house, and you destroy a bunch of stuff, lots of time you have to pay back the damage and then you get punished besides. You know, like you have to make restitution for the stuff you damaged and then maybe you have to go to jail because of what you did. You know what I mean? Can we agree that Heinz definitely has to pay for the stuff he took? Does that seem fair?

MIKE: I'm sorry, in my opinion . . . I could care less if we reach an agreement or not, so I don't know for ten minutes what we're gonna sit here.

MOTHER: I am just so— (*all three family members talk at once*)

STEPFATHER: Of course, it is very unrealistic, you know.

MIKE: It's ridiculous. I don't understand why we have to sit here and try to reach some kind of an agreement over something that's utterly ridiculous.

STEPFATHER: Well, I think the point of the study is that these are obviously difficult and hard questions, and we're gonna have to sit and try and comment. And the study doesn't give a damn whether Heinz goes to jail or not. You know, it doesn't care about Heinz's wife, you know it doesn't care about the judge, the jury, or anything else.

MIKE: Christ! (*very loudly*) Christ, but you'd at least think the story would be something. . . . You know, the kid who's on laetrile that went to Mexico.

STEPFATHER: Uh-um.

MIKE: Something like that. Or the lady who wanted the—This is completely far-fetched.

Mr. Wary persists in his calm, rational responses to Mike's challenges. Yet his essential failure at engaging Mike in the task at hand is clear. He cites several aspects of the dilemma and urges Mike to realize that the point of the discussion is not the *actual* answer. Such a request for Mike to step back and reflect over the rationale is meaningless, and confusing, to Mike. At his level of development, it is the immediate and concrete that capture his attention and drive his arguments. Mike's discomfort mounts. And with his growing unease Mike intensifies his hostility and mocking of the task itself:

MIKE: (*sighs*) I don't even know half the words you've been saying.

MOTHER: I mean how can he [Mike] possibly . . .

STEPFATHER: (*interrupting*) Restitution means pay back, you know. You know, like when you break a window you have to pay for it.

MIKE: (*in high-pitched voice*) Where do you fools—this far-fetched . . .

In contrast to Mr. Wary's persistent presence is his wife's absence. When she does reenter the discussion, it is in an unusual way. She does not offer her own opinion, but indicates that she will say whatever people want her to:

If you want me to agree with you [to her husband] I'll agree with you. If you want me to agree with Mike, I agree. I agree with whoever wants me to.

Besides offering to "help" anyone who wants her agreement, Mrs. Wary supports Mike's claim that he doesn't understand her husband: "I mean, how can he possibly know [half the words you've been saying]?"

Perplexed, Mike reinvolves himself in the discussion around concrete matters, such as amounts of money, length of jail sentences, and fights. After the interviewer announces that Mike and his stepfather are opposed to his mother's opinion about Heinz's stealing, that both he and his father favor stealing, Mike says, "All right, now we get to fight against her." But as soon as Mr. Wary indicates that he wants to expand upon the issues, Mike becomes uneasy:

STEPFATHER: Well, I'll tell you what I answered and see—see if any of you share my feelings.

MIKE: Oh, no, not another speech.

Mr. Wary nonetheless continues and describes how "Heinz is between a rock and a hard place." Mike responds, bringing up how if Heinz "does steal it, he gonna hate himself for stealin'." After a brief exchange between Mike and his stepfather about Heinz's guilt for his wife's death versus breaking the law, his mother presents the more gloomy view that Heinz's wife will probably die anyway, so if he steals the drug, he'll simply sit in jail. With this slim thread of dialogue broken, plus his mother's gloom, Mike reacts to his stepfather's question of why he favored stealing by saying he couldn't "pick one [answer] and finally decide on it."

Mrs. Wary emerges more clearly as she responds to her husband's criticism of her willingness to agree with anyone in the family: "You're more afraid of punishment than of your own conscience." This attack leads to Mike's retreat from the discussion, while Mrs. Wary, provoked by her husband, energetically returns, newly involved. She shows the difficulty she has remaining with the discussion at hand, as she associates to turning off life support machines and being a murderer. Two other characteristics of Mrs. Wary become visible, her stubbornness and her sense of oppression:

That's it, that's my position. . . . We can sit here and discuss this one all night, and I'm not going to change. Do—do we have to agree . . . to let us out of here?

Except for an extended monologue on life support machines, Mrs. Wary remains aloof from the family discussion. Mr. Wary, on the other hand, repeatedly reaches out to Mike and occasionally succeeds in making brief, tenuous contacts. It is in the final discussion of the evening that this reaching out is most apparent. Mike, now pitted against both parents, argues that it is morally wrong for Heinz to steal the drug:

STEPFATHER: (*to Mike*) Do you want to answer first? Then we'll give our reasons.

MIKE: You didn't give me that question. . . . I don't even know what to say.

MOTHER: Was it morally wrong for him to break in?

STEPFATHER: (*to Mike*) Do you know the difference between morally and legally, as they asked it here?

MIKE: What does "morally" mean then?

STEPFATHER: Okay, well—

MIKE: (*interrupting*) And watch me be right.

STEPFATHER: (*sighs*) Boy, I wonder if I can define this. (*laughs*) I'm sorry I asked the question. Ah, morally means it (*pauses*) . . . Is it better for all concerned as opposed to . . . ?

MOTHER: Shhhhh!

MIKE: I didn't say anything.

STEPFATHER: You know, is it better for all concerned? Well, let me, you know what a Blue Law is? Have you ever heard that expression?

MIKE: A what?

STEPFATHER: A Blue Law.

MIKE: Yeah, like, yeah, stores bein' open on Sundays?

MOTHER: Yeah.

STEPFATHER: That's one of them.

MIKE: Alc—, drinking and sold on Sundays.

STEPFATHER: There used to be a law, a Blue Law, that said on Sunday you weren't allowed to drink any carbonated beverage.

MIKE: I'd drink it.

Mr. Wary goes on to tell how ice cream sundaes originated from ice cream sodas made on Sundays, without the stimulating, intoxicating soda water. He uses this example as a way of showing how something could be legally wrong (sodas) but not morally wrong. Mike attentively listens and does not complain this time of his stepfather's "lectures." But he pulls away when Mr. Wary begins to apply the principle derived from this example to the moral question of whether Heinz should steal the radium. Mrs. Wary immediately follows the ice cream sundae example with a confusing tangential contribution:

MOTHER: That's why he had to be punished, but he wasn't really a criminal. Do you want to agree? . . . Why don't you agree if morally? Why, if it's morally wrong?

Not unexpectedly, Mike again departs:

MIKE: Aah . . . forget it!

Not to be discouraged, Mr. Wary once more turns to Mike, this time with a more meaningful example: "Do you think it's . . . morally wrong to smoke marijuana?" The example works, and Mike returns to the scene. In the midst of Mike's reentry, Mrs. Wary intervenes, upset about her husband's introduction of this new topic:

STEPFATHER: . . . You know it isn't legal, right to break the law, but it was his [Heinz's] need. And the reason for his doing that was so compelling . . . that it exceeded the need to obey the law, and I agree. I think that the marijuana laws are so stupid, so trivial and so stupid—

MOTHER: (*interrupting*) We're not here to discuss marijuana.

STEPFATHER: —that are obviously morally wrong.

MIKE: Hmm.

STEPFATHER: I mean, if that isn't legally—

MOTHER: (*interrupting*) Shall we go on and list especially alcohol and prostitution and all that?

STEPFATHER: Sure, that's all and the same thing. I think we pretty much agree, that it's probably morally right but legally wrong for Heinz to have done that. Do you agree, Mike?

MIKE: Yeah, I agree with you on that!

STEPFATHER: Okay, terrific!

Undaunted by his wife's objections and diverting comments, Mr. Wary persists in elaborating this new and more engaging example with Mike, who eventually connects ("Yeah, I agree with you on that!") with his stepfather.

Mrs. Wary's interruptions and objections are noteworthy. On the surface, she objects to the content of the discussion, marijuana. Yet when we look more closely, we can see that this objection is but an aspect of her tenuous participation in the family's exchanges. Recall her intermittent and peripheral involvement in the discussion. In a disconnected way, she first introduced and nervously presented her concerns about life supports. She later announced her "I'll agree with anyone" position. Outside the discussion she is visibly out of "synch" with, oblivious toward, Mike and his father. This detachment is shown in her unawareness of his having slipped back home instead of attending school, despite the fact that she was in another part of the house. Her sentence completions, with their signs of distractibility and rapid shifts from reflectiveness to evasive concreteness, parallel her unstable connection to the family discussion.

These dramatic differences between Mike's parents are also apparent when we look even more closely at the family's interactions. Mike directs almost all focusing, explaining, *and* distracting speeches to his stepfather. In fact, in addition to distracting, Mike devalues his stepfather and withholds from him much more. Overall, there is unmistakably more engagement between Mike and his stepfather. His mother is, at best, a bystander.

What part do Mr. and Mrs. Wary have in these strong differences in how Mike speaks with them? Mr. Wary is enabling—focusing and curious in his speeches toward Mike, often reaching out, as noted earlier. But Mr. Wary is also more distracting, frequently interrupting Mike. In contrast to Mr. Wary's balance between affective and cognitive constraining (some devaluing and distracting), Mrs. Wary's strong suit is inappropriate support, often excessively and seductively gratifying Mike. She jumps from prolonged detached silences to overinvolvement.

As we saw in Charlie's and Ellen's families, these relationships are hardly promoting of development. While Mike's stepfather repeatedly tries to connect with him, the overall family atmosphere is *not* one that encourages autonomy, self-assertion, or mutuality. In particular, Mrs. Wary's isolation and unpredictable involvement are confusing and not conducive to cumulative engagement on Mike's part.

Through these cases, we see individual adolescents who are seriously arrested in their ego development. Besides our prolonged look at these teenagers, we see their parents and the activity within their families. Features consistent over the three families include sharp differences between the parents, and abundant mocking and irritability. There is clearly much disrespect and only occasional acknowledgment of one another's ideas and feelings. Each family expresses impatience with sustained discussion, eschewing opportunities to forge deepening and differentiated connections with their sons or daughters.

Steady Conforming Ego Development: Amy Wright, Lou Provo, Sheila Paine

Amy, Lou, and Sheila were at the conformist level of development in the first and subsequent years of our longitudinal observations. In following their stories, we shall hear about caution, a compelling concern that organizes many of the family's views and actions. Parents insist on conformity, uncomfortable over the possible separateness and separation of their adolescents; they are intolerant of novel ideas introduced by their sons and daughters. Differences are minimized or not acknowledged at all. Often, even more dramatically, family members denigrate and dismiss opposing views. We also will hear how the adolescent's conformist style influences parents and their relationships with one another. Teenagers actively participate in the family's conformist style, as they provoke arguments and escalate parental insistence on the "right" way.

AMY WRIGHT

By the middle of her freshman year, Amy was feeling increasingly comfortable at her new school. At first she was lonesome and felt "lost" in this large high school, despite the help of her older sister, who had graduated the previous year. As she gradually felt more settled in her new classes, she became aware of specific, sometimes pressing, problems involving friends, school, and family. What emerges as Amy speaks about these parts of her life is her attentiveness to social rules and perceived conventions. Other people's nuances, or unexpected experiences with them, are either undetected or dismissed by Amy as "weird." Early in the interview, she describes her way of meeting new classmates:

AMY: You have to look around 'til you find somebody that looks like the person you want to meet. And it's not bad; it's not bad . . . just go in and sit next to somebody and start talking. . . . If they're really strange looking, I probably wouldn't go over and talk to them, but not just anybody. Sometimes, they're not even my type.

INTERVIEWER: What is your type?

AMY: I don't know, I can't explain it. Average, I guess.

Amy expresses her concerns about appearances in her sentence completions:

My main problem is "I worry too much about my appearance."

When a child will not join in group activities "they look left out."

Amy has many friends; a few are close ones whom she trusts with her secrets. Many of those secrets involve being left out of parties or other gatherings. Being part of the group, included, is an overriding concern for Amy.

Powerfully shaping how Amy organizes her schoolwork and handles classroom difficulties are her perceptions of prevailing social standards, of how others expect her to behave. One of her classes is especially "boring," yet Amy rejects the possibility of transferring to another class:

. . . I don't want to switch out, because I don't want it to be too hard. I'd rather get a better grade in the classes. . . . I don't know why, but [grades are] important to me . . . to go to college.

This goal, "to go to college," is not one that Amy thinks about very much. When asked why she wants to go to college, or what she expects to gain from college study, she replies that she doesn't know.

Closely related to her dedication to following social rules and being accepted is Amy's unease over expressing anger or other feelings that are, in her view, disruptive. If she calls too much attention to herself and behaves in unexpected ways, she risks being excluded by family and friends. When alone, Amy yells at whatever or whoever is frustrating her: "Oh, you're so stupid, I hate you. Why am I doing this? It is so stupid. Forget about it." But when her parents or friends are with her, she refrains from showing her anger, for fear that these other people will react by disliking her, by telling her not to yell. Being "nice," being acceptable, and being accepted are prominent concerns for Amy that appear everywhere: in daily thought, in the interview, and in written sentence completions:

When they avoided me "I walked away."

Rules are "good to have."

A wife should "be nice to her husband."

The generally restricted muted quality of Amy's feelings and beliefs is also visible in her relationships with her teachers. She gets along "good" with them. "I don't cause trouble for them." She does not discuss different teachers or explain how she manages not to "cause trouble for them." Similarly, Amy provides sparse detail and expresses little excitement when describing her visions of the future. Long ago, she wanted to be an actress. But then she decided that she could not carry out this plan, since the chances of success would be so slim:

I decided that [becoming an actress] probably wouldn't work. So I don't know; I have to think about it, for the next few years. . . . There's so many people who want to, so it's not really. You have to be really lucky and everything. I would rather . . . you know . . . get by and things like that.

AMY'S FAMILY

Amy's older sister, a freshman in college, is unhappy and preoccupied with her weight: "She's so picky, she's always on a diet. . . . It bothers me a lot. . . . She complains all the time. She thinks she's really fat, and she's not at all." They fought when both lived at home, and the quarrels have increased since her sister started college. Amy has little insight into her sister's new experiences and visions of the future. For the most part, Amy feels undermined by her sister and unhappy when with her:

AMY: Awful, awful mad at her and at, I don't know, at me too. Because she picks on me a lot. Like she makes me think I'm a nut, I'm bad, you know. She makes me think that I am bad.

INTERVIEWER: How does she do that?

AMY: Just the way she looks at me, and she makes little comments that really bother me, so I try not to hear her.

Amy and her sister fought less when they were younger. As her sister grew older, Amy recalls her emphasizing her superiority because of being older, and the successive fights they had with one another. Now that her sister is away at college, Amy misses her: "It's boring; there's nobody to talk to or fight with." Amy's description of her sister is relatively limited, focusing on the fighting and her sister's unhappiness. Amy is fuzzy about her sister's career plans—possibly teaching—and the rest of her sister's life.

Amy's pictures of her mother and father are similarly vague. In Amy's eyes, her mother is preoccupied with Amy's "chores," especially with her not performing them, because Amy is so "forgetful." Amy feels scapegoated by her mother: "Like she gets mad because she doesn't feel good, and she takes it out on me." Amy portrays an unhappy mother, engrossed with household chores and harassing Amy about these tasks. Amy's sentence completion responses hint at her sense of what she doesn't get from her mother (a satisfactory height and fair treatment):

If my mother "was taller I would be too."

A good mother "should treat kids as equals."

Amy also touches on more agreeable feelings toward her mother:

My mother and I "get along well when she's not yelling at me."

When she thought of her mother "she smiled and sighed."

Amy talks with her mother more often than with her father and, without being asked, insists that her mother is "not mean." She discusses certain matters, such as her recent dissatisfaction with her science teacher, with both parents. Both encourage her to "stick it out and not drop the class." Amy also tells her parents about the many problems she has with her sister. They talk with her sister, but ineffectually, and then counsel Amy to "not listen and things like that."

Mrs. Wright completed undergraduate training in education but does not currently teach. Her ego development stage (self-aware) is slightly higher than Amy's but is in the same conformist range. Mrs. Wright's attention to pleasing others, her concern with satisfying conventions, and her inhibitions certainly parallel Amy's wish to be accepted by others:

A woman should always "smile and try to do her best."

A good mother "tries to make her family happy."

When people are helpless "I try to assist whenever possible."

Women are lucky because "they have to be many things to many people—nurse, teacher, driver."

A wife should "be kind and considerate."

Rules are "important—we all need guidelines."

When they talked about sex I "listened, but did not ask questions or speak up."

Mrs. Wright also points to her experiences of being burdened and to her painful conscience and consequent regrets:

Men are lucky because "they take their freedom to come and go so naturally."

Sometimes she wished that "she could take the day off and do something different for a change."

My conscience bothers me if "I have not done a task well that I have undertaken or am slow in completing it."

My main problem is "I worry too much."

When I get mad "I'm sorry afterwards."

These responses match Amy's self-imposed restrictions about expressing anger, choosing a career, and changing classes.

Mr. Wright, a college graduate, is a salesman. Amy has great difficulty describing her father's work. Although provided with several opportunities, she says little about him, other than reporting that she talks with him less often than with her mother, and she "goes places" with both her parents—to restaurants, to visit her grandparents, and on long family trips. In her sentence completions, she portrays him as "really nice to my mother and sister."

Her father's ego development score is exactly the same as her mother's. Yet the *content* of his sentence completions decidedly differs from those of his wife and daughter. He resembles them in terms of the importance he attributes to conforming to conventions, but juxtaposed with this dominant family theme is the more optimistic view that people can change their destinies:

Rules are "made to be bent and broke."

If I can't get what I want "I try harder and look for other ways to get it."

When I am criticized "I rebel slightly and resent it."

These strands of complexity, flexibility, and perhaps rebelliousness in his thinking also surface in his other sentence completions:

A man's job "is something he should enjoy as well as make money at."

When people are helpless "I like to help them as much as I am able—sometimes!"

A good father "—that's what I think I am, and I don't think simple sentences can explain it properly."

Amy portrays her mother as restricted in her views, and Mrs. Wright supports this picture through her sentence completions. But Mr. Wright reveals more awareness of complexity and expresses a broader spectrum of feelings than either Amy or her mother. There are, for example, his visions of greater freedom to change and to challenge rules. These differences show up in the family's discussions and significantly shape the family dynamics.

AMY WITHIN HER FAMILY

From the outset, the Wrights show an intense and pervasive concern with social regulations. On occasion, as we shall see, the family tolerates—painfully—introductions of new options and initiatives.

The Wrights fasten their attention and energy on rules and answers—on "shoulds" and "oughts"—as they search for a message or "moral" to the story of Heinz. Mrs. Wright struggles to explain why she believes Heinz should steal the drug to save his wife's life. She finally voices her view of the "moral solution" at the end of a prolonged and confusing speech. She then becomes relieved, and clearer:

. . . If he [Heinz] came to me to ask me what to do, I would say, "Legally it's wrong and you shouldn't do it." (*Speaking very quickly and animatedly*). Because you should go to every avenue, because tomorrow you don't know. Someone may come forth to help you. You never know. But, morally, I said, "You have to think about it." I would say, "Okay. Go ahead and do it. But . . . morally . . . then tell the druggist that he was wrong and that he should pay." He can pay 'em back—of course. If he was in jail, it would be difficult, but he could do some sort of a work situation, (*her voice gets faster, and the pace quickens*) and maybe the druggist would realize that (*louder*) what he was doing was morally wrong. So there's the moral! I thought the moral was that the druggist was being mean and he could've helped the woman!

Mr. Wright, who thought that Heinz should not steal the drug, continues to address the moral question:

That may be true. The druggist was not morally wrong in charging $2,000, but he *was* morally wrong in not allowing the man to give him a thousand as down payment and letting the man pay off the balance at a later date.

The family becomes self-conscious about their deliberations, illustrating the importance they attribute to rules, this time in terms of the ongoing discussion:

AMY: I think that [the druggist was wrong in not allowing Heinz to give him a down payment].

MOTHER: Right! So what are we supposed to say?

FATHER: What are we supposed to say? I don't know.

AMY: We are supposed to decide.

As the Wrights debate whether or not Heinz should steal, Mrs. Wright brings in a new angle, revealing unexpected openness and flexibility. After restating her earlier view about how important it is for Heinz to pursue "all avenues," Mrs. Wright introduces ideas about Heinz's state of mind and what could happen to him:

MOTHER: Because sometimes you know, legally, you know, legally [stealing] is wrong. He sounds like a nice man. (*laughs*)

FATHER: But it was legally wrong, so accept the consequences!

AMY: But he could be under pressure, and under pressure—

MOTHER: (*interrupting*) He might have been going crazy. But at the last minute, I would say "yes," but not to plan in advance, "I'm going to steal, I'm going to steal." Go every avenue you can.

Amy presses her mother about how Heinz must steal "under pressure, at the eleventh hour," leading Mrs. Wright to raise yet another contingency, one quickly opposed by Amy and Mr. Wright:

MOTHER: What if he got killed in the process? Then he wouldn't be of any value to her [Heinz's wife].

AMY: How would he get killed?

MOTHER: Well, the guy might have set a trap.

FATHER: (*interrupting*) That's not part of the story.

AMY: Yeah, yeah, it's not, Ma! (*pleadingly*)

MOTHER: Well, but you don't know! (*loudly*)

FATHER: I'm going by what the story is that they read to me. It's not an issue.

MOTHER: Well, I know. You're cut-and-dried!

FATHER: It's not an issue. It's not something that sort of happened.

Clearly, Mr. Wright wants to *restrict* the discussion to the exact terms of the story. But Mrs. Wright continues to remind the family that there are unpredictables, circumstances not yet considered, making the discussion ever more unsettling and complex, thereby frustrating her husband and daughter:

MOTHER: Well, if we haven't come to a decision, I would say, yes, he should go ahead and do it [steal the drug], and let's hope he'll come out of it. But first and foremost, I said he shouldn't because maybe tomorrow some nice guy will come along, who'll come up with the money.

FATHER: But how can you say, "first and foremost" and then change your mind?

AMY: Yeah, you can't!

MOTHER: You mean he has just one day left that he has to—

FATHER: (*interrupting*) Make up your minds! He either has to go ahead and do it and takes the consequences.

MOTHER: But it's wrong, and I have certain things about right and wrong.

An important sequence has unfolded. Mrs. Wright initiates, challenges, and more fully explores the issues, while Mr. Wright, with increasing irritation, insists on being consistent and holding the discussion to "the facts." Later in the evening both parents are more willing to veer from the "exact" details of the story. But such straying from the point continues to be problematic for each of them. For instance, as Mrs. Wright expresses more openness to new possibilities, she at the same time firmly insists that her husband not change the subject. The family is now discussing whether Joe should refuse to give his father the money that he has earned as a newspaper boy. Mrs. Wright and Amy believe that Joe should refuse to give the money and are stunned by Mr. Wright's equivocating about such a self-evident principle:

MOTHER: (*to father*) I have to know why you said that. There's no question in my mind. But let's listen.

FATHER: I did say in the discussion that it all depends on the kinda guy Joe's father is.

AMY: A little chauvinistic, isn't it? No? (*laughs*)

FATHER: (*louder*) I simply said that if his father was the kind of guy that if Joe refused, the father is going to pick him up by the scruff of the neck . . . and take the money from him, what's the point of refusing? . . . He [Joe] should not want to give him the money.

AMY: Oh no!

MOTHER: Why?

FATHER: Because it's his money. He earned the money—

MOTHER: (*interrupting*) But that's the whole point!

AMY: Right. That's what I say!

FATHER: It was in his possession, whether it was given to him or he earned it.

MOTHER: He earned it. Now that was more important!

AMY: I said "yes," because he earned it.

FATHER: Earning is, you know—you know, a stronger argument for his not wanting to give it up! But even if he hadn't earned it, if his father had given it to him—

MOTHER: (*interrupting, and angrily*) That wasn't the point!

AMY: But his father promised him! He could go [to camp with the money he earned]—

MOTHER: (*interrupting*) He promised he could go if he earned it, and he kept his part of the bargain.

Mrs. Wright later responds to one of Amy's ideas, that Joe's father wanted the money for *his* pleasure. And, again, she provokes her husband by speculating and straying from the story line:

MOTHER: That's true. I hadn't thought about it from the point of view of the father. But I was all for it! After all, if he [the father] has friends who want him to go, and it's a few dollars. . . . It can't be that much . . . but obviously, he could probably get it unless he was destitute. And if he was that destitute, he wouldn't be going on a fishing trip. . . . He'd be working. He'd be out working steady somewhere.

FATHER: (*gruffly*) That may be so, but that wasn't the question!

Repeatedly, Mrs. Wright's reflections and new scenarios about the stories are angrily opposed by Mr. Wright's, "But that's not the question!" Although it is Mr. Wright's impatience that is most apparent, there are also signs of Mrs. Wright's irritation and impatience with her husband. Several times she breaks into the discussion, definitively predicting how Amy and Mr. Wright will react in imagined future situations:

FATHER: (*to Amy*) Let me, let me, let me ask you the question because you're in the same circumstances. You earn your own money.

AMY: That's right, Dad!

FATHER: And if I came, if I promised you something [and] then a couple of days later before you were ready to go somewhere, and I said, "I want that money you earned. I know you earned it."

AMY: For what?

FATHER: For my pleasure! I want that money, and I was very strong about telling you that I want that money. You think very carefully now. How would you answer me?

MOTHER: Well, she wouldn't. She's very firm. Just like you.

AMY: I would say, "No!" I would say, "No!"

FATHER: You might say that now, but in the circumstances you might not . . . because you might be afraid to say "No."

AMY: No, you wouldn't hit me.

MOTHER: (*more loudly than Amy*) She wouldn't straightly outright say no. She would argue you to the floor! You wouldn't come to her asking for money for your pleasure either.

Mrs. Wright and Amy plead with Mr. Wright to agree that Joe should refuse to give up his money to his father: "Say yes, Dad; say yes." Mr. Wright resists their pleas: "It's not black or white. You require more background." Yet in the face of mounting pressure, he finally backs down, concluding, "That [Joe should refuse to give the money to his father] answers that."

Eliminating ambiguity, not wandering from the story, and searching for definite answers are major priorities for the Wrights. While they show some evidence of being open to each other's ideas and encouraging separateness, such openness is indeed limited. Family discussions tend to be driven by a need for closure, which is often premature. The consequences of such premature closure include discouragement of exploration or curiosity and denial of uncertainty.

A closely related family characteristic is the Wrights's heightened attention to conformity, vividly displayed when Amy, directly opposing her parents, states that Officer Brown should not report his friend Heinz. Both parents audibly sigh, shocked by Amy's outrageous position:

MOTHER: There's a generation gap in there somewhere! Oh, that's the problem. Okay, (*to Amy*) give us your reasons.

AMY: [Officer Brown] shouldn't. Oh, okay. He shouldn't . . . because [Heinz] did it for a good cause.

MOTHER: NO! NO! NO! NO! That wasn't the question. The question was should he report him. That was the question, right?

FATHER: Should he report him?

AMY: He shouldn't because he did it for a good cause.

FATHER: How does [Officer Brown] know?

AMY: He knows, because [Heinz] asked everybody for the money and . . . was a friend of [Officer Brown].

MOTHER: But do you think he's doing something wrong, the policeman is doing something wrong by—?

AMY: (*interrupting*) Well, if nobody else saw the guy do it, then why should the policeman turn the guy in? And get him in trouble?

FATHER: (*firmly, angrily*) Because it's the law. And a policeman is sworn to uphold the law. He's paid to uphold the law.

MOTHER: (*speaking at a brisker pace*) And he might be able to help them in the long run. Because somebody else may be a witness, and could have seen it happen and the policeman would get into trouble and—

FATHER: (*interrupting*) As opposed to a private citizen.

MOTHER: (*to Amy*) I'm supr—You don't—you don't usually think that way. That's surprising! (*her voice becoming louder*)

AMY: (*embarrassed and hesitant*) I wasn't sure.

MOTHER: (*raising her voice*) That's all right! You were . . . you were. No, it's not all right. It's not a yes or no, pointedly; but I think—

FATHER: (*interrupting*) Oh, you [Amy] can think that way if you want.

At this point, as her parents are retreating, Amy begins to vacillate:

AMY: No, I think he should have reported him. Because it was wrong

MOTHER: If you were Mr. Brown, you might have said, "I won't."

AMY: If I was Mr. Brown, I would say, "Maybe not," because his wife was maybe dying.

MOTHER: Oh, Mr. Brown didn't see him, did he? I don't know about that.

FATHER: No, no, but you just answered the question in two different ways.

AMY: (*sighs*) Oh, I know. I said, "yes and no." (*laughs*)

MOTHER: I'm surprised . . .

FATHER: No, no. You said, *if* you were Mr. Brown, you might not report him. But you think, not being Mr. Brown, you think he should have.

AMY: Yeah, I think I should have reported him.

MOTHER: Because you do . . . know right from wrong, don't you? That's all it is!

FATHER: You mean, you mean you simply—?

AMY: Well, just because somebody stole something doesn't mean that I would report them.

FATHER: (*upset*) You wouldn't report them?

MOTHER: You mean it depends on what they were stealing? (*laughs*)

AMY: If I saw a friend—

MOTHER: (*very quickly and interrupting Amy*) If you saw a friend or or a compatriot?

AMY: —stealing some gum, I wouldn't report them.

FATHER: No, we're only talking about Mr. Heinz.

MOTHER: I know. That's very difficult . . .

FATHER: If I knew, if I was a friend of Mr. Heinz's! (*very loudly*)

AMY: If I was a policeman, I would have reported it! (*loudly*)

MOTHER: Well, that's the whole point!

FATHER: Well, that's the whole point!

MOTHER: You missed the question then, you weren't listening carefully.

FATHER: Your turn! You can go and get them [the interviewers].

AMY: You go get them.

In this revealing excerpt, Amy first startles her parents as she suggests that Officer Brown should not report Heinz's crime, even though he saw it. Then she wavers. Both parents become wary and angry over how she has deviated from her "normal" way of thinking: "I'm surprised, you usually don't think that way," said by Amy's mother, could be heard by Amy as "What's wrong with you? You usually know right from wrong" Eventually, Mrs. Wright offers Amy the possibility of imagining herself as Officer Brown. Amy considers the imaginary role. But Mr. Wright becomes angry and impatient with Amy's inconsistency. Both parents are alarmed over their daughter's apparently faltering moral sense. Mrs. Wright pleadingly questions Amy, "Because you do . . . know right from wrong, don't you? That's all it is!" Amy clarifies her point, describing the reasons she would use to determine whether or not she would report the crime. Yet the Wrights insist that Amy focus her thinking on being a policeman (Officer Brown), and acknowledge that she would, *without question,* report Heinz's violation of the law. The discussion ends with Amy's parents impatiently scolding her about "missing" the question, not "listening carefully." As if to say she has not *completely* capitulated, Amy then refuses to tell the interviewers that the family has "resolved" their differences of opinion.

This unfolding discussion dramatically illustrates how a family may strive, and for the moment succeed, in maintaining their adolescent daughter as a "steady conformist." We see that Amy's deviations from the usual, her explorations of new territories, elicit quick, decisive responses from her parents. Amy's self-assertiveness with her parents is episodic at best. While the Wrights, on occasion, accept her different opinions and feelings, they are usually troubled by these differences and try their utmost to draw Amy back to their views.

The ways in which the Wrights maintain an ambience that discourages or directly opposes expression of novel ideas are apparent in their specific interactions with one another. Amy redundantly explains her ideas, yet she is seldom curious about her parents' thoughts and only occasionally focuses the discussion or encourages either parent to concentrate on the problem at hand.

Amy's distracting and devaluing statements are major constraints she imposes on the discussion; many of the distractions are directed toward her father. We have already seen that Amy's parents, particularly Mr. Wright, were frequently irritated with any deviations from the story line or with Amy not expressing conclusions that she "should" be arriving at. In more detailed speech-by-speech analyses (based on the Constraining and Enabling Coding System), we see how Amy may be reacting to her father's strictures, by interrupting (distracting) and undermining (devaluing) his speeches. This pattern— together with her "you get them [interviewers]" remark to her father— suggests that she may be upset over his opposition and for a brief moment combating his pressure to embrace the accepted family position.

Mr. and Mrs. Wright, like Amy, offer many explanations. They are only sporadically curious, focusing, or accepting in their speeches to one another or to her. Instead, the Wrights constrain the discussion by distracting, judging, devaluing, and expressing indifference. Surprisingly, it is *Mrs. Wright* who is more constraining toward Amy in the family discussions.

More important, though, than this difference between the parents is the entire family's tendency to limit the discussion and to discourage exploration of alternatives through several different processes, such as devaluing and distracting, a tendency much stronger than we observe among the families of adolescents who show accelerated or progressive development. This constraining reflects the family's reluctance to change and intolerance of independent initiatives.

Amy and her parents illustrate how the individual members may act to constrain change in one another, in specific relationships, and in the family group. Although we can see inklings of challenge and awareness of complexity in each of the Wrights—Amy sometimes opposing her parents in the family discussion, Mrs. Wright introducing new scenarios, and Mr. Wright's occasional unconventional sentence completions—their overall impact on one another is restrictive. Rather than synthesize, enhance, or stimulate, the Wrights heighten one another's tendencies to self-limitation. Dangers are brought to center stage. Her parents are dismayed by the first signs of "rebellion" by Amy, and gently—later harshly—rein her in from making new points or possibly offering new perspectives.

In the next two portraits, of Lou and Sheila, we find other ways that families may oppose the differentiation of their members, especially an energetic and sometimes challenging or combative teenager. An important point to keep in mind is that not all the adolescents who grow up in such families stay arrested at the conformist stage. There must be a match between the adolescent and these powerful strictures toward conformity. As we shall see, some adolescents appear to welcome the strong rules and definitive realities imposed by their families. This embracing of conformist pressures is well illustrated by Lou, to whom we now turn.

LOU PROVO

In the early spring of his freshman year, Lou is amazed and conflicted over the freedom that he has in high school. In his grade school, tight rules and control had been the order of the day:

> I went to [the North School] and I had Dr. Doe as a principal, and the school was run . . . almost like an institution. He was . . . like an excellent principal, and . . . very strict . . . if you would do something wrong, they'd send you to The Bench. And The Bench is a big wooden bench like that [pointing to a bench]. . . . You would have to stay after school. And, it's, like here [high school] I run around all the time, go up the wrong staircases, two steps at a time.

Although Lou was overtly critical of this "strictness," his overriding reaction was a welcoming one. It was a relief for him to have his time so well structured by outside authorities. The emphasis on *rules* inside and outside the classroom was also helpful to Lou, since it gave him "a head start" at his new high school:

> I have a lot of work, like, if I get lax, my grades go hshoopt. I mean, I really have to work hard to get my grades and. . . . [the North School] helped. It helped a lot. . . . The jump was too big from North School to the high school. I mean the freedom here is unbelievable. . . . Like I have a free period right now, I don't have any classes, I don't have to do *anything!* I can go down the hall and stare at the walls. I don't have to be anyplace. And there isn't really anybody. . . . I never heard of skipping a class, or, um, playing hooky, or anything. Or, in my school, smoking, smoking cigarettes was a crime. I like the freedom, except I think that the transition should be less. I mean . . . it's such a big jump. And I don't think it should be that big.

It is easy for Lou to specify the troublesome details of this "big jump." On the surface, there is the largeness of the new high school, its more complex schedule, with free periods and teachers who didn't collect your homework or "check your notes." Beneath this surface is Lou's discomfort with more independence. Lou feels more confident when watched over, when told what to do, and when clear actions followed his violation of any of these clear rules (being "grounded"). His family is run much like the North School. Lou is immediately grounded the moment his grades slip:

> And, uh, my parents immediately took action. . . . No telephone calls, uh, uh, uh, uh. I don't have any TV anyway. I'm sort of used to it. I'm not allowed to watch TV on school nights.

Lou's grades were lower than the family wished for in his first term of high school. Predictably, his parents "took action":

> I was . . . relaxed, and I was, you know, taking it easy the first term and I got a C in English and a C in social studies, my worst subjects. And I was grounded. . . . I couldn't go to parties, no telephone calls, had to come home right after school, no plans with friends, which I was used to doing in the fourth, fifth, and sixth grades. But none of that. . . . Second term I got three A's and three B's. I was out of hot water, but still, some of

the restrictions helped. And the third term I did, I got five A's and one B.

In Lou's eyes, then, this firm discipline led to his better performance. Through careful regulation of his time, Lou raised his grades, a significant accomplishment for him. As his grades improved, Lou's parents decided that he should nonetheless continue adhering to restrictions, a position that he readily accepted. These rules serve as a powerful link between Lou and his parents. His belief, "If I do something [to violate the rules], I'll get creamed," reflects the significance of parental monitoring in Lou's relationship with his parents, a relationship in which separation and self-control are surely not applauded. Lou proclaims his belief in the effectiveness of parental control in one of his first sentence completions:

Crime and delinquency could be halted if "parents watched more carefully over their kids."

A significant force behind Lou's dependence on rules is his fear of losing control. It is important to be "cool," not "emotional." Lou worries about the dangers of erupting when upset by others:

If I'm really upset . . . I'll start yelling. Maybe I've gotten really really upset . . . if my brother keeps bothering me and . . . I got really annoyed with him and started screaming. But most of the time . . . I'm just cool. . . . I don't like to get annoyed. I don't like to get very emotional, cause I think you sort of make a fool of yourself when you're very emotional.

Also disturbing is the "nervousness in my stomach," the "butterflies," when a test is returned. But Lou's foremost worries are over possible "outbreaks" of yelling, appearing hurt, or sensing that he may become violent:

What gets me in trouble is "when my brother annoys me and I feel like punching him."

A man should always "keep cool, not get riled up."

My conscience bothers me "if I scream at my little brother."

Lou also has a less visible but perhaps even more troubling worry underlying his emphasis on managing feelings and accomplishing his daily tasks. He sees himself as not that "smart," as someone who needs to work very hard at academic subjects. Without such work, he imagines plummeting grades and failure to reach medical school, an ambition he holds throughout the four years of high school. Lou's vision of the long-term consequences of control, hard work, and perseverance is aptly conveyed through another of his sentence completions:

I feel sorry "for people who goof off in school and find themselves 'nowhere' when they get out. Even if they deserve it."

Clear rules, with explicit rewards and punishments, will restrain or counteract violent feelings, as well as the desire to avoid work, or "laziness":

My main problem is "sometimes I don't try hard enough."

In contrast to how much he talks about academic success, control of feelings, and pleasing his parents and teachers, Lou speaks very little about his friends. At the time of his first-year interview, he does not have a girlfriend, is not "going out," and has not "gone to a party for a long, long time." He has one close friend, a relationship that appears to be sustained primarily through proximity and a shared musical interest. But the relationship is waning, as Lou notices his differences from this friend:

He's a different kid than I am . . . well, not trying to be conceited, but he's . . . stupider than I am . . . he smokes, smokes and everything, and he's a different kid . . . you know, if he hadn't lived near me, we wouldn't be friends. . . . Very important point to him is . . . to be cool and to be tough, and I don't really think that's as important to me. But I don't really like kids calling me fag and all that kind of stuff. I get annoyed. . . .

What eventually surfaces in Lou's narrative about his friend is how much Lou worries about his own appearance (being "cool"), especially his physical strength and prowess. Lou is doing "physical activities" and karate so that he can "cream these people" who push him around. Lou's conflicts over expressing anger, especially through violence, probably contribute to this unease over being "pushed around." But he is also fearful of being unable to respond physically to "these other guys." Further alienating him from his friend is their competition, yet another feeling with which Lou is both familiar and uncomfortable:

We're in pretty, a lotta competition, but I am better than him. . . . I play the piano better than him. . . . And I'm, I'm smarter than him. . . . We have a constant competition. And one time he was with a friend and this friend was calling me names and things and he started to—He has to compete with me and

he has to do, have something that he's better at. And I think
that he has more friends than I do, and it doesn't bother me. I
don't really have time for a lotta friends. But he has more
friends than I do and . . . I try to compliment him on how he
gets the girls and all that kinda stuff too, to show him that he
has something better than me so that . . . I don't lose him as a
friend, cause he's a good kid, that's all.

Lou sees that the combined strains of their competition and increasing differences may lead to the rupture of their friendship over
the next few years. He has a new friend, with whom he feels more equal
and doesn't have to "worry about competing with him, because we're
both equal off."

Another major figure in Lou's life during this first year of high school
is his biology teacher, a "jock" who has been helping him with a
physical fitness program. In part because of his insecurity about his
appearance and physical skills, particularly in contrast to his "athletic" younger brother, Lou has become involved in an after-school
program with his biology teacher. A by-product of this program is that
it will also lead to extra "points," to "help me for an A." Lou, one of the
few teenagers to mention a teacher in any detail in the first-year
interview, cites the varied ways that she has influenced him:

Like my biology teacher's a fanatic, and she's, one of these, she's
a jock. You know, she's one of these runners and swimmers,
and, health foods she's aware of, you know, sugars and all that
kind of stuff. . . . It's sort of rubbed off a little on me. And my
mother, my mother thinks, knows she's crazy. She says, "She's a
fanatic. Forget it." But she's let me do this stuff and I got
weights. I work out with weights.

In later years, all the high school adolescents described teachers in
great detail, as they became more familiar with and less intimidated by
these important adults in their lives. Lou's yearnings for regulations
and structure draw this teacher into his life even sooner.

Through Lou and Amy, we begin to discern outlines of the steady
conformist path. Both place high priorities on academic performance
and future ambitions, and both are exquisitely sensitive to prevailing
standards, restricting themselves where necessary, in order to be
accepted, to fit in with friends and with family. But there are important
differences between Amy and Lou, which illustrate the multifaceted
nature of steady conformists. While friends are extremely important to
Amy, Lou is conflicted about how much he values his friendships,

which are more strained and competitive. As we have seen and will observe even more vividly in his family relationships, Lou seeks external controls to buttress the self-discipline he needs to accomplish his goals. He relishes rules and "strictness." Finally, there is Lou's image of his physical inadequacy, a less prominent concern for Amy. Lou tells of many ways that he connects his family with these preoccupations and conflicts.

LOU'S FAMILY

Lou is the oldest of three brothers. Bert, seven years old, is the youngest and a "brain," "the number boy." Lou thinks that Bert received special gifts from their parents: "My parents are both intelligent people. I'm, I'm sure that my brother Bert inherited both of their intelligences." His second brother, Jay, eleven years old, is "an athlete." Lou is awed by Jay's prowess and envious of him:

> He's incredible, he's got complete body control. I compete with my brother Jay, because he's ten and can do . . . head stands. He can do everything, and he used to put on little shows in the living room with head stands and he's in perfect form, unbelievable form. And I could never do that stuff. I mean never!

Lou feels inferior to both of his brothers:

> Me . . . I feel sort of in the middle . . . 'cause I'm not really really smarter than everyone. . . . I'm not the smartest kid. And . . . when I was younger, . . . I couldn't even do a somersault. But I've been improving myself.

By his own report, Lou's parents are a pervasive presence in his life, assisting in his program of impulse control, time management, and goal-setting. These are certainly ways that many parents participate in the lives of early, and at times late, adolescents. What is different here is the *extent* of parental influence and Lou's awareness of it. Besides his parents' impact on his daily activities and academic performance, Lou is also conscious of less tangible influences:

> You know . . . my parents have a lotta influence on the way we think. . . . I'm constantly joking towards my brother Bert, I mean I can drive him crazy. I'll have a joke for everything and then, because my parents say, "You joke all the time," I feel that I have to joke.

Lou describes his parents as "highly intelligent" and preoccupied with school and grades, documenting this preoccupation through his detailed accounts of their reactions to his flagging grades. Lou predicts that their inordinate concern with academic success will again surface in his parents' reactions to Jay, the "athletic" brother:

> [Jay's] a little less conscious about his schoolwork, I don't think it means that much to him . . . my parents are gonna find out what they think his ability is. And if he doesn't live up to that ability, they'll get him. The hardest part of it, I think, will be for them to find out how smart he really is and what his capabilities are. . . . My parents will, will bring the pressure on, and they'll give him restrictions like they gave me.

Not surprisingly, in response to the interviewer's conclusion that school is "a high priority" for his parents, Lou emphatically agrees: "Um hum. It comes first. It comes over piano lessons, guitar lessons, uh, Hebrew school. It comes over everything."

Lou's mother, thirty-nine years old, has an undergraduate education degree. In his characteristic way of labeling others, Lou describes her as "The English Person" who "deals with reading, writing, and spelling . . . she can spell any word in the world." When he is troubled, she is the first person he approaches:

> I can talk with her most of the time. . . . I usually go to my mother with problems. I think it's basically because she's home most of the time. . . . She works in the house. . . . I will come to her with things that are going wrong, or, she'll be the first . . . to know good things and bad things.

Mrs. Provo functions at the postconformist ego development level, a significantly higher level than Lou or his father. Perhaps it is her higher ego development stage that Lou is referring to when he describes her as "The English Person" in the family, as he acknowledges her greater facility with abstract ideas and language, as well as spelling. Lou's choice of her as the person he comes to "first" can be further understood as his response to her attitudes and actions about family and children, characteristics she expresses in completing sentences:

> Raising a family "is time-consuming, sometimes exhausting, sometimes fun, sometimes brings you pride and joy."
>
> A wife should "be a partner."
>
> A good mother "is sensitive to her children's needs, all needs, all the time, 24 hours a day!"

For a woman, a career is "wonderfully stimulating and productive, if she can handle it plus social life and family responsibilities."

Mrs. Provo also treasures her family of origin:

My mother and I "are good friends, she respects my judgment and areas of knowledge and I hers!"

When she thought of her mother she "saw a beautiful lady: (a homemaker)."

My father "and I understand each other better now than we ever did when I was younger—we have found we have a great deal in common—to our surprise, we talk!"

At the core for Mrs. Provo are her conflicts over her dual commitments to family and envisioned career. Lou occasionally alludes to these issues, as he portrays his mother as highly intelligent *and* working at home, *not* in the outside community. He also points toward her dilemmas in reacting to the stem, "If my mother," completing it by writing, "went to work, it would be interesting." Mrs. Provo first poignantly expresses her struggle as she writes about men and women:

Women are lucky because "they have the ability to give life, and in 1978, to fulfill all of their needs."

Men are lucky because "they always have had the ability to attain any goal they were capable of reaching for."

And in later stems Mrs. Provo reiterates this message, in case the reader had overlooked its significance:

My main problem is "obviously from previous answers—conflict between career and family."

The worst thing about being a woman "is housework is expected to be done by you."

Sometimes she wished that "she was born in a different era—earlier by one hundred years or later."

Possibly, Mrs. Provo's own career conflicts have contributed to her intense emphasis upon Lou's *performance* (Lou's achieving all that is conceivable for him), as she vicariously expresses her own—for the moment—seemingly thwarted work ambitions. Her beliefs in planning, anticipating future goals, and complying with rules are certainly among the important lessons that Lou reports having learned She writes about these beliefs:

What gets me in trouble is "speaking without thinking."

If I can't get what I want "I wait and plan how to get what I want."

Rules are "to be followed, if you disagree, discuss calmly and logically."

Mrs. Provo also stresses her high esteem for the mind and education, a lesson so clearly learned by her son:

The thing I like about myself is "my mind."

Education is "Is one of the most important things for the future of all mankind."

Mr. Provo, a forty-year-old health administrator, is characterized by Lou as "basically The Science" in the family. Lou emphasizes his father's high intelligence and Ivy League education. But Mr. Provo is also the more "moody" parent:

Well, I can talk to my mother most of the time. My father, if he gets into a bad mood, can't talk to him . . . everything you say to him, he may get really annoyed. . . . If I, if I bring an A in biology and a B in Math, he'll all of the sudden get really proud and happy.

Paralleling his description of spending more time with his mother, and her greater accessibility ("She works in the house"), Lou spends considerably more time in the interview talking about her than about his father. Our picture of Mr. Provo must rest largely on how he completed the thirty-six sentence stems. Mr. Provo's ego development stage, self-aware, is at the conformist level, identical to his son's. Mr. Provo first signals the importance he ascribes to achievement, "doing well," by entering his advanced degree in the space on the form for "education" on the sentence completion form. All other parents entered number of years of school attended or the type of school, rather than their credentials. His focus on performance is also conveyed through his feelings about completing the sentence stems:

My main problem is "trying to answer these damn questions."

He felt proud that "he finished this questionnaire."

Praise, success, and failure surely matter for Mr. Provo:

A man feels good "when he is praised."

When I am criticized "I feel indignant."

The worst thing about being a man "is being criticized for being one."

I feel sorry "for the failures."

At times he worried about "financial failure."

Other important themes are being accepted and liked by peers and authorities:

When I am with a woman "It's like being with a person, I want her to like me."

When they avoided me "I avoided them."

Being with other people "Can be important to insecure people."

Crime and delinquency could be halted if "People thought they would have to explain and justify their behavior to someone important."

Only thinly veiled are Mr. Provo's anxieties about his "strength":

What gets me in trouble is "my softness."

A man should always " 'be strong.' (so should a woman)."

My conscience bothers me if "I don't act firmly when I believe in a certain action."

Supporting Lou's perception of his father as "moody," Mr. Provo tells of his episodic anger, sensitivity to criticism, and intolerance of others:

When he thought of his mother "he became angry."

If my mother "would not use guilt, she would be more pleasant to talk to."

When his wife asked him to help with the housework "he resented it, and felt guilty about the resentment."

I just can't stand people who "are stupid, and don't believe it when told that they are."

Finally, Mr. Provo is clear about the place of rules and parental obligations:

Rules are "necessary."

When a child will not join in group activities "a parent may be concerned."

A good father "loves his children and lets them know it."

Both Lou's descriptions of his parents and their own sentence completions point to striking differences between Mr. and Mrs. Provo. She is at a higher level of ego development, articulates many complex perceptions and conflicts about herself and others, and is experienced by Lou as the more receptive parent. Mr. Provo appears to be conventional and rigid. Moreover, he is less empathic toward Lou and reacts more strongly when disappointed by Lou's performance. These parental differences appear in the Provo family's discussions.

LOU WITHIN HIS FAMILY

The Provos' strong consensus about their basic values is powerfully illustrated by their common idealization of education, as they separately complete the stem *Education is:*

"Necessary." (Lou)

"Vital, the most important life attribute." (Mr. Provo)

"One of the most important things for the future of mankind." (Mrs. Provo)

This convergence of values corresponds to a basic feature of this family: the requirement that its members closely adhere to the same beliefs and values. Family members occasionally depart from the group, experimenting with new views or "fantasies." They are at times especially adventurous, opposing the family's known "logical" understanding of the surrounding world. But a confluence of powerful familial forces always leads each member to return to the family's established views, through either a blunting or a rejection of their deviant ideas. Although this dynamic is most visible in Lou's negotiations with his parents, it is important to recognize that consensus and opposition to intrafamilial differentiation are prominent characteristics of the Provo *family*. In other words, we would be overlooking a basic dimension of this family were we to view Lou's frequent conflicts with each parent as representing only a parent–child conflict or a transient phase in the life of this family occurring while Lou is an oppositional "teenager."[1]

Early in their deliberations over the moral dilemmas, the Provos express their discomfort with differences. Mrs. Provo thinks that Officer Brown should *not* report Heinz's stealing the drug for his wife, while Mr. Provo and Lou both believe that the policeman should report him. A revealing dialogue follows the family interviewer's announcement of this difference:

MOTHER: Can I please talk since the two of you agree? All right?

LOU: We'll get her Dad! (*laughs*) This is it, pal . . .

MOTHER: Be quiet!

LOU: Okay, right, I won't say a word. You have the floor—

MOTHER: (*interrupting*) I have the floor . . . I have the floor.

FATHER: I've been alone before, so don't get too uptight about it.

MOTHER: All right . . . I'm not uptight!

FATHER: (*laughing*) Okay.

LOU: (*laughing*) She'll beat us both bloody okay.

Mr. Provo's comment about his wife's unease over being isolated from the other family members, and Lou's "joke" about her "beating us both bloody" are connected with the intense feelings that are set off when Mrs. Provo clearly differs from both of them. Eventually, after persistent arguments from Mr. Provo about the "logic" of a policeman's fulfilling his duties, Mrs. Provo renounces her original position: "I agree . . . I give in. We give in."

Alongside, and opposing, the strong pressures for conformity and family agreement are family members' yearnings for self-assertion and separateness. These opposing wishes lead to heated arguments. Mother, father, and son actively participate in protracted discussions, fueled by many barbs and provocations. We can see the pressure for consensus and the tensions surrounding this pressure in several of the family's discussions, where Lou's actions illuminate the Provo family's wishes for separateness, together with their terror over individual differentiation or distance. Lou provocatively opens discussions, joking, changing the subject, and devaluing both parents. At the same time, then, he succeeds in highlighting his differences from them *and* drawing their reprimands and criticisms. He takes a seemingly separate stand and connects with his parents through his provocativeness.

A more subtle way that he separates and reconnects is by bringing up disquieting topics. For instance, Lou becomes too "personal" in defending his position that Heinz should steal the drug to cure his wife. Although Mr. Provo disagrees with Lou's conclusion, he insists upon Lou's right to take this tack. But—within moments—he is put down by his son:

LOU: All right, let me ask you the question, Dad. All right, Mummy is now dying of an incurable—

MOTHER: (*interrupting*) You're making it personal . . .

FATHER: That's all right, he can make it personal, he's allowed to say anything he wants to say.

LOU: I know, okay, but if Mummy, . . . wouldn't you, wouldn't you . . . wouldn't you do everything, wouldn't you murder, wouldn't you do everything for Mummy? (*said with much involvement*)

FATHER: No!

LOU: (*sarcastically*) Oh, just because it's morally wrong, just because it's, uh, illegal?

As the discussion evolves, each of the Provos offers alternative solutions to the dilemma. But the Provos show few signs of openness to each other's views. Neither parent incorporates his or her own, nor others', prior ideas in subsequent speeches. And Lou is ultimately forced from his "personal" framing of the problem, a perspective so offensive to his mother:

MOTHER: Forget the fact that Mummy (*loud*), forget the fact that it's Mummy and Daddy. Make it somebody you think a great deal of. (*said more softly*)

FATHER: Yeah, that you've gotta do . . .

MOTHER: Anybody in the world that you really would not want to see hurt, and would not want to see die.

As Lou enthusiastically engages in the discussion along the less personal lines favored by his mother, both parents begin to feel pushed aside and try to quiet him, expressing this new difficulty through joking. But the humor does not fully mask their displeasure and struggle with Lou:

LOU: I have an example. It raises a perfect example—

FATHER: (*interrupting*) You're talking too much.

MOTHER: I have not had a chance to talk.

LOU: I'm allowed. (*voice becomes high*) All right, you talk.

MOTHER: Yes, you're allowed to talk, when I'm through. Okay? It's my turn now.

LOU: They're overpowering me. They're overpowering me, but go ahead. (*laughs*)

FATHER: (*spoken directly into the microphone*) He always talks a lot.

In his interview, several weeks before the family meeting, Lou described his experience of having his parents force him ("creaming" him) to conform. Surely his provocative actions trigger his parents' forceful reactions. But more is involved. The Provos consider it crucial that Lou align his ideas and actions with their own. They express mounting impatience as Lou insists that Heinz should not steal the drug for his wife if he doesn't love her:

LOU: Well, all right, let's say . . . they're on the grounds for divorce. Let's say they . . . couldn't stand, let's say they . . . almost killed each other. Let's say that—

FATHER: (*interrupting*) You're mixing apples and oranges, Lou—

LOU: (*interrupting*) All right, but you don't know that. It could have been a—

MOTHER: (*interrupting*) It doesn't matter!

LOU: It could've. They could've been forced to get married, because, um, the husband made her pregnant.

FATHER: Look, the way you just said it . . .

LOU: All right, let me just say something.

FATHER: Wait, wait, excuse me—

Eventually, Mr. Provo angrily announces, "We're getting off the whole subject." He offers a monologue about the nature of marital obligation, launching both parents into teaching Lou about the special nature of marriage, impressing upon him the "right" principles:

FATHER: The two of you are both confusing two things. You're confusing a person's immediate actions on the basis of emotions versus their actions after considering carefully and weighing all the alternatives. Lou, you're right, if somebody just deals with emotions, if he doesn't like her, he's not gonna steal the drug.

LOU: Right.

FATHER: All right? But the fact is, if he carefully weighs the situation, he'll know he has just as much obligation to the woman as he would if he did like her. So—

LOU: (*interrupting*) Why? You're unfair.

FATHER: Again, what I'm trying to do is get you . . . to sit and think about it—

MOTHER: (*interrupting*) Because marriage is an obligation.

LOU: Well, I don't know that, because I don't, I haven't been married yet.

MOTHER: We're trying to explain that to you!

Lou interrupts more and more, a pattern his parents call "playing" and "not trying." Yet accompanying his irritating antics is his steadfast view that he would not steal for a wife, or anyone, that he disliked. Despite their annoyance, Mr. and Mrs. Provo respond with tenacity, urging the importance of obligations:

FATHER: (*to Lou*) You're acting, you're on a stage. Relax.

MOTHER: All right. Forget the tape recorder and listen to me carefully. I've just explained to you something that you couldn't possibly know, that I couldn't possibly know until, not even—

LOU: (*interrupting*) You're married!

MOTHER: —the first year I was married.

LOU: Right.

MOTHER: But marriage is an obligation, it's a moral obligation as well. And I don't think it matters one bit whether, in fact, their relationship is. . . . This is his wife. He may not like her, he may like her, it doesn't matter. I think that to save a life, any life, (*voice softens*) any life, is the most important thing you can do.

FATHER: I see, even if you have to break a law, or injure yourself—?

MOTHER: (*interrupting*) To save a life!

FATHER: Or injure the person you saved? To save—

LOU: (*interrupting*) You saved a life! Anybody's? Even the kid that just punched me? . . . But why should I risk my neck for him? No way. I'm not morally obligated to him.

MOTHER: We're not talking about your kid in the hall. We're talking about a man and wife . . .

LOU: But if they're morally obligated from the marriage, I agree with you, maybe.

Mr. Provo tells Lou that he's not being very "logical" in his thinking, a familiar accusation that both Lou and Mrs. Provo dislike. Spurred by his father's challenge, Lou elaborates his "logical assumptions," leading to charged confrontations between him and his parents, together with Lou's observing how they are ganging up on him:

LOU: You're saying that I think all emotionally about it?

FATHER: Absolutely! If you hate her, you're not going to save her. If you don't hate her, and she's your wife, you're going to save her . . . I mean, it's crazy!

LOU: All right, let's think about this logically. Logically—

MOTHER: (*interrupting*) It's an emotion. You're talking about love and hate. Hate is an emotion.

LOU: Logically, if the earth was . . . a combined unit, and every single unit was a necessary function of the earth, then I would have to save that section of the earth—

MOTHER: (*interrrupting*) For yourself.

LOU: For my own good will. . . . I am a person, on my own, and it is logical that I—

MOTHER: (*interrupting*) Do you understand that?

LOU: —should have self-preservation.

MOTHER: You are—Did you just hear what you said?

LOU: What?

MOTHER: You are a person on your own. (*in staccato rhythm*) That is not marriage. A marriage is *not ever* a person on their own!

LOU: All right, then I'll have to look at the whole thing.

MOTHER: Hate is an emotion! Hate is an emotion like being cold and being hot.

FATHER: You could, you know, love and hate and not separate it too—

LOU: (*interrupting*) *Yeah.* But you see, you two, because you're teamed up, have morally influenced me, like you do in a lot of cases.

MOTHER: We do our best.

FATHER: (*laughing*) That's my job kid. (*lots of laughter and noise now ensue*)

LOU: Okay, we've settled that. (*happily*)

And Mr. Provo follows with the marriage message, one more time:

FATHER: I guess we have settled, in the sense . . . that whether the . . . guy liked his wife or not, or whether it was a good marriage, or not a good marriage, that we would like you to consider this: that they're acting like a couple, which is something you can't appreciate, but try to think of it that way. Acting as a couple, there's sort of a moral obligation to act as a couple, whether or not you like the other person. . . .

LOU: That's acting emotionally, but—

FATHER: (*interrupting*) But it's all right for you to be individual at this stage, because you're not thinking of what . . . you would be like with another person yet, okay? You are an individual, all right. And that's fine.

MOTHER: You are all set at this moment of your life.

The family tells the interviewer of their "agreement" that Heinz should steal the drug to save his wife's life, and Mrs. Provo, in a joking aside to the interviewer, reveals the parents' stake in Lou's embracing their outlook:

MOTHER: We didn't even have to hit him [Lou] very hard [to get agreement]. . . . It didn't matter . . . we hit quietly.

In the final discussion, Lou calls once again attention to his essential experiences within the Provo family: Being bullied by his parents; their resistance to his holding views that are distinct from theirs. In contrast to both parents, he is against Heinz's receiving a suspended sentence. The family's feelings surface immediately after the interviewer announces this newest difference:

MOTHER: Well, I think he's [Lou] gonna change his mind.

Both parents intensify their efforts to persuade Lou, emphasizing the importance of a judge's "humanity," and the cruelty of "throwing Heinz in jail." Lou experiences their combined pressure: "You're pushing me into a corner again. (*laughs*) They always do this. Yes?" Mr. and Mrs. Provo continue to press their arguments, telling Lou that jail is "for hardened criminals" and evoking images of the "bread and water" of jail. And they suggest that Lou consider the possibility that one day in extenuating circumstances he too may have to steal. Mrs. Provo cites "the balance of the scales of justice," while Mr. Provo reminds Lou of the importance of using "logic." Faced with these relentless pressures and images, all distant from his own, Lou eventually capitulates:

FATHER: Now you have a chance to save him [Heinz].

LOU: I'd like the judge to suspend the sentence.

FATHER: Okay. All right. Then we agree.

LOU: (*to parents and interviewer*) So I never win.

MOTHER: Right.

LOU: Put that down. I never win. I never win. Me.

MOTHER: (*laughs*)

FATHER: Were you the only, the only one that's been the minority opinion tonight?

LOU: No!

FATHER: All right. That's better.

LOU: I've never won *still*. Not on my own.

The theme that emerges is pressure to conform, both in thought and in action. The pattern is at times difficult to discern, camouflaged by Lou's provocativeness as he presses his parents to "cream him," to force him to behave more in line with the rest of the family. But the family, in more muted form, treats each of the members in similar ways, vacillating between conformity and separation, as members strain to be different, only to be drawn back to the family group through their own discomfort with separation and the strong pressure to return to the fold. This family dialectic of separation and connection is apparent in the way Lou speaks with both parents. In his provocative dialogues with them, Lou frequently distracts, changing the subject, making tangential and incendiary remarks. Although his efforts at distraction are distributed equally in the direction of both parents, he more often taunts Mr. Provo as they struggle over the significance of their opinions.

Consistent with the vacillation between separation and connection is Lou's dazzling mix of acceptance and empathy toward his father. In other specific family interactions, we see Lou engaging, often combatively, with both parents, as he connects and separates by offering provocative new ideas. What was not apparent in our earlier description of the Provo's family relationships was how Lou varies his interactions with each parent. There is a clue in Lou's own description of his parents. Recall that he portrays his father as more "moody," perhaps touching on emotional engagement between father and son, and Lou's precipitation of the engagement.

Lou's pattern of enabling with his mother is also consistent with his statement that he could "talk" with her her more easily than with his father. One meaning of this description is that Lou and his mother can connect more easily in various discussions. The greater proportion of explaining, problem-solving, and focusing speeches that he directs toward her reveal his greater ease of talking with her. So too, these interactions may reflect her higher level of ego development, indicating her interest in and greater capacity for complex thoughts and perceptions, which then elicit more complex thoughts and perceptions from Lou. The possibility that she draws more enabling from Lou is also supported by the fact that in speaking with him she explains more and frequently guides him back to the point of the discussion.

The more intense and erratic involvement between Lou and his father is evident in his father's speech patterns. Mr. Provo is both more devaluing *and* more indifferent (affectively constraining) *and* more accepting (affectively enabling) toward Lou.

Taken together, the interview, sentence completions, and family discussions provide a rich picture of the Provo family. The Provos' wishes for togetherness, heightened by their fears over Lou's differences from them, lead them to exert considerable pressure on him toward conformity with their views. On occasion, one parent (usually mother) allows that some of Lou's insights are legitimate. But in the end strong moral precepts and monologues are delivered either solo or in chorus by both parents. At the same time it is important to recognize that neither parent is ever directly abusive or even baldly unresponsive to or rejecting of Lou. Engagement is maintained, with strong pressures to connect.

On his part, Lou craves their attention, acceptance, and structure. In his interview, sentence completions, and actual family behaviors he repeatedly provokes his parents into positions where they "cream" him. In rare moments he suggests that he wants to express totally different ideas: the world and its components; being unwilling to save someone he doesn't love. Lou's tentative forays in the direction of more independent stands have two clear intents as they reveal his momentary experimentation with novel ideas *and* reflect his wishes to draw his parents back, provoking them toward once more imposing the heavy structure of their moral precepts.

Lou and his parents are locked into a dance of conformity, set to music appropriate for a marching band. Lou's experience of himself and his surroundings is constricted, shaped by his level of development and by the pressures of an intolerant family environment.

SHEILA PAINE

Sheila, a thirteen-year-old girl, was in her ninth month of hospitalization when she was first interviewed. In her interview she differed dramatically from the other steady conformist adolescents. To most questions she responded sadly or angrily, with one- to three-word answers. Few topics generated any interest, curiosity, or apparent reserves of energy. Almost all the high school or psychiatrically hospitalized adolescents who were beyond the preconformist level would eventually find a topic or interest that they could expand upon, and in some way would tell the interviewer about aspects of their life or experience that they had not yet disclosed. Sheila rarely expanded on any topic.

Immediately before being admitted to the hospital, Sheila had become increasingly withdrawn and anorectic. In a less severe form, these symptoms had been present for several years. After a brief admission to a general psychiatric ward at a nearby private hospital and an attempt at outpatient psychotherapy, she was transferred to the private psychiatric hospital, where she entered our project.

Sheila usually viewed the people around her, friends and hospital staff, as "nice." The hospital school was less demanding, with fewer requirements than the public school Sheila had attended before being hospitalized. Best of all, Sheila was no longer required to take gym for one and a half hours a day. The people that she liked on the unit were "understanding and friendly." The few people with whom she was unhappy with were "grouchy" and "got mad a lot at people." Overall, she had no public difficulties with others, because, "I keep to myself," (This style of coping with strong feelings was again described by Sheila in completing the stem: When I get mad "I like to be by myself.")

Sheila felt best about her pet and about babies. There were two moments during the interview when Sheila became more animated, actively introducing topics and speaking in sentences of more than a few words. The first of these exchanges was early in the interview, when Sheila commented on what is was like for her on the unit:

SHEILA: It's all right . . . I sort of miss my dog.

INTERVIEWER: What do you miss?

SHEILA: Just playing with him with his toys . . . dog toys.

Sheila later spoke of her unhappiness over her mother's "giving away" one of her pets without asking her, and also told of wanting to be a veterinarian in the future. The prominent place of dogs in Sheila's life was emphasized in her response to the stem: My husband and I "will live in a big house and have dogs." Along these same lines is her preference for animal stories about "Dogs, I like dogs . . . just like them."

Sheila's feelings about "babies" emerged at the end of the interview. Sheila described her wishes to "live in a big house . . . *maybe* . . . with a husband and some kids, babies, I like babies. . . . I like little kids, they're so cute." In both brief exchanges (about dogs and babies) there were fewer pauses than usual, and Sheila even seemed to enjoy answering the questions, despite the characteristic brevity of her answers.

Although Sheila prefers the company of dogs and babies, she is not completely isolated from peers. She mentions two close friends, one she has maintained contact with for six years, despite the fact that her friend now lives many hundreds of miles away from where they first met. A second friend, known since the second grade, is "quiet, friendly, and . . . plays games and stuff" with her. Like Amy, Sheila is vague in her descriptions of other people. Friends are "nice," "friendly," not "snobby." The few peers that Sheila admits to being on unfriendly terms with are "snobs," who bother her because of their "ignoring people." As Sheila describes her experiences with them, what emerges is how much she interprets their behavior as personal rejection. But she minimizes any upset:

SHEILA: Didn't bother me, 'cause I didn't like her that much.

INTERVIEWER: How did you react to her ignoring you?

SHEILA: Just ignore her.

Through the medium of sentence completions Sheila is most disclosing of how highly she values relationships:

Being with other people "is good company."

A woman feels good when "she's out with her friends."

I feel sorry "when someone is sad."

When they avoided me "I felt sort of left out."

When a child will not join in group activities "he or she must feel left out or shy."

When I am with a man "I feel shy unless I know him real good."

Independence is also important:

The thing I like about myself is "I can do things on my own."

A woman should always "keep her freedom and not let people boss her around."

Within these responses are themes touching on Sheila's shyness, yearnings for friends, and fears of being left out. She tells us of a sympathetic response to other people, and her conflicts over autonomy: her wishes to be independent and her related fears about being controlled or dominated ("bossed around").

Sheila also believes in the importance of conforming to social rules. There are definite rules to which she, and those with whom she has contact, should adhere:

Rules are "things you shouldn't break."

A wife should "do most—some—of the housework."

For a woman a career is "good and hard work."

My conscience bothers me if "I know I did something wrong."

SHEILA'S FAMILY

Sheila is definitive about the connection between her family and her unhappiness. She sees her family as somehow the "cause" of her difficulties. When the interview turned to her family, the first and most visible sign of her unhappiness pointedly appeared:

INTERVIEWER: How come you've been here? . . . You must have some ways you've figured that out by now.

SHEILA: It was family problems [I] don't talk to my family. . . . No one in the family, hardly ever talk to no one.

INTERVIEWER: Who is it that hardly talks?

SHEILA: Me and my sister do, and those two [mother and father] hardly do. . . . I don't like them.

INTERVIEWER: What don't you like about them?

SHEILA: I just don't like them.

INTERVIEWER: Can you put your finger on what bothers you about them?

SHEILA: (after long pause) Just don't like 'em. I don't know.

Again, Sheila is vague about the reasons behind these feelings and her attitudes toward people in her life, in this case her parents. Nonetheless, she is crystal clear about how much she dislikes her parents. The prime target of her dislike is her mother, an Asian woman who has been in the country for fifteen years. Sheila portrays her mother as chronically unhappy, preoccupied, and angry—"always mad and everything." Sheila reacts to her with anger and hurt feelings. For instance, there was the time her mother did not consult with Sheila about her dogs:

Like, my mother gave away one of my dogs and she didn't even tell me she was going to give it away. . . . That made me mad inside. She didn't like the dog, 'cause it shed too much hair or somethin'. . . . She just gave it away. . . . Gave away my favorite dog.

This incident is an exemplar of Sheila's belief that her mother is an unpleasant and difficult person:

She's nice to most people outside, but she's mean inside. . . . She's always grouchy, she's mad at one person, she's made at everyone.

It is again in her sentence completions that Sheila reveals more inner complexity than is apparent in her spare verbal statements in the interview. She conveys varied feelings toward her mother, as she expresses tender attachments to her, ones surely not acknowledged to the interviewer:

If my mother needs help "I try to help her."

My mother and I "go shopping together sometimes."

A good mother "is one who loves the kids and keeps a nice home."

When she thought of her mother "she missed her a little."

Mrs. Paine is forty-six years old and functions at the impulsive ego development stage. This unusually low level of ego development is in part a consequence of her difficulties with spoken and written English. Her sentence completions provide glimpses of an unhappy, nervous woman, not fully in command of English despite her fifteen years in this country:

The thing I like about myself is "miserable."

What gets me in trouble is "working so much."

I am "unhappy person."

Sometimes she wished "it hadn't happened this way."

If I can't get what I want "sad."

In contrast to this picture of her mother, Sheila offers few clues about who her father is or about the nature of her relationship to him. In response to the interviewer's summary about her mother, "You don't feel too good about her," Sheila introduces her father: "I like my father better. . . . He's pretty nice." But the problem is his un-availability:

> He's not hardly home, he wasn't before. Used to play a lot of sports. When he got home . . . then he'd leave and go.

Sheila's father, seven years younger than his wife, is American and has worked in the Army for most of his life. He functions at the transition between the conformist and conscientious ego develop-ment stages. Through his sentence completions, he conveys the plea-sures he experiences with others and his devotion to family. Like Sheila, he offers responses that are general and socially acceptable:

> Being with other people "is enjoyable."

> When I am with a woman "I enjoy conversing."

> I feel sorry for people who "are unable to care for themselves."

> My father and I "were very good friends."

> A good father "cares for his family."

He also highlights the importance of self-confidence, respect, and modesty, ideals that he awkwardly mixes with his self-restrictiveness and inhibitions:

> A man "should always be self-confident."

> A man feels good when "he is shown respect."

> Crime and delinquency could be halted if "people were better educated and showed more respect for others."

> The thing I like about myself is "that I don't talk about myself."

> I just can't stand people who "brag about themselves."

> If I can't get what I want "I accept that fact."

> When I am criticized "if justified I accept it."

Finally, he traces the burdens he carries:

> Raising a family "is a large responsibility."

> A man's job is "to provide for his family."

> The worst thing about being a man is "the responsibility of raising a family."

If I had more money "I would live a little better."

Sheila's sister is two years older. We have the least information about this older sibling. Sheila sees her as one of the members of her family in whom she can confide. She completes "I am," with "glad to have a sister."

The Paine family is a restricted and quiet group, with an unhappy, angry mother who does not yet feel at home in America, and an inhibited, conscience-burdened father, inaccessible to the family. The one ray of light for Sheila in her family is her relationship with her sister, a relationship she does not expand upon in the interview.

SHEILA WITHIN HER FAMILY

Several themes that we noticed in Amy's family are also present for the Paines. Most salient is the attention paid, particularly by her parents, to the social order. They worry over society's rules and the disasters that would follow if one did not comply with the existing laws and norms. The idea of a "generation gap" in the dilemma about Officer Brown again appears, as Sheila insists that a policeman does not have to report Heinz. As we shall see, Mr. and Mrs. Paine's reactions to Sheila's clear differences with them are far more muted than in Amy's case. In general, the discussions are more restrained, each family member rarely explaining his or her feelings or the rationale behind a given position.

Besides their greater restraint, a second way that the Paines differ from the other two families of steady conformist adolescents is the persistent alliance between Sheila and her father against her mother. In her individual interview Sheila showed little acceptance of or interest in her mother's ideas, positions, feelings, or conflicts. In the family, when not opposing her mother, Sheila is minimally responsive to her. What we would not have predicted from her interview, however, is the extent to which Sheila and her father "team up" or, perhaps more accurately, "gang up" on Mrs. Paine. This coalition can be seen as the family discusses whether Heinz should steal the drug for a stranger. Sheila and her mother begin in the same position, both having said "no," in contrast to Mr. Paine. As they open the discussion, each of the Paines acknowledges his or her opinion. More important, Sheila and her father explain their views, ignoring Mrs. Paine:

SHEILA: I said "no" [he shouldn't steal the drug] 'cause he doesn't even know the person.

FATHER: Well, the reason I said "yes" is because there's another person, another human being that needs help.

SHEILA: I said "no," 'cause he doesn't even know who the person is. What if he got cancer? He'd need the money for himself.

MOTHER: I said "no" too.

FATHER: No, but he stole the drug.

SHEILA: I know, but he might need the drug for him, in case something happened to him.

Sheila soon changes her position, and the family division—Sheila and her father pitted against her mother—emerges more explicitly:

MOTHER: I still say "no."

SHEILA: I say "yes," two against one.

MOTHER: I still say "no," that he should. If it come to my family, I'd store-break.

SHEILA: No, but there's no one else it's a stranger you know. She's desperate. She's gonna die unless you give her the pills. Would you give them to her or would you let her die?

MOTHER: No, I don't mean to die, but I'd try the best I can to—

FATHER: (*interrupting*) What would you do?

SHEILA: Would you get the pills for her or would you just let her suffer?

MOTHER: Yes, somehow, I probably try the best I can.

SHEILA: So?

FATHER: Yes, but how?

MOTHER: Well, I go and talk to someone.

SHEILA: Well, what if—

FATHER: (*interrupting*) What if everybody refused, you couldn't get nothin' done?

MOTHER: Well, then, I'd probably stole.

FATHER: Okay. In other words, and I go along with that. What I would say is that you try and talk to the other person that's got the medicine, or maybe some other medical people. And then if you can't get help from anybody, then you steal it and give the medicine to the person.

MOTHER: Yeah, I can't see, you know, people dying.

FATHER: (*to Sheila*) Yeah, that sound okay to you?

Sheila's answer to her father's question is to announce that the family has resolved their differences, since her mother has now changed her position. She then orders her father to bring back the interviewers:

SHEILA: Go tell them [the interviewers].

FATHER: I will. Just put my cigarette out.

The alliance of Sheila and her father recurs throughout the evening's discussions. Mrs. Paine responds similarly, shifting to her daughter's and husband's position, at times explaining that she probably "misunderstood" the ideas. There are also, although less often, episodes where Sheila opposes both parents. An important feature of the Paine family is highlighted as both parents argue with Sheila over their unmistakable differences with her. Sheila switches her position to agree with her parents, but her change is *not* recognized by either parent. Their obliviousness to the fact that she is now allied with them can be seen as they discuss whether Officer Brown should report Heinz's robbery. Sheila enters the argument opposed to *ever* informing on Heinz, or anyone else. By the end of the deliberations her position has evolved into a complex conditional one:

SHEILA: Like, if I had a friend and her boyfriend had cancer or somethin', she did something to get the money. If I knew the reason that she was gettin for her boyfriend, 'cause he was dyin' of cancer, then I wouldn't report. If I just thought she was stealing for no reason, then I'd report it.

(the family is silent for ten seconds)

FATHER: Well, I guess this is one we can't agree on. We'll just to have to keep a split on this one 'cause I can understand what you're saying.

(again, the family is silent for ten seconds)

MOTHER: Okay?

FATHER: Yeah, I guess so. I don't think we're going to be able to come up with a different solution.

Sheila has changed her position from a definitive stand against reporting Heinz. Under special circumstances ("she was stealing for no reason"), Sheila would "report it," following her "duty" as a policeman. Although she expresses this transformation in her thinking, neither parent seems to notice. In this restrained and intermittently combative family, partial agreement is not seen as agreement at all. Only total agreement—or disagreement—is noticed.

There are other circumstances where Sheila will not budge in her opposition to her parents' ideas. At these times of total disagreement, her parents have no difficulty in understanding her positions. Not surprisingly, Sheila's feelings about pets energize her impassioned argument that Heinz should steal for one. Her poignant monologue alerts her parents to her idea of how important a pet can be for a very lonely person. Eventually they almost fully agree with her position. The discussion is triggered by Sheila's defending Heinz for stealing a drug for his sick pet, in contrast to her parents, who believe that one should not steal to save the life of a pet:

SHEILA: Thought you liked animals.

FATHER: I do.

MOTHER: Just because animal?

FATHER: Yeah, I think a person's life is more important than animals' life.

SHEILA: Well, the way she told me, it's just the animal there.

MOTHER: That's it, Heinz's pet.

SHEILA: Talking about his pet, his friend, his best friend, man's best friend.

FATHER: Yeah.

SHEILA: And I would save him definitely.

MOTHER: Just like with people, happen to, you gonna let . . . he die?

FATHER: Yeah, I'd say, "tough luck, buddy."

MOTHER: You really think that?

FATHER: (*laughing*) I don't know, if I'm not really in that situation right now. I feel like, that it's not worth breaking the law to save an animal.

SHEILA: I do.

FATHER: No matter how much you love the animal. But a person it's different.

MOTHER: This is, talking about your, only your pet.

FATHER: Yeah, just like Skippy.

SHEILA: I say . . . I would save—(*said emphatically*)

FATHER: I had to think about that, I didn't know exactly.

SHEILA: Yeah, but you knew I was gonna say "yes."

FATHER: Well, yeah. I knew what you were going to answer to that one.

SHEILA: I'd say "yes", think "yes" would be the right answer. Save your animal, just like humans are animals.

FATHER: Well, I guess, I guess you'll look at it this way, too. You're not doing any harm to anybody by taking that medicine, you know. If you was going to kill the drug store man to get it, then I guess not . . .

MOTHER: I would take you there.

SHEILA: I would say . . . even if you did get caught, and it was your loving animal. Like having good things to tell the judge. Say you only had an animal, no one else loved you. That you would save that animal. Only one that gives you love and only one you could talk to, only one that lives with you, poor thing. Would you let it die?

FATHER: Hmmm. Well, I don't know. That's what I said. I don't know, a person I know for sure I wouldn't. An animal? I really don't know.

SHEILA: You mean the poor little thing, you let it die. You just sit and watch? And he'd keep you company, and kept you from burglars. . . . All that he'd do for you and you'd just let him die?

FATHER: Well, no I . . .

MOTHER: . . . Just like you say. Cross the street, dog gets hit. You'd just watch and let it go?

FATHER: Well, no, but that's not breaking the law to go and help that dog. You're breaking the law to go out and steal that medicine.

SHEILA: I say I would.

MOTHER: I don't know, if you own a pet, I think, yes.

FATHER: Well, as long as you wasn't going to hurt another person. I guess . . . I would probably change my mind about that, and uhh . . . go ahead and uhh . . .

SHEILA: Is "yes" the answer?

MOTHER: Half and half.

FATHER: Yeah . . . I probably would.

The Paines express many of the same themes that we saw in the other steady conformist families. They have definite ideas about the functions of laws; they are uneasy with ambiguity and wary of distinct intrafamilial differences. Sheila's father, for example, ends debates on several occasions, eliminating—for the moment—opposing positions and explicit conflicts. After Sheila finally agrees with her parents' opinion that punishment should be given even if the crime is conscience-driven, her father delivers a lengthy monologue that closes off further discussion:

SHEILA: Or maybe he should get a little punishment or some kind of punishment so he wouldn't do it again.

FATHER: Right, to let him know that he just can't do something every time his conscience tells him. . . . You know, my conscience might tell me to go over and beat someone along, along the side of the head, . . . and I think I should be punished for doing that. It depends on what you're doing. I say, even though I agree with all that he's done, that doesn't make it right. I think we also agree, you know, that what he's done was okay, but if you did get caught, he should be punished. I agree with you, that it shouldn't be a real bad punishment either . . .

Important, and by now significant, themes characterize the Paine family. The group is impatient with ambiguity. Members show striking unease with deviation from family values. They are unmistakably attentive to authority. Yet we have also drawn attention to features not apparent in the families of high school students. The Paines' family discussions distinctly differ from those of the high school families in terms of recurring cross-generational alliances; Sheila and her father repeatedly join together in opposition to Mrs. Paine. Their joining is usually in the service of Sheila's devaluing and distancing of herself from her mother.[2]

Yet another layer of observations about the Paines involves the ways they talk with one another. Sheila's interactions with each parent provide specific instances of the individual and family themes we described earlier. To begin with, she is rarely helpful to either parent separately, or together. Acceptance, empathy, and curiosity seldom characterize her speeches. In addition, and consistent with the way she reports relating to her mother, Sheila addresses many more enabling speeches to her father. In fact, there are three kinds of enabling she *never* expresses to her mother: problem-solving, acceptance, and empathy. Sheila's repertoire of constraining is more complex. Not unexpectedly, she speaks in more judgmental and devaluing ways to her mother. But there is one kind of constraining—distracting—that she expresses more frequently toward her father. We can understand Sheila's greater distracting to her father as representing her more intense level of interaction with him. Not only does she initiate more speeches to him and respond more to him after he speaks, but she also—in her more excited connection with him—frequently interrupts his speeches, actions that are seen as "distracting."

Turning to her parents, we see that Mrs. Paine's dialogues with her daughter involve much explaining but little curiosity, problem-solving, or focusing. Mr. Paine also directs much explaining toward Sheila. Yet, unlike his wife, he also engages in other types of enabling interactions with his daughter, notably problem-solving and acceptance.

With respect to constraining interactions, we again see strong contrasts between Sheila's parents. Mrs. Paine is more constraining to her daughter in numerous ways, particularly by way of excessive gratifying. Her blend of more excessive gratifying *and* indifference suggests that Mrs. Paine may be bewildered about how to react to her daughter, vacillating between offering wholesale inappropriate support (excessive gratifying) and ignoring (indifference) her daughter's unpleasant barbs and criticisms.

These interaction profiles closely reflect and extend what we already know about Sheila and her family relationships. Her persistent belief that her two parents can be seen as "good" (father) and "bad" (mother) caretakers is documented by these analyses. What they add to our knowledge of the Paines is important detail, as we see skewed relationships, represented by reciprocal enabling with father and mutual constraining with mother. Further, there is clear indication of her mother's reacting to Sheila's challenges and occasional outright assaults with indifference and excessive gratification.

The restrained, conflicted, and haltingly fragmented style of the Paine family is congruent with Sheila's sense of herself and her world. Arguments, thoughts, and feelings are rarely reflected upon, examined, or even visible for more than a few moments. Shades of gray are but sporadically noticed. One family member, Mrs. Paine, is persistently ignored or actively excluded. Within the discussion, Sheila voices the warmest and most tender feelings toward her pet—the nonhuman member of the family—who is not even present during the discussion. The fact that these feelings are taken seriously by her parents indicates some connection between them and her, some openness to recognizing her by them. Perhaps this modicum of acceptance and empathy is one reason for Sheila's being an exception, her *not* being among the adolescent patients who are severely arrested in their development. We cannot argue that this family's style of perceiving themselves and the world has "caused" Sheila's premature foreclosure at the conformist stage—or her depression. Yet we can see consistencies between her experience and the family's style. While perhaps not severely disturbing to her, it is also clear that this family is not promoting her continued growth, not "launching" her toward greater curiosity or skepticism about how she sees and understands herself and the surrounding world.

Progressions in Ego Development: Andy Lewis, Lois Weller, Larry Delta

In this chapter we look closely at adolescents moving forward in their ego development and at the early signs of their progressions present in the first two years of interviews. Three kinds of progression are possible. First, in the early progression path teenagers advance from unawareness of others' feelings and highly simplified understandings of themselves to a limited interest in in others, to wanting to "fit in," and new-found abilities to become members of various social groups. Teenagers following the second, or advanced, path change from conventional understandings and longings for acceptance to a new-found recognition of complexity, inner standards, and individual differences among people. Finally there are the dramatic progressions, instances of radical change, as a teenager remarkably advances from the earliest of stages—where immediate satisfaction and self-protection are uppermost—to the most advanced stages, involving delay, anticipation, concern for others, and understanding the unique ways that people differ.

EARLY PROGRESSION: ANDY LEWIS

Midway into his first year of high school, Andy is cooperative but reserved during his interview. He responds to questions with brief answers, amplifying them only if encouraged to do so. Andy's two older brothers have been students at private high schools. Andy, not admitted to one of those schools, reluctantly chose to attend the public high school. Although at first he felt somewhat lost and frustrated in high school, Andy quickly drew on friends and teachers for support:

ANDY: I met a lot of people [when coming to the high school]. And everyone was nice to me. At first, it was a big change because I didn't know . . . how to get around the high school, I didn't know where the rooms were . . . it was hard to find places, but everyone was nice to me. My teachers were good. So after the first semester—well halfway through—I really got to know the high school and it was really good.

INTERVIEWER: What was it like when you couldn't find your way around?

ANDY: Well, (*sighs*) like it was a little frustrating at first, but I just asked somebody and they helped me.

Friends are an important part of Andy's life. He retains old friends and adds new ones:

I have stuck with my old friends, but I've met a lot of new friends. But I didn't forget all my other friends. I still see them . . . you *should* meet new people. You shouldn't just stay with the same people.

Andy firmly believes in expanding friendship circles and throughout his interview illustrates how he's made these changes. Like many of the other fourteen-year-old boys we spoke with, Andy describes his relationships with friends in terms of shared physical activities—tennis and bowling. Difficult moments are apparently few in number and have to do largely with Andy's feeling pushed around or "bossed." He deals with such situations by avoiding the problematic person or people. Andy is also similar to the other adolescent boys in that girls are not yet major figures on his horizon. At this point his friendship networks and activities are clearly restricted to boys.

Besides the importance of friends, the other major topic in Andy's first-year interview has to do with why he is attending the large public high school, in contrast to both of his older brothers. Andy is more articulate about this point than almost anything else. He describes his uncertainty about the future and his plans. A large school provides him with many educational options:

I don't really have a preference [about what I'll be doing in ten years]. . . . That's why I thought it would be good to go to this school, because they have many opportunities. I can go anywhere I want to. In two years I think I'll probably have an idea of what I want to be.

Although Andy says he feels "pretty contented," his voice and manner suggest that he is edgy or nervous. Most prominent is Andy's pervasive uncertainty—he does not know what he wants to become or where he will be in the near or far future, or the kind of person with whom he would like to spend his life. He speaks with more certainty about activities and competition. He plays many sports competently and was a serious drum player for many years. He talks about these activities with more animation and detail than about any other area in his life.

Andy articulates a broader range of feelings and concerns through his sentence completions. The most consistent theme involves his view of the burden, the hard work, that lies ahead:

Raising a family "is hard."

A man's job "is hard work."

Women are lucky because "they don't have to do hard work."

The worst thing about being a man is "you have to do all the hard work."

Feelings about himself and others vary from pleasure to unhappiness and depression:

Being with other people "is fun."

The thing I like about myself is "I'm creative."

When they avoided me "I was angry."

When a child will not join in group activities "he is shy."

When he thought of his mother "he felt sorry."

Sometime he wished that "he was dead."

Two other themes surface in Andy's written completions. One is his sensitivity to others, expressed through his altruistic wishes to help them:

If my mother "had a lot of housework I would help her."

When people are helpless "other people should try to help them."

I feel sorry "for people who discriminate against other kids."

The second motif is Andy's belief in what can be gained from reason and reflection:

> When I am criticized "if it is constructive, I listen to it, if it isn't constructive, I ignore it."

> If I can't get what I want "I try to reason it out."

ANDY'S FAMILY

Throughout his first-year interview Andy tells us much about his family. He is the youngest of three boys. The oldest, who "watches more TV," is about to graduate from one private high school, while the second attends a different private high school. Andy tells of their sporadic skirmishes, of the fact that one of the brothers is "neater than he is," and how both brothers help him with school subjects, such as math, that they've already taken. Yet, consistent with the rest of his first-year interview, Andy's descriptions of his brothers and parents are limited in detail and depth.

Andy's father, Dr. Lewis, a fifty-four-year-old health professional, is "very helpful," giving Andy lifts to school, helping him work on projects, and sharing with Andy aspects of his "cases." He plays games (backgammon and tennis) with his family, and they watch television together, "so we have a very close family."

Dr. Lewis's ego development in the first year was in the conformist range, at the self-aware stage. In his sentence completions *helping others*, and *responsibility* stand out as major concerns, appearing in many guises throughout his writings:

> A man's job is "to make money for his family and be responsible as a husband and father."

> Crime and delinquency would be halted "if the federal, state, and local government were interested in same."

> When they talked about sex "I encouraged their discussion."

> When his wife asked him to help with the housework "he co-operated."

> I just can't stand people who "are disinterested in the welfare of others."

But Dr. Lewis also tells of how he can be overzealous in his wish to help and in his work:

What gets me in trouble is "that I keep trying to help people who don't want help."

My main problem is "that I overwork."

Alongside of his altruism are Dr. Lewis's many strivings for achievement:

A man feels good "when he accomplishes as many goals."

If I can't get what I want "I try to analyze why I'm not successful."

He felt proud that "he was successful."

Another strength expressed by Dr. Lewis is his sharply focused awareness on inner psychological forces of others and (on occasion) his own empathy:

When a child will not join in group activities "I try to understand why."

When they avoided me "I contacted them."

When people are helpless "they should learn to tolerate the feeling."

I feel sorry "when tragedy strikes people."

When he thought about his mother "he reminded himself of how she knew little about child rearing practices."

Dr. Lewis is uneven in his sensitivities to others. At times he is empathic. Yet alongside his thoughtful concerns about others are his attention to rules, his ambitious strivings for achievement, and his adherence to socially acceptable roles. (A wife should "try to please her husband.")

Mrs. Lewis, at forty-five, is nine years younger than her husband. Andy describes her, like his father, as helpful and "always looking out for me." She is now completing a graduate degree in education and also working as a substitute teacher. During Andy's recent uncertainty about whether to go to private or public high school, he cites his mother as the one who "let me come here [public high school]" despite his initial report of talking it over with both parents.

Like her husband, Mrs. Lewis's ego development level is at the self-aware stage. Although her overall level is the same, the content of her responses differ. She gives greater emphasis to feelings, particularly optimistic, hopeful ones. In contrast to her husband's affinity for rules and responsibilities, Mrs. Lewis values spontaneity and expression:

If my mother "were me she would be happier."

Being with other people "is fun."

The thing I like about myself is "my humor."

What gets me in trouble "is my spontaneity."

A wife should "try to add joy to a man's life."

When I get mad "I try to express feelings and get it out."

When they avoided me "I didn't like it."

A good mother "is a growing person who is prepared to work hard and has the ability to laugh."

Consistent with her minimizing of rule-bound views and simplistic understandings, and with her heightened awareness of feelings, is Mrs. Lewis's alertness to the many sides of people and of competing priorities:

I am "a wife, mother, and student in that order."

A girl has the right to "a career, marriage and the joys of life."

For a woman a career is "an additional joy when the children are grown."

This last point, Mrs. Lewis's career, is not a small one for her. She refers to career conflicts several times, most directly when she notes that her main problem is "making a career decision." This was the one facet of his mother that Andy explicitly remarked on during his otherwise impoverished descriptions of family life. In sum, while similar to her husband in emphasizing "helping others" and psychological understandings, Mrs. Lewis distinctly differs from him in having a greater awareness of complexity in herself and others. She apparently also feels less burdened by heavy responsibilities and by the restrictions imposed by rules and narrowly defined roles.

ANDY WITHIN HIS FAMILY

There is a striking contrast between what Andy says in his interview and how he speaks with his parents. In the interview Andy is responsive, describing his family in positive terms, especially the "helpful" aspects. But his descriptions are succinct. He is polite but reluctant to talk at length about his brothers or parents. In the first-year family discussion we hear a very different voice, one with many features of the more socially aware ego development stage Andy reaches during the following year.

Assertive and verbally clear, Andy is the primary work leader throughout the evening. Whenever a point is unclear or the discussion becomes at all tangential, Andy is on the scene, tactfully clarifying or steering the discussion back to the original point. His mother and father respond favorably to these efforts, showing no signs of resentment or struggle over his obvious leadership. Indeed, while his father comes across as somewhat mechanical or provocative at times, his mother often praises Andy's contributions as "creative" or superior to hers.

The discussion opens with the family in disagreement over whether Heinz should steal to save his wife's life. Dr. Lewis has concluded that Heinz should not steal, but Andy and his mother both argue that the theft of the drug will save the wife's life. Andy immediately clarifies his point, not requiring any encouragement to do so from his parents, as we've seen in other families:

ANDY: I think that life is more important.

MOTHER: I think that life is the greatest human value and that—

ANDY: (*interrupting*) You could always repay the crimes you did.

MOTHER: And that—

ANDY: (*interrupting*) You can never bring back a life, but you can repay.

MOTHER: Uh-huh.

ANDY: Really good.

FATHER: Yeah, but in this particular case the man was acting independently, as if he were an expert. And there was no physician involved. And he wanted to do something because he wanted to do it.

ANDY: (*excited*) Yeah, but the drug, the drug.

At first, when the question is at all unclear, Andy tries to recall the interviewer. Ever attentive to the rules, his father will not allow this deviation; Andy is not supposed to bring her back until the family has resolved their difference of opinion. Later, with his mother's encouragement, Andy doesn't even check with his father before bringing the interviewer back to clarify the question:

ANDY: I don't think that's the question.

MOTHER: But what is? Let's get the question reread.

ANDY: Let's get the question reread. (*knocks on the door to the interviewer*) We need to have the question reread.

Mrs. Lewis gives Andy permission throughout the discussion to take the initiative, to express himself, and to do so in clear and definite terms. In other words, she strongly encourages Andy to assert himself and to have a distinct voice within the family discussion, qualities clearly reflected in his advance in ego development the following year. This message is implicit most of the evening and becomes explicit in the final discussion of the evening.

Andy never takes over in a dogmatic or abrasive way. He consistently listens to the opinions of others, almost always catching the drift of the discussion. When the family is discussing a second set of differing opinions, Andy is alone in promoting the idea that one should steal to save a pet's life. Yet he thoughtfully responds to his mother's position, and then goes on to change his own:

ANDY: Listen, I felt that in this story it said that the person really loved the pet, and it was an important part of the person's life and that, you know, if you really love the person you would feel that it's more important to save the person's life. It's (*gets excited*) the same circumstance [with an animal], 'cause this person has love toward an animal as he has love towards his wife.

MOTHER: I didn't, I didn't, say . . . I did not say that Heinz should steal [the drug] on the basis of love. I said that Heinz should steal on the basis of saving a human life. And I don't think Heinz has the right to steal for love, only for life. And I separated those two issues.

ANDY: Uh-huh.

MOTHER: The issue with the pet. It's not, not a question about what a man, a man may love something, but he doesn't have the right to violate another man. He does for human life, and I didn't think he had the right to steal to satisfy his love wishes for an animal.

ANDY: (*in low whisper*) I see the point.

MOTHER: I agree.

ANDY: But I didn't look at it that way.

MOTHER: (*to father*) Do you agree on it?

FATHER: I guess. Surely.

The liveliest exchanges, those most illustrative of Andy's leadership, occur around the question of punishing a lawbreaker for acting out of conscience. Andy stands alone as he concludes that one should not punish a lawbreaker in these circumstances, while his mother and father offer conditional views ("Yes, it depends"). In a variety of ways, Andy clarifies vague or ambiguous offerings from his father and thereby helps the family discuss their differences more coherently. Sometimes Andy's clarifications are practical ones:

FATHER: This man was punished, right, when he was brought to trial (*Andy sighs*) and he did it only out of conscience.

ANDY: No, you're asking me about the trial. He's not being punished. He did break the law. If he would be punished he would be sent away to a jail term.

Sometimes Andy becomes impatient with his father's deceptive inconsistency, masking his provocativeness. In the midst of an example given by Mrs. Lewis, of a son stealing a diamond for his mother, Andy suggests that the son should be punished for the theft:

ANDY: And you think he should be punished for stealing a diamond.

MOTHER: For stealing a diamond. For stealing, it's a case, his mother—

FATHER: (*interrupting*) I don't think that everyone should be punished, period.

ANDY: But you said!

MOTHER: That's what I said, he should be rehabilitated or—

ANDY: (*interrupting, shouting angrily*) Okay!

MOTHER: To pay back the debt to society. But we usually—

FATHER: (*interrupting*) You're getting confused with something wrong.

MOTHER: He should be taught.

FATHER: Yeah.

ANDY: But you want to change the whole judicial system? By saying that—

FATHER: (*interrupting*) Yes I do, I do.

ANDY: —people shouldn't have to go to jail?

MOTHER: He [father] would like to teach people.

ANDY: Okay, but what are we going to do . . . let him out to society and . . . ?

Dr. and Mrs. Lewis now forcefully interrupt Andy, pointing out that society *does* have rules (Mrs. Lewis), and that you could put all the criminals in the hospital to be treated for a sickness (Dr. Lewis). Once again, Andy is receptive to the new perspectives:

ANDY: I agree. I agree that they should be rehabilitated. I mean, that there are some sick people, but the idea is—

MOTHER: (*interrupting*) Have certain rules of society.

ANDY: Keep them away from society to not—

MOTHER: (*yelling and interrupting*) *Shouldn't* you get a traffic ticket?

ANDY: So that they don't leak . . .

Despite these interruptions from both parents, particularly his mother, Andy sticks to his point, refusing to be distracted.

Andy clarifies his understanding of specific ideas and paraphrases each parent's muddled thinking at various moments, a role well illustrated during the following discussion about conscience. Both parents are arguing about whether fines are punishments, ways of collecting revenues or ways of "helping people behave according to the rules." Andy intervenes:

ANDY: I feel we're getting off the subject.

MOTHER: I do too.

ANDY: If the question was whether we think that man should be punished for doing something from his conscience, now you're saying—

MOTHER: (*interrupting*) But I'm—

ANDY: (*interrupting*) And you're saying that nobody should be punished.

FATHER: Right.

ANDY: So let's just say—

FATHER: (*interrupting*) Do you know why?

ANDY: Yeah, because they're sick. And you feel that they should be—

FATHER: (*interrupting*) Yeah, because if they had, you know, if they had the right kind of conscience, right? If they had the right kind of conscience, then most of the time you would have to obey by the rules and regulations.

ANDY: Okay, but—

FATHER: (*interrupting*) Now in the situation . . . the man felt guilty for doing something wrong, but he felt he had (*bangs fist on table*) done something wrong to save a life. . . . He couldn't do anything right, because he had no money, he got no money from any place whatsoever. So he had only two choices: the choices either to break the law or let his wife die. But he chose to break the law.

ANDY: Yeah, but—

MOTHER: Which was the highest . . . which according, I said that—

ANDY: (*interrupting*) So in that set of circumstances, do you think he should be punished?

FATHER: No!

ANDY: Okay, well . . .

FATHER: That's why I said it.

MOTHER: But it also depends on the *laws!* And that's society (*getting frantic*) for the—

ANDY: (*interrupting*) So you agree that people should be punished for their conscience?

MOTHER: No!

ANDY: Depending on—

MOTHER: (*interrupting*) Depending on—

ANDY: (*interrupting*) the circumstances.

Through his many interventions and interruptions, Andy steers the family back to the heart of the problem: conscience and the law. He engages his father in a continuing dialogue, but their conversation soon drifts to Dr. Lewis's position on the usefulness of punishment. Andy briefly responds before trying to return the discussion to its original theme:

ANDY: So we're in agreement that—

FATHER: (*interrupting*) That punishment doesn't teach anyone anything.

MOTHER: But I don't think that's the issue here!

ANDY: No, that's not the question here. Do we agree that under certain circumstances people should be punished for doing crimes on their conscience?

FATHER: No, (*lowering his voice*) I don't think we should punish them.

ANDY: You don't think anybody should be punished?

FATHER: (*coldly*) Yeah.

ANDY: But if you did feel—Now we're going to have to argue whether there should be punishments or whether there shouldn't be punishments—

FATHER: (*interrupting*) That's right.

ANDY: And that's not the question. Let's say that okay, if they do the crime—

FATHER: (*interrupting*) If they commit a crime, should they be punished?

Mrs. Lewis enters the discussion at this point, suggesting the term "rehabilitate" be substituted for punish as a way of getting through the seeming impasse that has developed between Dr. Lewis, preoccupied with punishment, and Andy, who wants to resolve the original question—one he is keeping a sharp eye on. Andy quickly grasps his mother's solution and is delighted with her proposal:

MOTHER: Well . . . should we agree to use the term?

ANDY: Rehabilitate.

MOTHER: Rehabilitate, or that society has the right to impose certain criteria to uh, rehabilitate the person . . . a certain lesson be taught to the person. We're not saying how the lesson should be carried out.

FATHER: Right, sure.

MOTHER: But let's now rephrase it. See if we can come to some agreement.

ANDY: But by just replacing the word "punishment" with rehabilitate.

MOTHER: (*with pleased voice*) Rehabilitate.

FATHER: (*almost mechanically*) When someone breaks a rule (*long pause*) every effort should be made to try to help that person. Period.

ANDY: So we agree.

FATHER: Yeah, whatever that may be.

ANDY: Okay, so we have an agreement.

FATHER: Yeah.

Even after this triumphant moment of agreement, Mrs. Lewis veers to yet another topic, a boy disobeying his father. Andy reminds her she has wandered off the subject.

The final discussion of the evening illuminates origins of Andy's effective skills in preventing the discussion from becoming scattered and diffuse. Until now, both parents have been receptive to his challenges, clarifications, and overview comments (e.g. "We're not discussing the question."). But in one of the last exchanges, Mrs. Lewis argues for the importance of a son's differentiating himself from his father and maintaining that differentiation, in the face of intense counter-pressure. The question on the floor is, "What's the most important thing a son should be concerned about in relationship to his father?" Mrs. Lewis asserts, "Having the guts to stand up to his father" (as opposed to Dr. Lewis's "loving, loving a father"). Despite many interruptions by Andy and her anxious husband, Mrs. Lewis amplifies her idea about a son and his father:

MOTHER: Standing up to the father and being his own person.

FATHER: (*meekly*) That question. That's this [question], can the son stand up to the father?

MOTHER: Be able to tell the father off.

ANDY: I don't think that's the question.

After Andy asks the interviewer to return and reread the question, Mrs. Lewis elaborates:

MOTHER: I think, I guess I put it in different words. I think the important thing to be concerned about in relation to his father is being able to be his own person. And being able to express his feelings to his father.

ANDY: And being open with his father!

MOTHER: Being open and comfortable with his father. . . . That's what I say!

FATHER: (*to Andy*) What did you say?

ANDY: I agree. I can see the point.

Dr. Lewis speaks of the place of love in the relationship between a son and his father, and Mrs. Lewis then clarifies her idea, becoming more specific:

MOTHER: And I guess . . . when I talk about openness, that I'm thinking about a big son . . . an older son would know he could answer back his father, and he would still be loved, you know? That he could separate from his father, and that he could be open and tell his father that he disagrees with him, and he knows his father loves him no matter what he says.

Andy struggles to unite the two voices: his mother's soliloquy about independence and his father's telegraphic emphasis on love. He insists that both parental positions are variations of one basic idea: "helping and loving." He probably is hearing his mother's encouragement of autonomy, endorsing his challenges and leadership in the family. It is likely that Andy has heard her clear message over the years, as he builds on it during the discussions and in no way blocks her call for independence and differentiation.

Rarely do we see, within a family session, so clear a vision of how a parent's values may underlie an adolescent's developmental path. Usually we infer these values on the basis of how parents and adolescent speak, or don't speak, with one another. Here we have a bold, involved picture of how one parent may advocate through word and deed the belief that self-assertion and separateness from the family are both desirable and safe. In the specific interactions of the Lewis family we find even more evidence of Mrs. Lewis's strong commitment to promoting her son's autonomy.

Mrs. Lewis, perhaps reflecting the clear endorsement she is giving Andy to differ and "be his own man," directs many more explaining speeches to him than his father does. She also guides and focuses Andy more actively in various discussions, paralleling his many efforts in that direction that we have already observed. Overall, Mrs. Lewis is more empathic toward Andy and his father, while Dr. Lewis's role is to ask many questions, of both Andy and Mrs. Lewis.

ANDY'S PROGRESSION

During his freshman year Andy reapplied to the private school that one of his brothers had attended. This time, his grades having improved, he was admitted and transferred from the high school. Perhaps stimulated by the change in schools and the demanding new academic setting, Andy was now functioning at a conformist level. His sentence completions were more substantial than the terse expressions, usually built around one dimension, characteristic of his first year preconformist level. Now, rather than monolithic rules or solutions, he refers to more complicated social norms and the approval of others, as well as more subtle feelings—his own and others':

A man's job "is to bring home money for the family."

Rules are "there for a good purpose."

When a child will not join in group activities "he should be helped."

A wife should "clean the house, wash the clothes, and make dinner."

A man should always "be physically fit."

The thing I like about myself is "I'm spontaneous."

I feel sorry for people "who feel sorry for themselves."

No longer at the preconformist level of the first year, Andy remained at the conformist level over the following two years, continuing to concentrate on rules, socially acceptable feelings, and traditional social roles.

In his second-year interview Andy is more relaxed and expansive, telling of many new experiences and interests. Most important, in

Andy's eyes, is his new family structure; he has become "an only child":

> Both my brothers have gone away to college this year. . . . So
> I'm alone with my parents and that's a big change. It's probably
> the biggest change.

Besides the specialness of now being an only child, Andy is feeling proud of himself and confident enough to reveal that he wasn't accepted at his new school the first time he applied. (In his first-year interview he implied that it was his choice to attend public school.) Being admitted to this selective private school means, to Andy, that he has performed more competently. Throughout the freshman year of high school he wanted to transfer to this small private school because of "the academic standards—it's supposed to be one of the best schools in North America."

Sports, band music, and friends continue to be the mainstays of Andy's life. But we also see first glimmerings of his struggles over being more independent:

> This summer my father wants me to work, so I will. . . . It'll be a
> good experience, 'coz I've gotta start to be a little more indepen-
> dent and do things on my own. . . . I try to be more than they
> [his parents] let me. . . . But they're pretty flexible about that.

Andy goes on to describe his parents' insistence that an older cousin stay with him while they were away one weekend. At first he objected, but then—in his usual style—he acceded to their judgment. Earlier in the year he had also complied with his parents' wishes by not playing football, since they were worried about his being unable to meet his school demands.

Other than those short-lived struggles over independence, Andy's life in the family and at school is without major difficulties or upheavals. He is optimistic, minimizing serious conflicts or unhappiness, describing how he tries to avoid disruptive experiences. He avoided a bully in the new school, for instance, and did not let himself become too upset, since this bully bothered all the kids, not just him. The steadiness of life reported by Andy is consistent with that of the steady conformists.

It is noteworthy that signs of more advanced ego development already appeared in Andy's participation in the family discussion: his responsiveness to others, his self-confidence in clarifying other's thoughts and feelings. In the second year and beyond, what we see is evidence that Andy is now extending this way of experiencing and expressing himself outside of the family, with friends and with the interviewer.

ADVANCED PROGRESSION: LOIS WELLER

Uppermost for Lois is other people, their support and understanding. Her connections with them are pervasive and constantly on her mind. From the first minutes of the interview with this fifteen-year-old high school freshman, the significance of friends and family members and the continuity of relationships with them is apparent. When we asked other students about their transition to high school, most of them commented on "being lost" and "getting adjusted" to the new classes or to the new freedom. For Lois, the fundamental change has to do with friends:

> It was a big change, because I don't see all my friends as much as I used to. I used to hang around with a bunch of kids . . . we had all been pretty close, 'cuz we went to the same school for eight years, and there have been certain additions and subtractions, but basically it was the same, the same nucleus. And I thought it was going to be . . . that was the end of the group. But apparently it was a strong nucleus, 'cuz we managed to stay together and I see them almost every day. . . . And I also made a lot of new friends. That all made my transition a lot easier.

Lois emphasizes the support and longevity of the relationships within her "nucleus": "So we just stayed close friends all over the years, and I . . . just think it's nice to have a bunch of kids you can turn to." Lois also extols the value of people in her sentence completions, as she proclaims that being with other people "Is *terrific!!!*" and the thing she likes about herself "is my attitude towards people."

Much of Lois's pleasure with others has to do with being accepted and acknowledged by them. She describes, in great detail, several friendships and group "antics" on weekend nights. Contact and consistent companionship are basic components of Lois's experiences with her friends. On the less favorable side, Lois's need to be with others leaves her particularly vulnerable to feeling slighted or left in the lurch. The humiliation of being left out is certainly a major theme for many teenagers. What is especially noteworthy in Lois's case is that she brings up this painful experience early in the interview, detailing both her suffering and her coping:

One of the boys had a party that I wasn't invited to. So . . . one of my friends told me nobody to her knowledge had asked [about me]. "Well didn't anybody notice I wasn't there?" And she said [to me], well, that a couple of kids had gone up to her, but to her knowledge nobody had said anything. And that got me even more upset because I didn't know who my friends were.

Added to the injury of not being invited was the fact that nobody noticed Lois's absence. At first, Lois was stunned and dismayed:

. . . I was very depressed. A lot of crying. I did a lot of yelling at my mother, but she knew why. I told her . . . so I talked to her for a while, and I told her that I was going to be real crabby because I was really in a bad mood, and she said she understood.

Lois turned to her mother, her older brother, and her father. At the same time, she began to discover that she really was not as friendless as she had imagined:

LOIS: But that all worked out, and I discovered that more people that I had known about had asked and had made me feel really good that a lot of kids were wondering where I was, and I was just kinda wondering why he hadn't invited me. So we talked, but I really don't think I found [out] exactly. (*laughs*) I still haven't figured it out . . . he excluded some other people. I found that out later, that he had excluded more people than I had known about.

INTERVIEWER: Did that help you, to find out from others too?

LOIS: Yeah, because it had sounded like all my friends were there except for me and then when I had found out that a group of girls wasn't there, [it] made me feel all right. Maybe he didn't have enough room [in his house] and he decided he's trying to broaden his friends too, and maybe he knows we're . . . always gonna be there. So he just invited the kids he wasn't so sure about. . . . It made me feel a lot better to know I wasn't the only one.

Lois surmounts this familiar, and nearly always dismaying, moment of feeling rebuffed by the social world that is so dear to her. Friends (and her family) help in this episode in at least two ways. First, there is the support that she receives directly from her family. Second, there is the information that she gains, as her friends tell her that others were also missing and that others had noticed her absence. In her sentence completions Lois points out the importance of direct support from others and obtaining information as ways to cope:

When a child will not join in group activities "they should be asked personally, they might be shy."

When they avoided me "I tried to find out what I had done."

As was true for many of the boys and girls in these early adolescent years, sexual relationships are not yet salient. Yet Lois suggests that these matters are already problematic. She openly discusses boys and her "body changes" with her mother. Several times in the interview Lois describes, with relief, the pleasure she has with boys who are "not boyfriends." A more indirect, but telling, sign of her unease in this area was the single sentence stem that Lois did not complete (by a student who conscientiously filled out all forms and never missed an appointment). "When I am with a man" was followed by a large black dot, suggesting that Lois had taken a long pause with her pen, a pause that led to an amorphous blot rather than her usual distinct words.

Lois's skills and pleasure in relationships are also apparent with teachers. These adults chose her to participate in a host of activities, including the town band, a multischool magazine, and a special leadership conference, all oriented to the transition to high school. Through each of these special involvements, Lois connects with many new students and gains increasing recognition from her teachers. She is clearly pleased with herself as she describes the many people she knows in her high school, demonstrating the extensive new networks she has developed through her special activities.

Lois's visions of the future build on these strengths and satisfactions. For many years, in addition to cherishing being with people, she has wanted to help them. Often she expresses this wish directly. But in her sentence completions, she also reveals a tension between giving to others *and* giving to herself:

A woman should always "be good to herself as well as other people."

A good mother "should love her family but not neglect herself."

When people are helpless "I want to help them."

Two of Lois's career ambitions spring from this blend of skills and wishes. First, in the fifth grade Lois decided she wanted to be a psychoanalyst. More recently, in her freshman year of high school, she has decided to be a pediatrician. Once again, Lois is clear about the roots of her plans:

I basically want to help people. That's one of my main goals in life. Because I figure if I can't help people it's not really worth it. . . . I'm pretty much decided I want to be a doctor and I've pretty much moved to being a pediatrician. I really love children. I've always loved to work with children.

LOIS'S FAMILY

With more convincing clarity than many of the other adolescents show, Lois builds a strong case for her family's contribution to the clear advance that we shall see in her development and to her generally high self-esteem, optimistic visions of the future, altruistic wishes, and resilience—her "bouncing" back from her dismay over feeling rejected by friends from the party, and from her dejection over no longer being academic "top dog" as a freshman in her high school. Lois provides rich narratives of each family member's contribution to her progression. She also reveals an emotional brittleness that was evident to her in the years before we ever met her. These more problematic issues have important meanings within her family.

Mrs. Weller plays a dual role in Lois's life: mother and best friend. In the opening moments of her first interview, Lois introduces her mother as she tells of the upsetting party incident:

A lot of crying [about not being invited], I did a lot of yelling at my mother but she knew why. I tell my mother just about everything. It's natural to share everything with my mother. . . . I don't keep anything from her . . . even the things like bad grades and the coming home from lunch [period at high school] when I'm not exactly supposed to yet, and things like that. Even when I tell her that, she says, "Well don't do it again." She doesn't get mad. She's accepting to a point. I mean, she wouldn't let me run around, and I don't go taking drugs or something. But she is very accepting. She's very helpful for things like that. . . .

Later in the interview, Lois portrays this special relationship in more poignant detail:

Well, my mother and I have a very unique relationship . . . and this is the kinda relationship she had with her mother. It's the kind of thing that seems to be passed down in our family. My mother and I are very close, we're closer than sisters. . . . I like her, I love her as a mother, and I love her as a person, and I think that's the key to the whole thing, because we respect each other and we tell each other everything. I mean my mother doesn't tell me as much as I tell her, because she doesn't have the same kinda problems I do. But my mother went through everything that I'm going through now, and so she understands and she's willing to talk. . . . I can tell her anything, and I know that if I say, "Look, I don't want anyone else to know this," I know that nobody else is going to know this, even my father, who she would tell most things to.

Reliability, acceptance, and a persistent commitment to being available to her daughter make Lois's mother a staunch ally:

She's somebody I can rely on, and it's very important to have somebody I know I can rely on and I know that somebody's always there. And it's important to know that somebody thinks the same way as me. . . . We have a very special relationship, and I don't know that many people who have that relationship with their parents or their mother. . . . Most people are saying they're glad to get out of the house . . . they're so mad at their mothers, and I'm just not usually mad at my mother. There are occasionally little mads, but by the end of the day, the two of us are making up. It's a very special relationship, and that's very important to me.

Lois brims with adoration, warmth, and recognition of something "very special" as she describes her bond with her mother:

My mother and I "are very close. I can tell her *anything!*"

If my mother "is upset it affects the whole family."

When she thought of her mother she "was happy."

Mrs. Weller is forty-eight years old, has completed her master's degree, and works at a nearby college. She functions at one of the highest ego development stages, autonomous, a level that is evident within the family discussions. In her own sentence completions, Mrs. Weller lucidly communicates the extraordinary importance she attributes to family relationships:

Raising a family "has been a most stimulating and enjoyable experience."

If my mother "would continue in her current frame of mind it would be great for us all."

My mother and I "are very close—she is my stepmother. My natural mother died when I was three. Dad remarried when I was seven."

When she thought of her mother she "recalled many incidents of their life with pleasure."

My father "was a very wonderful man who adored me and was very helpful."

My husband "and I will continue to enjoy each other and life."

Mrs. Weller also celebrates life and good feelings about herself:

The thing I like about myself is "my flexibility and my life style."

Women are lucky because "they have the best of both worlds: The option to work and the pleasure to stay home if they want to."

I am "so grateful to be alive and to have the opportunity to live each day with my family and friends."

Other people, beyond family members, are also of much interest to Mrs. Weller:

When I am with a man "I am interested in assessing his reaction to me and in finding out as much as I can about him."

Being with other people "is very important to me, but I also need to be by myself."

When they talked about sex, I "Was interested in others' feelings."

Finally, Mrs. Weller expresses altruistic concerns that are also reminiscent of her daughter's values:

I feel sorry "that the world has so many problems and that our children will not have an easy time."

When people are helpless "they need all the support one can give them."

When a child will not join in group activities "it is helpful to find out why he or she is shy and to stand by him/her until he/she can risk venturing into the group"

Lois's father, Mr. Weller, is a forty-nine-year-old executive in a large institution. He has completed graduate studies and functions at the transition between two advanced stages, conscientious and autonomous. Lois portrays him as available to her when she is upset, such as when she was not invited to the recent party. She feels close to him, "but we're not close the way I am close with my mother. I can't confide in my father." Although her relationship with her father does not have the intensity and openness that she experiences with her mother, there are several distinctive features that Lois appreciates. He values her observations and understandings: "He confides in me . . . he respects me in a different way than most people do. He respects my opinions and he's willing to listen to me a lot of the time."

She also has fun with her father, sharing baseball interests and shopping sprees with him. Lois is delighted as they buy new stereo equipment together, based on special information he has obtained for her from colleagues. Yet his time with her is more episodic, often concentrated in the summers, when they have lunch together or go to baseball games.

Lois is clear about the differences in her relationships with her parents, and she expresses some unease about whether these differences might imply a problem or weakness in her tie with her father:

LOIS: . . . So we do fun things together and he also respects me as a person, but I don't confide in him [her father] the way I confide in my mother. I wouldn't be as comfortable confiding in a man.

INTERVIEWER: Why do you think that is?

LOIS: Because he's a man, because he didn't go through the kinds of things I'm going through . . . changes in my body and stuff like that . . . feeling certain ways about boys, for instance, and my mother remembers stuff like that. And my father . . . could only give me . . . advice from a male point of view, which is always helpful. But . . . the two of us don't have that kind of relationship. And I don't think it makes our relationship any weaker because I confide in my mother like that and I don't confide in him. . . . It's just a different. . . . I don't ever think you can have the same kind of relationship with two people, it's just not the same kind of thing.

Lois's reluctant recognition of feeling more distant from her father is hinted at in one of her sentence completions:

My father "is very important but that doesn't keep him from me."

In Mr. Weller's sentence completions we see why Lois may feel more detached when she is with him. In his world of abstract principles, matters of responsibility and morality are of the utmost importance:

Women are lucky "because as a group which has been discriminated against, they will now have great opportunities."

A husband has a right to "expect his wife will remain faithful."

The worst thing about being a man "is the expectation that everyone has about your being responsible for their welfare."

Mr. Weller also reveals his preoccupations with the demands of work and leadership:

A man's job "is to provide for his family and to provide moral leadership as well."

He felt proud that "he has accomplished his task which aided some group of needy kids."

The thing I like about myself "is my capacity to foresee needs and the capacity to make constructive change."

The casual, spontaneous exchanges that Lois has with her mother do not occur so easily with Mr. Weller, the parent who attends to responsibilities and goals.

A man should always "strive to accomplish major goals in life."

A man feels good "when he has achieved his objectives."

My conscience bothers me "if I do not complete necessary assignments."

I feel sorry "for young people who are educated and cannot get jobs in their field of interest."

In contrast to his views on work, goals, and long-range planning, Mr. Weller experiences less confidence about feelings and relationships:

What gets me in trouble "is being open about my feelings in situations that call for more tact."

My main problem is "not being able to roll with the punches and taking things too seriously."

When I am criticized "I used to become very defensive."

Being with other people "brings me pleasure or sometimes is very tiring."

The other two members of Lois's immediate family are her older brothers. In contrast to most of the other adolescents, Lois speaks at length about the importance of her siblings, about the special ways that they have influenced her development and continue to do so. She recalls how they reminded her about her overreactions when she was younger:

> I used to get really upset without finding out exactly what was going on, so I decided to change. My brother and I used to complain all the time. We spent a weekend with a family. The youngest daughter complained every single second. I could not think that anybody could think of so many complaints. And my brother said, "I'm glad that you were so . . . aggravated by that, because that's what we lived for, for quite a few years of your life." . . . I knew I had complained a lot. . . . I had tried to make it less and less, but I knew that I wasn't getting very far. . . . I didn't think I complained as much as the boys thought I did. And they said, "You've gotten a lot, lot better. And then I just decided, "This is ridiculous, there's no reason for me to keep complaining all the time." So I just try and figure things out before I complain.

Although the two brothers are mentioned together in this narrative, most of the time Lois clearly distinguishes between them, giving more prominence to Ted, her older brother by five years. For example, she points out how Ted was a catalyst for the change in her outlook as she transformed herself from spoiled baby to valued sister:

> It probably happened in the seventh or eighth grade. . . . My brother went to this place called Mystery Islands, and he came back totally changed. He was a different person, and nothing meant anything any more. . . . Nothing material mattered. I've always looked up to my oldest brother . . . and so when he changed completely it was just such a big influence that I had to change too. 'Cuz when I saw how terrific he was, I couldn't bear thinking he had to live with a crabby little sister. (laughs) . . . I think Ted's made a big difference in my attitude towards life.

Her brother Joe, two years older than Lois, is less idealized. Nonetheless, he too has pressured Lois to change:

> My other brother helped a lot because he was the one who could say, "Lois, you're kvetching, or "Lois, you're complaining, you shouldn't do that." I think I'm probably closer to him now. . . . I think he considers me more of an equal.

As Lois suggests here, and elaborates even more fully in her interview, her relationship with Joe is fraught with competition, curiosity, and occasional pitched battles. Lois describes how she was recruited by Joe's girlfriend to help her end the relationship. The experience served to correct Lois's exaggerated view of Joe's specialness to women and made her more curious about him. Lois's competition with and fear of Joe are also apparent in the story that she tells of a recent fiery argument over household chores. It was a quarrel that Lois eventually took to her parents' room, seeking their protection from his size and temper. In contrast to Ted, Joe has strong mood swings and an easily triggered temper.

Lois provides a remarkably full portrait of her family. This presentation is consistent with her general articulateness and openness. Although we might speculate about the contribution of siblings to the maturation or arrested growth of each of the adolescents, it is Lois who affords us detailed perceptions of these other family members. Lois's elaborate description of each family member and her relationships with them represents an even broader theme: the importance of her family and the security she feels within it. This is a family that is so aware of itself as a unit that for many years "Family Council" meetings have provided a forum for members to raise questions or problems, with safeguards from the intrusion or domination of other (older) family members:

> My family's very important. And even when Joe's mad at me, I still . . . don't think it really makes that much difference. Because the things we argue about a lot of times are really silly, and when I have a problem that involves family, we have a Family Council at the dinner table, discuss it. And it's how we decide whether or not to buy things. It's just so I get a chance to say what I want to say uninterrupted. . . . In our family we all interrupt each other all the time, and half the time you're interrupting an interruption that interrupted somebody else's interruptions, (*laughs*) and so this way you just get to talk constantly about your subject . . . and if you feel it is straying into another matter you can say, "Look, we're having a Family Council about this subject, and I want this discussed." Whenever somebody wants to say something we just say "Family Council"
> (*laughs*) . . . and anybody can call one or anything like that.

Lois offers one of the most complete descriptions of a family in our study. We see aspects of her family ranging from the individual members to the special functions of the whole unit (Family Council meetings). Outstanding strengths cited by Lois include the appreciation and respect that the members of her family have for one another, and

the trusting relationships that Lois has with her mother and, sometimes, with her older brother and father. Given these ingredients, plus
her strong motivation to "improve," it is not surprising that Lois's ego
development has progressed over the years. Yet important questions
remain. To what extent are these features of Lois's family visible in their
interactions with one another? *How* has Lois's family promoted her
progressive ego development? And how does her family differ from
families of teenagers who begin the study at the most advanced stages
(accelerated development) or those who reach them from the earliest
stages (dramatic progression)?

LOIS WITHIN HER FAMILY

The Wellers discuss two different dilemmas, with Lois initially opposing her parents' conclusions. Both sets of discussions provide an
excellent vantage point for seeing how the Wellers promote and con-
tend with Lois's differences and with her trial separations from them.
We also see her influence upon the parents' interactions.

With great tenacity, Lois clearly presents her ideas, which at times
verge on immovable opinions. Her parents are initially curious and
consistently accepting. Their many murmured "okay"s and "um"s as
they react to her ideas signal their openness with her. Lois at first
concludes that Heinz should steal to save his wife's life. Both her
parents think that he should not steal:

LOIS: Oh, I'm going to have to be alone against both of you.

MOTHER: Okay, that's super! How come you said yes?

FATHER: Lois, why don't you tell us why you think he should steal it?

LOIS: Well, I didn't really say, "Yes, he should definitely steal it." I said
that he should go and look for help and see if someone else can help
her. And he should go to other people and say, "Can you help me
with this, can you work on this drug . . . ?" He should go to the
government and ask them to help him get the drug for him. I didn't
say definitely, "Yes." But then—

MOTHER: (*interrupting*) Well, that's a very good idea.

LOIS: (*interrupting*) But then . . . [the interviewer] said, "Suppose he
couldn't get any help, he either doesn't get the drug or he steals it,
and there's no other alternatives, nobody else can help." Then I saw,
in a case like that it is more important for him to steal it, because it's a
person's life and a human life is a human life—

MOTHER: (*interrupting*) That's true, but what about the quality of life?

LOIS: What do you mean about the qual—

FATHER: (*interrupting*) Well suppose everybody stole. What do you think the society would be like?

LOIS: But it's not a question of everybody stealing. It's a question of one person stealing to save someone's life. I'm not saying that everybody should go around stealing. . . . I mean he should steal because it's his wife that's dying. That's the big difference.

Lois clarifies her position in response to her parents' points. It is not that she simply is more verbose as a way to evade their questions or mask her resistance to their challenges. Rather, what we see is her growing engagement with them, her inclusion of their ideas in her ever more complex contributions to the unfolding discussion. Yet in the midst of what seems to be a series of challenges and responses between Lois and her mother, Lois's father suddenly begins to direct the group, pressing his wife to describe her thoughts.

Mrs. Weller persists in questioning Lois, countering her husband's pressures, but Mr. Weller does not want this exchange between mother and daughter to continue. In the apparent spirit of wanting to protect his daughter, he warns his wife to stop trying to persuade Lois to change her mind. Lois has just reminded the family that it's Heinz's wife who is dying:

MOTHER: But what about, what about—

FATHER: (*interrupting*) Well, don't, don't, lets not try to convince Lois. Why don't you share, why don't—

MOTHER: (*interrupting*) No, I'm just—

LOIS: (*interrupting*) She's just—Go ahead.

MOTHER: Well, what I'm asking you is, what do you think about the druggist's rights? Is it all right for his product, for which he has worked to save? Now . . . granted he's not such a great character to make some money on it. . . . He still has the right of not having somebody take that away from him.

LOIS: I know. But he shouldn't be selling for ten times. I mean, this woman is dying.

MOTHER: Oh, I agree with that.

LOIS: And if this guy says he'll pay him, he should let him pay him . . .

FATHER: Mmhm, hmmm. But it says here, it says he offers to pay him.

MOTHER: (*interrupting*) Well, I certainly agree with that.

LOIS: (*finishes*) To pay it later.

Not only does her father intervene to shield Lois and orchestrate the situation, but Lois then intervenes to protect her mother and encourage her to express her position, as if to say, "Let her continue with me; she's not going to push me to her position. Let her speak." And her speaking leads to further agreement between Lois and both parents.

Mr. Weller's attempt to restrain his wife from pressing their daughter allows Lois to maintain her special connection with her mother and elaborate her ideas. Of further interest is Lois's parallel protective response to her mother, as if to shield *her* from Mr. Weller. In her interview Lois dwelt at length upon the specialness of her relationship with her mother, perhaps explaining Lois's efforts to make sure her mother is in no way cut off from this connection with her.

In a later phase of the discussion, Lois's influence upon the family dynamics is even clearer, as she questions the logic of the discussion and clarifies her stance on the individual versus society. Her points are taken very seriously by both parents:

LOIS: I think that life is the only thing that is important!

FATHER: Well, I know, but it's a question of an individual's needs versus, in effect, society's needs. And you have to weigh those.

LOIS: How does this get into society?

FATHER: Well, because in fact if, if people just stole, then the structure of society would break down.

LOIS: Well . . . the thing is, I don't think he should steal; I think he should get help. But if he can't get help, then I think he's driven . . . to stealing. The guy, the druggist, is bringing it on himself. [Heinz] offered to pay the whole thing, if he could pay it, you know, in bunches. . . . In effect, the druggist has the right to say this woman dies. And I don't think any person has the right to say who dies and who lives.

FATHER: Well, that's true, but on the other hand there's a higher, higher issue, or a higher standard that you have to think about, and that is you can't justify people stealing. Because if people can steal no matter what their reason . . . then the whole structure of society falls apart . . . and life, the quality of life isn't worth anything.

LOIS: . . . I can't think of this one case on such a large scope, because it's—

MOTHER: (*interrupting, and to Lois*) Okay, that's very plausible. I can understand your saying that.

LOIS: Because, I mean, this is a person's life. When you say the quality of someone's life, it's a life!

MOTHER: Well, there is quality of life.

LOIS: But who's to decide what's good and what's bad?

The bond between Lois and her mother is illustrated in their exchange on the quality of life and ultimate decisions, an exchange launched by her father's more abstract point about society. Another sign of Lois's special connection to her mother is the very high level of important enabling processes—namely, problem-solving and accepting—that she engages in with Mrs. Weller. Moreover, Lois frequently jumps in to interrupt or complete ideas begun by her mother.[1]

Eventually Mr. Weller returns to take a more active role in the discussion, introducing a somewhat tangential idea about the "quality of life associated with the drug," which leads to an exchange with his wife about a topic they undoubtedly have discussed before. His points are unrelated to Lois's. She continues to insist on the "woman's life," while her father offers his more sociological-ethical stance. Lois underscores their divergent perspectives by teasing him about his abstractness:

FATHER: Well, it isn't even the druggist's rights, it's, it's the druggist—

MOTHER: (*interrupting*) It's true, but you just—

FATHER: (*interrupting*)—is really, in my judgment, a representative of society.

LOIS: Uh, oh, deep meanings! (*said with sarcasm*)

FATHER: Well, no, really.

MOTHER: Well, all right, that's true.

LOIS: (*interrupting*) I know, but—

FATHER: (*interrupting*) It's not the the druggist. [What is] important is pitting breaking the law versus saving someone's life. . . . Whether it be a wife or stranger does not make a difference, although you would be more motivated to steal for your wife than you would for a stranger but that—

LOIS: (*interrupting*) I said that too.

FATHER: Those are the critical issues.

Once again we witness the family's protective style of interacting, as Mrs. Weller supports her husband's position following Lois's sarcastic remark about "deep meanings."

Ultimately the family agrees that the druggist should in some way make the drug available to save Heinz's wife. In another family this might signal a consensus and a stopping point, permitting the members to sidestep their original differences. Mr. Weller seems to recognize this possibility and directs the family to confront their differences yet again:

MOTHER: Well, well, I agree and as far as [making the drug available is] concerned—

FATHER: (*interrupting*) But that's not the issue that's confronting us. We have to deal with the dilemma they have laid out for us . . . can you see—?

MOTHER: (*interrupting*) In other words you have to—

FATHER: (*interrupting*) Can you see? I mean, if we're supposed to come to some consensus, can you see the point we're trying to make?

LOIS: Oh, I understand what you're trying to— Is it a question of one person's life and of society's rules?

FATHER: That's right.

LOIS: But I don't see that society's rules are as important as life.

FATHER: I see.

LOIS: I mean, it's important to have rules because otherwise everything would fall apart and. . . . It's a human life. I just can't see pitting rules against a human life.

FATHER: So you're saying that . . . it's not possible then for us to come to a consensus as a family?

LOIS: Well, I don't think we're gonna get very far, because I think life is more important, and you guys think that society's rules are more important.

FATHER: Mmm.

MOTHER: . . . Well, I guess it is really a question of that.

In this last series of linked exchanges Mr. Weller is respectful of Lois but does not retreat from his difference of opinion with her. It is of interest that Mrs. Weller also accepts Lois's new conclusion. Mr. Weller's sensitivity to unresolved issues coupled with his assertive style lead to significant results: Lois perceives and articulates his point, and he clearly identifies the depth of their differences.

In several ways, then, both parents promote Lois's engagement in the discussion (and continued growth). They acknowledge and accept her points thoughtfully, in full recognition of the differences between her views and theirs. Her father's insistence on remaining with the issue at hand not only helps Lois develop her arguments but also exemplifies an interactive style that she can incorporate within her repertoire. The additional features of mutual protectiveness between Lois and her mother, and the family's ways of summarizing, which do not close off the flow of discourse, further enhance the family's contributions to Lois's development. In fact, following her summary statement about society's rules and needs, Lois goes on to recommend how the judge should respond, that he should address the wife's dire circumstances. Both parents applaud Lois for articulating this idea, since they had not attended to Heinz's wife in their conclusions: "That's interesting. That's very good" (Mother); "That's good" (Father). Another family quality illustrated in these excerpts is the persistent interrupting, something Lois recognizes in describing her family as "interrupting interruptions." It is important to see that these interruptions are not usually disruptions or distractions, as the speaker returns again and again to his or her point, often incorporating the ideas of the interrupter. Far from distractions, these interruptions reflect the close active engagement of the three Wellers, their excitement in the evolving views being expressed.

In a later discussion of Joe and his father, Lois again opposes both her parents, now arguing that Joe should not give the money to his father for a fishing trip. The family drifts away from the point, as Mr. Weller discusses how ideal it would be if Joe would, as an act of devotion to his father, "give up the money." After remarking how "selfish and self-centered" Joe's father is, Lois reminds her own father of the question at hand:

LOIS: But do you think he should give up the money, under the circumstances?

FATHER: It's not whether he *should* or not. It's a question—

LOIS: (*interrupting*) Yeah, but that was the question.

FATHER: —of it would be a good thing if he could do it.

MOTHER: Oh, but Lois is absolutely right.

LOIS: The question is should—

MOTHER: (*simultaneously*) Right. *Should he*, should he give up the money, not will he, not—

FATHER: (*interrupting*) If he is an entirely, highly moral person, he'll give up the money.

LOIS: Well, he isn't.

MOTHER: Well, you don't know whether he is. And he's only fourteen years old. But if the father—

LOIS: (*interrupting*) How many fourteen-year-olds are gonna give up like that?

FATHER: Very few.

LOIS: Exactly.

As the family begins to question whether Joe *would* give the money to his father rather than whether he *should,* Lois once more intervenes:

LOIS: *Should* he give it to him?

MOTHER: No, that's what I'm saying, that if the father puts the son in the position, then the son is unlikely to have seen the model of the other kind of behavior, and therefore I don't think that realistically he would be able to do this. But I think he should.

LOIS: The question isn't would, the question is should. Do you think he should give it up?

MOTHER: That's right, yes, I do.

LOIS: Why?

MOTHER: Because I agree with your father. I think that that's the highest form of selflessness.

LOIS: That it's morally correct.

In this excerpt we see the influence that adolescents can have on their families. As Lois pushes for greater clarity, her parents respond by articulating their positions more precisely. Sometimes Lois encourages the emergence of her parents' implicit assumptions. For instance, following Lois's insistence that they "stick to the point" about Joe, her mother expresses her view about a "scale of values" and its "two moral portions." While she may have been silently entertaining this idea, it is through Lois's interventions that she first airs it publicly in the family and then offers a more complex formulation of it:

MOTHER: If you're looking at it in a very practical point of view, the son owes a loyalty to the father, and granted the father gave [the promise] to the son too.

LOIS: Yeah.

MOTHER: But I think on the higher scale of things, the way things go in this solution, the son should give [the money] up. But I can't imagine a father ever putting his son in that kind of situation, that was where I was.

LOIS: I can't see the son giving it up. I don't think he should give it up. I think that in a situation like this, he's not the person who should have to give, because he's been planning for so long and his father just, it's whim. I don't think he *should* give it up. I don't think he would either. I think we've agreed on that. He's not gonna give up the money. But I don't think he *should* either, because he's worked hard for the money, and I can understand where you're coming from. I mean I can see that . . . it's high in moral and everything like that. But I don't think that in this case he really should give up the money, because he worked hard for it and he planned.

MOTHER: Well, of course, you're looking at it from—

LOIS: (*interrupting*) I knew you were going to say that.

MOTHER: —the highest moral point of view. The father shouldn't ask it, and the son then—

LOIS: (*interrupting*) Shouldn't have to give it—

MOTHER: (*interrupting*) If you're looking at it, the *two* moral portions, most moral (*voice gets higher*) then, the father should not ask the son—

LOIS: (*interrupting*) Right.

MOTHER: —but the son should give it to the father.

Here then is a complex interweaving: Lois pressing her parents to stay with the point, taking on their perspectives, and encouraging them to be even clearer and more complex in their articulation of issues being discussed. She incorporates her mother's helpful summary of the two moral dimensions and builds her own position still further, providing an excellent example of how an adolescent's discourse can become progressively more complex while interacting with her parents.[2]

After joking that the father should "get a paper route" if he has no money, Lois presents her most clearly defined, multifaceted position, leading to expressions of lively interest and understanding by her parents:

LOIS: Yeah, but when you think about it this is a fourteen-year-old kid. A fourteen-year-old . . . [with] hard-earned money. And I know the father is working and making hard-earned money, but when you're an adult you expect that. . . . He accepts the responsibility of having a family. He's saying, by having a family I will accept the responsibility of feeding them, give them clothes, give them shelter, and giving them an education. That's what he's saying by becoming a father. Now the son didn't ask to become a son. He just became a son. So if he works hard for his money, it's not for his father, it's for himself. And I agree with you that the highest moral thing would be for him to give it up. But I don't think he should. Because I don't think . . . it's his calling to give up hard-earned money.

There are examples throughout the evening's exchanges of how the Wellers' very high levels of ego development shape these discussions and provide "multiperspective" stances for Lois to emulate. Elsewhere in their deliberations about Joe, Mr. Weller acknowledges the two points of view (Lois's and her parents') and concedes that both are acceptable ("two different points and I think there's obvious validity for both points"). This is followed by Mrs. Weller's description of how different life experiences (Lois's and theirs) might contribute to the "generation difference" that Lois pointed to, since the parents have lived longer and have known of many situations in which laws were broken. The idea that their views are colored by their histories, other beliefs, and perceptions recurs a number of times and obviously conveys yet more complexity to Lois.

The dialogue between Lois and her parents demonstrates a wide range of dynamics surrounding progressive ego development, dynamics that go in both directions: from parent to child and from child to parent. It is important, but by no means critical, that both Lois's parents function at such high levels of ego development. We know from our other individual and group portraits that not all parents of progressively developing adolescents function at these high levels.

LOIS'S PROGRESSION

In the spring of her sophomore year, Lois looked back with amazement over a year that had been filled with departures and serious illness within her family. Her second brother had left for college, her father had unexpected surgery, and her mother was about to have an elective operation. As in the past, Lois continued to be active, working at her first part-time job, joining her youth group on trips to nearby states, and going to Europe with the school orchestra. Characteristically, she dealt with her new difficulties through all this activity and by drawing support from friends and family. Although relationships remain prominent features of her landscape, she experiences a new autonomy and a new intimacy with her friends. While Lois has always felt at ease with other people, peers and adults, she now feels more open with others, more confident about their presence:

LOIS: I feel not only a lot more open. . . . Most of the things I need to discuss are my feelings or my relationships with people in the band, because that is who I have most of my relationships with. And even if I am talking to them about them I feel comfortable. It's a really good feeling. Nice.

INTERVIEWER: Can you give an example of what you would talk over with one of them that is helpful and meaningful to you?

LOIS: There are so many. I find the most helpful is just knowing that they're there, so that when I have a problem . . . and not even just telling them about problems, but about your everyday things . . . knowing that if I have a problem, they're there. So it's not a specific thing we talk about; just that we talk, sort of communicate. And . . . I know that even if my entire world falls apart, they'll still be there.

Lois is aware of changes in her relationships with both parents, changes she traces directly to these new experiences with friends:

I think a lot of the fact that I have [close friends] here is that I don't have to unburden myself as much on my mother. I can sort of spread it out more thinly . . . no one has to really carry my burden. Which means that I can, instead of just going to my mother and father to talk about the heavy stuff, I can just go and talk . . . because I can tell more people about my problems, [my parents] don't just have to hear about my problems, they can hear about other stuff too. And I think that strengthens our relationships.

Lois reveals one consequence of this growing independence from her mother. When visiting her father in the hospital, while distraught over his operation, she was nonetheless able to leave his hospital room with her brother, allowing her mother to remain with her father.

In her new sentence completions, written shortly after the interview, we see that Lois's concerns about support and the significance of her mother in her life continue to be central:

My main problem is "most of my friends come to me for guidance and I don't always feel I have someone to go to."

My mother and I "are more like sisters than mother and daughter."

If my mother ever fell apart "I think the whole family would."

Lois is also more acutely aware of how people are different from one another. What is satisfying and important for her may not be for someone else:

For a woman a career is "one of the most important things, if she wants one."

Describing her mother's anticipated elective surgery, Lois says "I'm scared for her, but she's scared for herself and that is a lot harder."

Paralleling Lois's growing recognition of how people differ from one another, and from her, is an increasing ability to empathize. In the midst of her upsetting visit to her father, Lois considered both her own and her mother's distress:

I certainly wasn't dealing with [the visit] very well. . . . My mother was sort of stuck because she wanted to be by his side. But she also needed to be with me. I just felt that for her sake, if not for my own, I should leave, because she was stuck. She didn't know what to do.

A second component of Lois's progression in development is her experience of greater coherence, which she refers to in her interview and new sentence completions:

It's been a hard year, but I've not been lacking in self-esteem. I sort of have an idea of where I am right now, which is a nice feeling. I feel much more comfortable than I used to, in everything.

The thing I like about myself is "I'm pretty together in these screwed up times."

Connections between new relationships, new-found self-confidence, and integration are aptly illustrated as Lois joins these major points of her life:

I have an idea of what I want out of life . . . of what I want out of my life that's going on right now. . . . I know what I want to do with myself and what I want to—it's hard to explain—just I know where I am and I know. It's not like I am still going through the "there's something wrong with me" phase, because I feel accepted by my friends, my youth group friends, my girlfriends.

Earning her own money adds to Lois's new feelings of independence, feelings not leading to any form of rupture from her parents. While in Europe she used this money to buy presents for family and friends. "[It] made me feel good that I was independent enough to say, 'This is my money. I have been working for it, you know.' "

DRAMATIC PROGRESSION: LARRY DELTA

Larry was discharged from the hospital several weeks before his first interview. We did not then know that his ego development was to change so radically over the next year. But there were already signs of important strengths and specific ways that he differed from many other patients who were functioning—as he was—at very early stages of ego development. His vision of the future was more coherent and optimistic than that of most of the other patients. For instance, after remarking that his mother dropped out of school in the tenth grade, Larry tells the interviewer, "I'll make it through high school. I'll even make it through college. I'll be a lawyer."

Related to his optimistic vision of the future is Larry's pride in himself. Many of the patients alternated between verbally abusing or undermining others and expressing intense self-hatred. But Larry recognizes his strengths, first telling the interviewer of his academic successes, then his athletic accomplishments, and finally his mechanical prowess:

LARRY: If I see somethin' I can pick it up and I can do it, really good. Like . . . I started putting small engines, one-cylinder engines together, and I got 'em to order bodies and I got into frame work. And now I can tell you a car backwards, inside out, upside down, and I can take one apart and put it back together again—better.

INTERVIEWER: You're quick to pick up on things.

LARRY: Yeah, like I can remember somethin'. I can remember the first thing I learned. We used to put, ah, one-cylinder engines together from every step there is to it. Now I'm up to V-8 and piston jobs.

Larry does not tell of his achievements in the spirit of self-aggrandizement or boasting as a cover for more deflated feelings about himself. It would be a mistake to dismiss his pride as simply a way of bolstering his low self-esteem. As he expounds upon his ambition to become a lawyer, Larry's self-confidence and pleasure with others are clear:

INTERVIEWER: How come you want to be a lawyer?

LARRY: Um, 'coz I can talk to people. Some people, I can . . . I can sit down with a friend even if he's in a bad mood. I can get him back into a good mood and I can sometimes, I can even tell what a person's like just by what he wears, how he looks, and—I did that while I was here [at the hospital]. . . . My roommate, I told him exactly what he was like; I didn't even know him. . . . I was there for two days and I told 'im. . . . I like law. I like talking with and to people.

Larry's view of himself is more differentiated than that of other adolescents who remained at low levels of ego development. He describes his shyness about speaking in front of groups when receiving awards or in class. It is the fact that his praise of himself is not global or overblown that suggests we are observing genuine pride rather than an effort to quell deeper feelings of inadequacy.

Yet another context for this theme is Larry's sentence completions, communicating his optimism, generosity, and ambitions, all relatively infrequent emphases in the responses expressed by other adolescents functioning at low levels of ego development:

Being with other people "is easy for me."

The thing I like about myself "I can do what ever I'm told to do."

Education "is something I'm glad to have."

When people are helpless "I help them."

He felt proud that "he went through high school and college with not major problems."

Accompanying this hopeful voice is a violent one. Like the other male patients, Larry is aware of his violent impulses and responses, and on occasion he allows them to disrupt his relationships. The most serious episode involved his stepfather:

. . . after he, who is not my father . . . come and hit me and I broke his arm. I would have killed him . . . I would of. . . . It wasn't something to be proud of, but then again I'm not gonna be sorry for doin' it.

It was after several months of sudden mood swings, fights, erratic eating, and irregular sleep (staying awake all night), that Larry was admitted to the hospital. In the weeks before his admission he felt confused and depressed. His fights with others had grown more frequent, he was unable to control his temper, and he was upset about losing his girlfriend. He slept during the day, while at the same time fearful that boys from school might come to his home and beat him. At times he carried a knife when roaming the streets at night, looking for his biological father. Larry was becoming terrified of his suicidal ideas, fears of others, and surprising mood changes.

When he first arrived at the hospital, Larry didn't like being locked up. He "got really mad, and then hit things and people." But he soon realized that he got hurt each time by being restrained on the ward ("four points") and was threatened with being sent to the adult part of the hospital. Furthermore, he learned that his fights would extend his stay in the hospital. Although Larry insisted in the first moments of the interview that he hadn't changed, his narrative of how he now controls his fighting argues against that conclusion. He has more control over his impulsive outbursts and considerably greater awareness of himself. After noticing the results of his ward fights, Larry ended those self-destructive struggles. In preparing for discharge, after two months, Larry decided that the "kids" he had hung around with before could bring out the difficulties that led him to the hospital in the first place. His solution was first to recognize his potential and reputation as a fighter, *but* at the same time decrease the chance of his being violent by self-restraint and by changing environments. An illuminating exchange occurs during the interview, as Larry describes his increasing mastery over the "fights":

LARRY: The kids I used to hang around with give me a lot of trouble now.

INTERVIEWER: Like what kind of trouble?

LARRY: Fights, things like that.

INTERVIEWER: So what do you do when they want to get into a fight with you?

LARRY: Walk away.

INTERVIEWER: Is this new for you, or is that what you usually do?

LARRY: It's new.

INTERVIEWER: What did you used to do?

LARRY: Fight . . . it was [hard to walk away from a fight] 'coz I have a reputation in Jonesville. In two years no one here bothered me. But then I don't go lookin' for fights. I just mind my own business. You know, be with my friends and I think that if anyone gets into trouble, I go with them if they want me to. I think it's their fault not my friends', and I'll fight with them even, if I have to. But it's not that I'm gonna go out there and beat them up just because they given my friend a hassle.

INTERVIEWER: Now is this new for you? Did you used to go beat them up anyhow?

LARRY: In a way . . . yeah, because before my friends would get in trouble with those kids and we'd go back and we'd fight; they'd be six or seven of us and I'd be gettin' into trouble, the police and people, all those kinda things. Now, those kids I fight with and fought are fightin' with me so now I'm like, I don't hang around with anyone in Jonesville because I'd either be beatin' them up or hang around with them.

Larry wavers between grasping the importance of controlling his inclinations to fight and thinking that he must control the powerful "influences" of his surroundings. In his sentence completions he aptly expresses this vacillation between believing in the potency of his environment to disrupt and his worries about losing control:

Crime and delinquency could be halted "if everyone was evaluated here."

What gets me in trouble is "my old friends."

My main problem is "the kids in Jonesville."

I just can't stand people who "fight people for stupid reasons."

Women are lucky because "they don't have to worry about getting in fights (physically)."

A steady girlfriend in another town and an older store manager ("older than my mother") represent two other important supports in Larry's life, contributing to his feeling less vulnerable:

You just know there's someone there [his older friend], which is probably one of my best friends. He's probably my best friend. I mean, if I need him, he's there. If I ever run short of money he'll—[3]

Larry distinguishes himself from the profoundly arrested teen-agers—both patient and high school adolescents—in his flexibility, self-awareness, and sporadic interest in applying insights about himself. He is frequently clear about the people in his life, his responses to them, and how his responses have changed in recent times. In the first year of the study, Larry's tendency to blame the environment for his difficulties, not taking personal responsibility, is certainly consistent with his functioning at the self-protective ego development stage. An alternative view is that he anticipates the impact of his environment and accordingly modifies his behavior in these situations. His self-awareness is evident during the interview as he describes the fact that he has begun to *like* (to his surprise) the hospital and is sorry to leave. Larry shows his self-awareness at the end of the interview, when he describes his difficulty in asking questions:

INTERVIEWER: Do you have any question that you want to ask me?

LARRY: No . . . see, there's one thing I'm not very good at. It's asking questions, 'coz I don't know what to say.[4]

LARRY'S FAMILY

Larry's penetrating observations and articulateness are particularly striking as he describes his family. We already know that his relationship with his stepfather is problematic. Larry speaks openly, intensely, of his dislike for this new man in his life, one who disrupts Larry's close bond with his mother and interferes with the more tenuous one he tries to maintain with his biological father.

Mrs. Delta is extremely important to Larry. Not surprisingly, he is acutely aware of her impact on him, repeatedly observing that he has lived with her for more than fourteen years, that "if she's not important to me then no one is. . . . I wouldn't do anything to hurt her." It was because of his wanting not to upset his mother that Larry only broke his stepfather's arm and "didn't kill him" during their recent clash. Larry is very different from the teenagers following early arrest and early progression paths in his open acknowledgement of intense attachments to his mother, disclosures that also appear in his sentence completions:

> If my mother "wasn't there when I needed her I wouldn't be so good now."

> When he thought of his mother "He remembered the love he had for her and she had for him."

Mrs. Delta is thirty-six years old and has been remarried for the last four years. Her ego development level is in the upper end of the conformist range, self-aware. Her sentence completion responses suggest reasons why Larry feels so very warm and attached to her. Mrs. Delta expresses generosity and consideration in dealing with others and has many concerns about family members:

> If my mother "were not very ill I would probably tell her how much she is imposing on me."

> I feel sorry "for any person with a mental or physical illness. I would like so much to be able to help."

> When I get mad "I keep my anger pretty much to myself, knowing what I say when angry could hurt the ones I love."

> When a child will not join in group activities "it's probably because he or she feels unwanted."

> At times she worried about "my son getting hurt in some way."

> I am "happy to have a good family."

My main problem is "not being able to communicate with my son."

Larry was two years old when his biological father abruptly left the family, not having told his wife he planned to leave, or of his whereabouts. He suddenly reappeared when Larry was four and lived with the family for the next nine months. Then his parents again separated and soon divorced. The biological father lives in a nearby town, and until Larry's hospitalization, which his father opposed, Larry saw him regularly. Once he entered the hospital, his father rarely visited or phoned, yet he continues to be a very strong presence in Larry's life. On numerous occasions Larry compares himself to his father with respect to his gregariousness, his extensive social network, and the kind of house Larry intends one day to live in.

Mrs. Delta remarried two years before Larry entered the hospital. She had known her new husband, Mr. Bolton, over the last five years. Larry rarely mentions his stepfather, and when he does, it is usually with much conflict: some gratitude, mostly anger and criticism. Larry sees how his stepfather has supported his mother in setting clearer, more consistent limits for him. Alongside this more rational and measured evaluation is Larry's overt disdain for and distance from Mr. Bolton.

Through the stepfather's sentence completions, we see a more differentiated picture of this man, who probably contributes to the striking changes that occur in Larry between the first and second years of the study. Mr. Bolton is forty-two years old and, like his wife, functions at the self-aware level. He has completed several years of business college. In his concentration on family concerns and broad altruistic ideals he parallels Larry's mother:

A good father "tries to keep his family together."

My main problem is "the health and welfare of my stepson."

Raising a family "is harder then I anticipated."

If I had more money "I would do more for my family and with the rest I would use it to help them."

In the last completion, Mr. Bolton brings together his commitments to family and altruism. In several other responses he writes of generosity and his concerns about hurting others:

The thing I like about myself "is my concern and effort to help others whenever possible."

I feel sorry "for people who are suffering from any illness, emotional or otherwise."

I can't stand people "who don't see the problems and needs of others."

He felt proud that he "could help them with their problems."

My conscience bothers me if "I do anything to hurt anyone."

Besides the belief in helping others, particularly family, Mr. Bolton reveals a degree of insightfulness that was not evident in the responses of either his wife or Larry. In Larry's interview there are suggestions of his sensitivity to other people's feelings and thoughts. This sensitivity is more fully developed in Mr. Bolton's responses and may possibly encourage Larry's budding inclinations in this direction:

When a child will not join in group activities "I feel there is problem that should be looked into."

When they avoided me "I feel I am doing something to offend them, and try to find a reason."

Sometimes he wished "he could have more knowledge."

Counterbalancing, and sometimes contradicting, Mr. Bolton's leanings toward psychological explanations and insights is his tough stance on taking responsibility, leading to his "law and order" attitudes:

Crime and delinquency could be halted if "more severe punishment were used."

Rules are "made to be upheld."

When people are helpless "(it is usually) because they refuse to seek adequate help for themselves."

This last response was even more definitive at first. It was as a second thought that Mr. Bolton inserted the qualification "it is usually" before his stronger statement "because they refuse to seek adequate help for themselves."

His mother's marriage to Mr. Bolton was most disturbing for Larry, threatening an end to the closeness he had with her and serving as well to remind him of his father's absence. Adding to Larry's difficulties with his stepfather are Mr. Bolton's swings from an understanding and thoughtful attitude to the imposition of rigid rules and force.

The other member of the family is Joe, Larry's eight-year-old brother, whom Larry has cared for since his birth, while his mother either worked or dated. Joe was born between his mother's marriages. For a long time Larry imagined that his biological father was also Joe's father. Just as Larry tends to idealize his biological father and his older friend, Joe looks up to Larry:

> . . . like Joe's looked up to me, because I'm his big brother and I've taken care of him since he was born and, I mean . . . I don't think he likes anyone the way he likes me, or loves the same for me. 'Coz if anything ever happened to him, I'd pity the person that does it. I'll stop at nothin'.

Despite some occasional irritation, Larry admires and praises Joe:

> . . . He's at the stage now when he's a real pest. You know how you have to listen to him. If you're talking someone he'll start talkin', and if you don't listen to him he'll start scream- ing. . . . But he's smart. My whole family's pretty smart. My brother's eight years old and he's in the first grade or second grade . . . and he's smart enough to go into the fifth grade.

Compelling feelings pervade Larry's family relationships: warmth and closeness toward his mother and Joe, disappointment with his father, and unsettling—at times stormy—conflicts with his stepfather. By observing his family, we have the opportunity to see how Larry interacts with two of these family members and to consider how these transactions may contribute to the course of Larry's dramatic progres- sion.

LARRY WITHIN HIS FAMILY

Distinctive features of the Delta family's discussions are the atten- tiveness, humor, and engagement of each family member. Like many of the other families we watched, members challenge one another's positions. In sharp contrast to families of teenagers who remain at low levels of ego development, however, Larry and his parents change their ideas after hearing meaningful opposing views. For instance, Larry's mother and stepfather raise several new ideas early in the discussion of whether Heinz should be sentenced to jail. Larry, hearing each parent change, is then remarkably flexible and reflective in his deliber- ations about this issue. At first he disagrees with them, insisting that Heinz should be sentenced. His mother and stepfather engage in a long dialogue about the nature of Heinz's crime, concluding that it was a crime of conscience, not passion. They consider the druggist's immorality:

STEPFATHER: I think the druggist should be—ah—punished for charging—

MOTHER: (*interrupting*) Yeah, but you can't change society . . . what you can do to change society is to go by your own conscience. If you're a good person to begin with . . . I think in this particular case [Heinz] was trying to help somebody, but he's not trying to get away with anything.

STEPFATHER: Mmm.

MOTHER: And he'd be more than willing to pay.

STEPFATHER: Larry wants him sent up for life. (*mother and stepfather laugh*)

LARRY: No, I said that he should be sent because he did it and he should face the consequences. But then we're seeing everything from different—

STEPFATHER: (*interrupting*) Yeah, that's right.

MOTHER: That sounds right, but I didn't see it from that. I saw it from the point that—

STEPFATHER: (*interrupting*) He broke the law.

LARRY: Yeah, but he *did* commit the crime and he should be sentenced.

MOTHER: Right.

LARRY: Because if everyone got off—

MOTHER: (*interrupting*) That's right.

LARRY: Then that's—

STEPFATHER: (*interrupting*)—True.

LARRY: There wouldn't be any law enforcement and—

MOTHER: (*interrupting*) That's what I said. I mean under these particular circumstances. I think I still feel as though the guy shouldn't be sentenced—not a jail sentence and not a prison sentence of any kind. I think the most sentencing that he should be given—

LARRY: (*interrupting*) I think that. I think I'd agree. . . . Pay back what he did steal.

STEPFATHER: Pay back.

MOTHER: You know, even though it was unreasonable.

Besides illustrating Larry's capacity to change his ideas and the circumstances that may enhance this flexibility, this family excerpt illuminates several other important features of the Delta family. They are clearly responsive to one another. A long dialogue between his parents preceded Larry's entry. He has been observing each parent listening to and wondering about the other's ideas. The appreciation that Larry shows for multiple perspectives is unusual for someone functioning at his low level of ego development. What we are seeing is more evidence of Larry's uneven development. On the one hand, his sentence completions and interview discourse are replete with signs of uncertain impulse control and a tendency to blame others. Yet there are hints of more thoughtful perceptions and understandings within the interview and now in the family exchanges, as Larry displays his awareness of multiple perspectives, as opposed to single-cause explanations of behavior and events.

Larry's parents directly and indirectly encourage his openness to varied ideas and complex explanations. They provide him with clear models of such thinking as they express their own perspectives. They explain, focus, and are respectful to one another. Rarely do they obstruct or undermine each other's ideas or perceptions. Such exchanges set the stage for Larry's engagement and growth during these discussions, and over the ensuing years.

A consistent focus is maintained within Larry's family. His parents are especially committed to remaining with the task. Numerous questions are raised by different family members, all aimed at bringing the discussion back on track. There is an interest in recognizing solutions and obtaining closure on the task, but *not* prematurely.

Turning to the family's specific interactions, we see that Mrs. Delta directs *more* enabling speeches toward Larry than does her husband. She explains more and is more focusing and more curious. Often it is Mrs. Delta who asks Larry what his idea was or challenges him through a question to explain himself more. In light of the greater overall input from his mother and his devotion to her, it is likely that Larry experiences more comfort and an easier channel to her in these exchanges. It is also important to notice that Larry is not simply reciprocating the specific types of speeches expressed by Mrs. Delta to him. For instance, although his mother expresses much more curiosity than his stepfather, Larry's pattern is to direct more curiosity toward his stepfather.

The possibility that Mr. Bolton is being excluded from the communications between Larry and his mother and is reacting to this exclusion is suggested by his strikingly higher distracting scores. It is as if he is clamoring for the floor, trying to make his presence known, by interrupting, changing the subject, and drawing attention to himself. Finally, our impression of a high level of positive engagement between

Larry's parents is certainly borne out in our analyses of the exchanges between them. They consistently express high levels of enabling (explaining, focusing, accepting) toward one another, suggesting the presence of a close and responsive connection.

LARRY'S PROGRESSION

One year later, Larry's insights about himself are no longer so unexpected and sporadic. In the first months after his discharge Larry was absent from his community school for many days. The situation worsened when, after repeated warnings, the school began legal proceedings. He then began to attend regularly, thankful for their setting limits. Larry returned to school, deciding it was in his best interest, as he had decided before, in the hospital, that it was in his best interest to control his impulses. He was pleased with his performance:

> When and if I got to school I did do all my work and got A's for the day. And my teachers liked it. They thought it was good for my age group. So I started going. It can't hurt. It will get me out faster.

This degree of articulateness and sensitivity to himself was an audible but minor chord during his first year in the study. In the second year he expresses this voice more consistently, extolling the benefits of understanding ongoing experience, being able to reflect on his and others' actions. We hear this change as he describes how he is trying to help his new girlfriend:

> She's quiet at times. . . . A lot of times she'll have something happen in the family like I used to do before I was [hospitalized] . . . the advice I got from here was to talk about it with people when I never used to. And now I'm trying to help her and tell her to talk about it. I told her she could talk to me. My mother will listen to her, and my mother's listened to a lot of things . . . and gave me advice.

Getting advice is a major result of Larry's talking about his problems with others, receiving support through relationships. The meaningfulness of relationships was touched on by Larry in his first-year interview, even while functioning at the lowest ego development stages. In the second year he expands upon this theme, now reminding us of Lois. Larry's main relationship is still with his mother. Added to his circle of relationships are several close friends, a new girlfriend, and a deepening connection with his biological father. During poignant moments of the interview in this second year, Larry expresses his yearning to speak with his father when angry with others. He tells of his disappointment over his father's inconsistent availability. But those disappointments do not immobilize Larry. Ever resourceful, he reaches out to older friends and adult men:

> I can talk to older people and have them understand me better than I can talk to kids my age. I've always hung around with kids older than me. I'm fifteen now. I'll be sixteen in June. And my best friend's eighteen.

And he will also call Jack, the adult friend of whom he spoke in the first year, when unable to reach his father:

> [Jack] is a friend, you know. If we—I—have nothing to do one night I'll give him a call and see what he's doing. . . . He's almost like a father-type, you know.

Other indications of his deepening relationships with others are Larry's perception of inner connections with his father and his greater empathic understanding of his mother:

> My father knows a lot of people. And I take after him that way because I know a lot of people. . . . When I was [at the hospital] I thought about my father and my mother . . . and maybe the reason my mother used to yell at me a lot was because she saw points in me that reminded her of my father. She couldn't handle it. But it's different now.

And Larry puts his disappointment over his father's recent unavailability in more perspective through his new idea that his father might have felt hurt when Larry's mother brought him to the hospital over his father's objections. Yet his visits with his father are marred when his father includes his new wife and stepson, thereby interfering with Larry's time:

> Sometimes if I have problems he will come down and see me, just the two of us . . . just very rarely he'll bring his wife and my stepbrother. And I like my stepmother and stepbrother, but at times I just want to go out with him. But it makes me feel better. Because I grew up seeing him. And the way I saw him it was just us two.

Larry's enhanced understanding of family relationships is also reflected in one of his new sentence completions:

> Raising a family "would be very hard to do right now. But eventually I would like to and probably will."

Another facet of Larry's progression is his greater sense of independence, his feeling more like the master of his actions and impulses:

INTERVIEWER: So [your mother] made changes?

LARRY: I don't think it's her that's changed. I think it's me, and the way I was toward the family. Before I was always out, never home. Never did anything with the family. Now once in awhile I'll do something with the family and I will do it because I want to, not because I want my mother to think that I'm gonna do it because she wants it. I'm gonna do it because I want to do it. . . . My temper's been pretty good lately. Well, pretty good period. I haven't been in a fight in I don't know how long. . . . It's just that things happened to me in the past . . . but [now] I take it in a different way. I don't know why. . . . A person says something to me. Why should I fight over it? If it's not gonna help me, I could get hurt. . . . If somebody says something, even if it's my girlfriend . . . and I get mad, I will think about it and I will think if she had a right to say it . . . and if I think I did it just to aggravate, then I'll talk to my mother and ask her about it and what she thinks about it, and she tells me something. She tells me what her answer is. I'll think about it, and think about whether that's the right answer. Usually it is. . . . I find it's a lot easier for me [by thinking about things before acting] to stay out of trouble, stay out of fights.

Larry also writes about autonomy in his new sentence completions:

The thing I like about myself is "I can do what I want within reason, and be who and what I want to be."

When people are helpless "I try to help them help themselves."

He felt proud he "was doing and being what he wanted to do and be."

Larry's interviewer also commented on these striking changes and her awareness of strengths already evident in the first-year interview. Without knowing that Larry's ego development had dramatically advanced from a preconformist to a postconformist stage, his interviewer dictated this note immediately after the second-year interview:

He looks good, . . . more mature, more serious. He continues to be an articulate, sensitive, introspective teenager. And I think it's markedly clear how he has changed in terms of better impulse control. . . . I expect some of these changes would help him to be . . . more stable and able to use his many strengths.

Accelerated Ego Development: Aaron Winger, Judy Movine, Sarah Resilie

Unusually mature teenagers evoke delighted and sometimes perplexed reactions from adults, as these adolescents express remarkably insightful perceptions about themselves and their surroundings. Far earlier than most of their peers (and many adults), they seem to appreciate the complexities of personal relationships and subtle aspects of their inner lives. These children may be considered "gifted," but not in the usual sense of academic or artistic talent. Rather, their gift is their ability to discern and articulate "shades of gray" and paradox. They express novel observations and ways of understanding, being aware of many, often inconsistent, feelings. Differences among friends are welcomed, not simply tolerated or rejected in favor of more palatable stereotypes. Aaron, Judy, and Sarah were functioning at high levels of ego development (above the conformist stages) when they entered the study. Aaron and Judy remained at these levels in subsequent years, while Sarah functioned at a slightly lower stage (transition to postconformist) over the following two years before returning to her initially high postconformist stage in the final year of the study, four years later. Through their interviews and sentence completions, each of these adolescents provides us with an intricate picture of their usually advanced development. Our direct observations of these adolescents with their parents enhance these understandings and suggest ways that such advanced teenage development may shape aspects of family life.

AARON WINGER

When we first met with Aaron Winger, he was in the early months of his freshman year at high school. The third of four children, he had received advanced warning of what to expect from this large new school. Those scouting reports, from his older brother and sister, were helpful to him in adapting to the somewhat frightening new setting. But those contributions did not prepare Aaron for a new problem, a change in his awareness of himself and his "outlook toward things":

> I always used to know how other people felt, what to say to them, and now sometimes I don't. Some people will call me insensitive now. I mean they know that I mean well. I don't seem to know exactly what they feel or what to say sometimes. . . . That seems to be a change for the worse now.

While others have noticed the change, Aaron thinks it is he who is most conscious of it: "It's mostly me, I just know I've changed." Within the first minutes of his interview, Aaron expresses less certainty about how others feel and is no longer so sure about "what to say to them." Such a shift reflects his new recognition of the difficulties of knowing exactly what others are thinking, let alone how to react to them. Moreover, his source of knowledge about this change is himself, not others. In completing the sentence "When I am criticized," Aaron introduces another aspect of his experience with self-knowledge and how he uses it: "I usually take it very well and use it to help me. I am growing out of defending myself."

It was during the summer before high school, while convalescing from an athletic injury, that Aaron began to feel "more adult": "I felt like I was reaching the personality that I would be for the rest of my life. I felt a little more learned or experienced." His more complex perceptions of himself are lucidly illustrated in his sentence completions. For instance, for "My main problem," he writes "is recently sharing confidential (to my sources) things to my friends. I fail to see what is personal." Paralleling Aaron's greater awareness of his inner life are his more complex views of other people and how they affect one another:

> I just can't stand people "who never think of what they're doing, think only of what good they can do for themselves, and never what good they can leave behind."

> Being with other people "can greatly change one's actions."

> When people are helpless "there is much less to live for, if no one helps them."

Aaron is also aware of his own recent physical growth spurt, accompanied by a blunting of his mood swings. He has become wary of friends whose moods are more turbulent and has distanced himself from a recent girlfriend who "kept being depressed." Aaron's friends include teammates and girlfriends. He spends time with male friends in athletic activities. He believes it would be inappropriate for him to introduce comments about his "changes" when talking with these male friends. "[I] talk about the newest thing in school, or something like that. Never really had any philosophical conversations. (*laughs*) Boys don't get philosophical for some reason." His attitude about sex differences surfaces in another sentence completion:

> Men are lucky because "they don't have to worry about having a baby or menstruating, and at my age he doesn't have to worry about ruining his reputation like a girl when he makes love."

Finally, commitments—sports, school projects, college, and clarinet playing—are intense, yet clearly pleasurable for Aaron. His visions of the future are shaped by his wish to be competent, "good at something and have fun." This could include "something in the arts," singing or trumpet, or professional sports.

Striking about Aaron is his restricted range of feelings, He admires stable moods and shuns mood swings. Aaron also thinks highly of rational, thoughtful discussion, often rejecting friends who openly display their feelings, especially unhappy ones. This emotional impoverishment contrasts sharply with Aaron's pride in his rich perceptions and ideas. Such richness is not apparent in his affective life. In his first-year interview, Aaron makes few comments about his own feelings, his attitudes about those feelings, and how he manages to hold them in check. He is more disclosing in his sentence completions, where we discover that his affective life may not be so calm. In these responses we find yearnings to be cared for and disquieting feelings, especially about girls and sex:

> When I am with a woman "I find myself wishing to cover my faults."

> Women are lucky because "At our age they can sit and wait for an embarrassed scared young man to try and ask them out."

> A man feels good when "He knows he's got a woman who cares for him."

> Usually he felt that sex "was a scary dangerous subject."

Sometimes he wished that "things would always go right, so-cially."

As the reader will soon see, we do not have to turn to sentence completion responses to discover affective currents in the lives of Judy and Sarah, two girls who also follow a path of accelerated development. Their sentence completions certainly amplify the feelings that they express and reflect about in their interviews, but those responses do not reveal the feelings *de novo*. It is along these lines, conscious awareness of feelings, that Aaron most sharply differs from the other two accelerated teenagers.

AARON'S FAMILY

Aaron portrays his parents as "busy" with professional commitments. His father has a law practice, and his mother acts in local theater companies. When the parents are not working, "They play tennis all the time." Although they do find time to talk with him (when their schedules coincide with his), it is his older sister who has recently become an important family consultant for Aaron, advising him about how to break off his relationship with his girlfriend gently:

> She's the foremost authority on social relationships, I guess. She told me things that wouldn't hurt her [his girlfriend] or some-thing, and not to be honest because that would hurt her too much, because that would be a really bad thing to do, and I would be a real jerk for saying those things. But I did anyhow. *(laughs)*

Aaron very briefly describes his two brothers. His older brother, now a senior in high school, is occasionally helpful to Aaron, introducing him to new circles of friends and to new opportunities. On the other hand, his younger brother, "little brother," imposes many demands on Aaron's parents and indirectly on Aaron because of his problems at school.

Aaron thinks his parents are aware of the changes he is experiencing but that they devote most of their attention to his little brother, who (together with his older sister):

> . . . really don't get along with teachers and they tend to be loud; and they have it [intelligence] upstairs, but they don't use it in school. . . . So they [mother and father] just pay attention to my little brother. They just trust me and my big brother. We've always done well, so they leave us alone.

Through his sentence completions Aaron gives a more extended account of how he sees these family bonds, their impacts and demands:

Raising a family "At sometime in my life, raising a family will absorb all of my energy."

He felt proud that "he could get along with all members of his family."

If my mother "were not so artistic, I may never have been interested in dramatics or even started playing the trumpet."

When he thought of his mother "he saw an obstacle to things he really wanted to do."

A good father "understands and remembers his feelings as a child, or when younger."

My father and I "can talk about almost anything, except specifically my personal life."

Aaron's mother's level of ego development is in the same range as Aaron's (postconformist), but at a lower stage (conscientious). Through her responses she expresses an awareness of paradox, some regrets, and recognition of many sides of herself:

If my mother "had married 'better' I might be more of a bitch than I am."

What gets me in trouble is "when I get overwrought from too many conflicting obligations."

I am "fairly content most of the time."

I feel sorry "about my not having a good relationship with my daughter."

My main problem is that "I lack confidence and can easily be intimidated."

She emphasizes development, autonomy, and multiple possibilities as she writes about the family and the wider social world:

A good mother "allows her children to grow away from her."

A woman should always "be able to take care of herself."

My husband and I "will probably go off into the sunset together."

When a child will not join in group activities "it can mean many things."

Education "should enable people to have better control over their lives."

Rules are "guides for behavior but are meant to be bent or even broken under certain circumstances."

In contrast to Mrs. Winger and Aaron, Mr. Winger functions at a conformist stage of ego development. For the most part, his sentence completions reflect the socially acceptable and conventional. Sporadically, he suggests an appreciation of complexity, within himself or others:

The thing I like about myself is "my inventiveness, both with ideas and people."

When I am with a woman "I enjoy talking about ideas."

What gets me in trouble "is my occasional lapses in diplomacy."

If I can't get what I want "I feel thwarted."

Mr. Winger's views of his family and others are also marked by their relative simplicity and hints of rigidity, revealing even more strongly his conformist stage of development:

Raising a family "has its ups and downs."

A man's job "is to provide support (physical, emotional, financial)."

Crime and delinquency could be halted if "families are strengthened."

Women are lucky because "if they become housewives, they are protected from the competitive world of business."

A good father "is loving, but punishes when a lesson must be taught."

A man should always "maintain a consistent role as a father."

Rules are "important as a cohesive force in a social group re the family."

Usually he felt that sex "was not a topic to be discussed in mixed company."

He felt proud that he "(my son) set a school-boy athletic record."

The perceptions, feelings, and thoughts that Aaron's parents express in completing the many sentence stems reveal their distinctly different subjective worlds and levels of ego development. These differences between his mother and father are certainly not apparent in the sparse family descriptions Aaron presents during his interview. However, our observations of the family members as they engage in resolving moral dilemmas give us more insight about how the differences between Mr. and Mrs. Winger affect their interactions with their son and may contribute to his accelerated ego development.

AARON WITHIN HIS FAMILY

Both parents and Aaron become quickly immersed in the family discussion as they argue and challenge one another. Each of them also listens carefully to the others, often incorporating or developing more complex understandings based on ideas expressed by other family members. A persistent pattern is the seriousness with which both parents reflect on Aaron's new ideas. For instance, in discussing whether or not Heinz should steal the drug for his wife, if he does not love her, Aaron's father initially concludes that Heinz should not steal, since "if he doesn't love her, is that still a family? Because it's officially in name only." Aaron disagrees, arguing that the husband and his wife have had a long life together and a sustained, loyal relationship. Responding to his father's continued skepticism about whether Heinz and his wife even have "a family," Aaron urges him to think about their attachments to one another, not simply the label "family":

But their lives together, and they've spent—obviously if they're married, they have spent much time helping each other and such . . . If he spent so much time with her . . . I'm sure that he's known her for quite a long time, and you are also dealing with somebody dying. I thought that (pause) if you have been with somebody for so long, and if you have known them so, how could you just, you know, let them die? I mean, you can do something to help, of course.

After at first reiterating his commitment to "the family and people working for each other," Mr. Winger becomes less abstract and introduces a new dimension:

FATHER: So that's why, I guess we have to talk about their relationship, supposing he doesn't love her. It's like in *Fiddler on the Roof*, they never loved each other but—

MOTHER: (*interrupting*) Right. Right.

FATHER: —they were loyal to each other. Okay, so I'll change it. As long as there is loyalty, some sort of base for loyalty, that should supersede the law.

Listening carefully to their son's views, Mr. and Mrs. Winger modify their own thoughts, help Aaron clarify his, and even at times defend his ideas. While Mrs. Winger engages in more problem-solving and empathic exchanges with her son, Mr. Winger challenges and focuses the meanings of Aaron's ideas.

Openness to new ideas and to change is a second theme in the family's interactions, one that can be seen in the exchanges of both parents. To begin with, there is the example of Mr. Winger's reconsiderations, based on his recognition of the importance of loyalty. Mrs. Winger later reveals her willingness to change her view that Heinz should steal the drug, after Mr. Winger brings up the possibility that Heinz's wife was "fooling around." Mrs. Winger then announces that were this the case, she would feel differently about her answer: "You'd have to consider extenuating circumstances."

A third salient feature of the Winger family is their tolerance of uncertainty. They question their previously expressed positions and explicitly recognize that definitive, absolute answers are unavailable:

AARON: Yeah, I wasn't sure about that one.

FATHER: I don't know, (*long pause*) it's a hard one.

Yet their embracing of openness and uncertainty has its limits. As the discussion unfolds, it becomes clear that Aaron can differ with and question his parents only up to a point. At two moments in the discussion one of Aaron's ideas is overridden, as he is "told" by his parents that his rationale for his answers is irrelevant. The most dramatic instance wherein Aaron's argument is undermined and he is reined in happens when he decides that Heinz should steal the drug to save his dog's life, a conclusion vehemently opposed by both parents. Aaron is immediately confronted, as his parents insist that his conclusion, of course, implies that Aaron should be "willing to go to jail for the cat." Mr. Winger interrupts Aaron's explanation:

AARON: But you said a pet that you loved so I just felt—

FATHER: (*interrupting*) I mean, would you be willing to go to jail for the cat?

AARON: Of course not.

FATHER: That's what we're talking about!

Aaron tries to clarify his position:

> [What if] he didn't have a wife, and he spends all his time with his cat, and if the cat is the most important thing in the world?

Both parents continue to stress their belief that Aaron (or they) would have to "love the pet enough to go to jail for it." And after Aaron reverses his position, "Definitely not" steal the drug for the cat, the Wingers quickly close the discussion and call in the interviewer.

One of Aaron's strengths is highlighted in these more conflicted exchanges. He does not explicitly oppose his parents' view that all three should now agree, since his rationale was "wrong." But, at the same time, he does stay with his position, repeating and amplifying with increasing passion:

> I am simply saying, Christ, if you just had an animal who you spent all the time with and loved, of course, you should steal for it, because you would be miserable without it. Okay?

In this sequence we see the dynamic interplay between this accelerated teenager and his parents. Clearly Aaron's unusual development is not merely the consequence of passively "taking in" (or actively identifying with) parental models. Besides their ample enabling, Mr. and Mrs. Winger also suddenly close off discussions, or prematurely dismiss Aaron's position. In addition to their discomfort over the widening gap between Aaron's understanding and theirs, his parents may be eager to end the evening's long discussions. Yet Aaron is unwilling to allow them simply to overrule or dismiss his ideas. Such consistent resistance to domination is not apparent in the family interactions of the arrested and steady conformist adolescents.

Further evidence of Aaron's robust responses to his parents and overall functioning in the family can be found in his enabling and constraining profile. Two features are particularly outstanding. First, there is the contrast between his enabling and constraining speeches. We see few indications of Aaron's directing any constraining speeches toward either parent. In contrast, there are abundant examples of all enabling behaviors, particularly explaining, problem-solving, and accepting. Second, and also striking, is Aaron's tendency to direct speeches to his father. It is likely that this emphasis upon his father reflects Mr. Winger's greater involvement in the discussion. In our earlier observations of this family, we were aware of Mr. Winger's energetic participation in the discussion, particularly as he countered Aaron's moves toward differentiation. On the other hand, Aaron's mother is less insistent that Aaron conform to the family's values and positions. Perhaps this heightened sympathy on her part leads to the greater number of empathic speeches that Aaron directs to her.

Mr. and Mrs. Winger differ in their enabling speeches, with Mrs. Winger expressing more empathy and engaging in more explaining and problem-solving. Mr. Winger focuses more often and raises many questions. Thus, Aaron's addressing more speeches to his father is not simply a reflection of father's expressing more enabling toward Aaron. The picture is a more complicated one than reciprocal enabling between Aaron and his father. Aaron's mother directs many enabling speeches to him, while Aaron directs consistently more enabling speeches to his father. It is as if mother's efforts to enable are—so far as is observable—rebuffed by Aaron, as he persists in directing all kinds of enabling to his father, without wholesale encouragement by him. Although he does not always directly reciprocate his mother's enabling, there is nonetheless the possibility that she is providing background support, that without her contributions he could not continue in these many exchanges with his father. The importance of his mother's enabling speeches is suggested through the many empathic speeches she expresses to Aaron. It is here that we may have evidence of an important bond between them, acknowledgment that they perceive each other as being on the "same wavelength" during the discussion.

On the other hand, Mrs. Winger's constraining speeches to her husband may represent her reaction to Aaron's numerous dialogues with his father. Her interruptions and other distracting statements suggest that she may be vying for the floor, feeling "crowded out" by the swell of father–son interactions.

With respect to the whole family, it is explaining and accepting that are especially prominent for the Wingers. Both parents and Aaron are very similar in the extent to which they enable each other to voice, clarify, or defend their points of view. But this symmetry does not prevail for constraining speeches, those that indirectly interfere with (through indifference or withholding behaviors) or directly obstruct (through distraction or devaluing) the emergence of new ideas or differing points of view. His parents interrupt and oppose each other's statements far more than Aaron does with either one.

In the Winger family, then, we see openness and encouragement of expression and disagreement, along with an element of unease, especially on the part of Mr. Winger, that this openness may sometimes go too far. While various struggles occur between Aaron and his father, there are indications of empathy and support from his mother. This blend of emotional encouragement (empathy and accepting) and challenge may be a significant source of Aaron's accelerated development. And his accelerated development, in turn, may stimulate the serious listening, lively exchanges, and pervasive enabling in this family.

JUDY MOVINE

When we met Judy she was completing the first half of her freshman year of high school. Like several other students, she found the transition to high school relatively smooth, having anticipated much of the experience through her older friends:

> The reason why it [high school] is easy for me is because when I was in the seventh grade most of my friends were in the eighth, so when we went up to the high school, ya know, they, I'd still see them and they'd talk at the high school. So it wasn't really too shocking coming up here.

Judy is accustomed to transitions. When she was younger, her family moved many times, leading to Judy's experiences in varied school and family settings. In her early childhood the entire family moved to another part of the city. Another move followed shortly, this time involving only part of her family. Judy, her brother, and her mother moved to a nearby state after her parents' separation. Within the year, her father rejoined the family. Several years later, the entire family returned to her birthplace. Not long after this last move, her parents again separated. Judy's experience of the first separation was bewildering:

> When I was little I didn't know about my parents' separation until later, a couple of years later, when I talked to my mother and she said we had come to Elmtown without my father. I just didn't remember that because it seemed sort of, everything was sort of quick, and moving and all.

The second separation, when she was ten years old, was less confusing for Judy. When she visited her father at his apartment in a nearby city, she was clear about the different locations, yet she continued to be puzzled about her parents' relationship:

> But it was just a little strange, because it was like when my parents, my father, would . . . take us back to the house . . . it was never like they were actually mad at each other, or they snarled at each other when they saw each other. But they just kinda went their own way for a short while.

Judy's remarkable curiosity was already active during these earlier years:

> It was a little bit awkward, because I kept on wondering why he, why my father, just didn't move back, because it didn't seem they were having any trouble. And I didn't understand why they had separated, because they didn't seem to be having any huge arguments.

Judy is convinced that her parents would have "explained" what was happening:

> I've asked my parents questions before, and they've never been hesitant about telling me things I wanted to know. Because they always wanted to make sure I wasn't confused about something. I always had so many questions. I didn't know what was going on, and the only way I could find out was to ask questions, so it was a great relief to be able to talk to them about [their relationship].

Throughout the interview, Judy touches on how her parents supported her "always asking questions." Judy also writes about curiosity in her sentence completions:

> When they avoided me "I wondered what would make them not want to know an interesting person."

> The thing I like about myself is "I try to understand other people and not try to judge them before I get to know them."

Along with her curiosity and wish to understand is Judy's "caring a lot about people's feelings and stuff." Judy describes how she and her younger brother like to help friends with problems feel better. In recounting those experiences, her recognition of people's complexity emerges:

> Well, I try to help as much as I can, I don't know if, I mean sometimes I see results that seem to help them, but I don't

know if that inside they always feel like they've been helped. I just try.

Despite her wishes to help and understand people, she has difficulties in her relationships with friends. For instance, after she moved to another new school, Judy fumbled in an early try to make new friends. Her poignant memory of a disturbing incident, together with her speculations about her role in it and her motivations, is an excellent example of Judy's high level of development and her grasp of internal as well as interpersonal nuances:

> I kind of made a mistake at the beginning of the year, because there was just getting to know other people, and no one really knew who I was, and I didn't know who they were. . . . So I called one of the boys a name, and the rest of the year he would go around trying to bother me and call me names and all of that. And so it wasn't too pleasant. I don't know why I called him a name. Maybe I was testing people to see how far they could go, but, um, I felt kinda rotten, because it was just like I really wanted to get to know people a lot, and I really wanted to have friends.

Judy's awareness of others and altruistic wishes underlie sympathetic, often compassionate, responses. In describing her parents and friends, she focuses on their perspectives, experiences, and wishes:

> When people are helpless "they tend to get angry at people who are in a better situation than they are."

> When my mother spanked me "which was only once in my life, she was so upset by the incident she never did it again."

> I feel sorry "for people who shut out other people who try to help them."

In emphasizing the importance of other people, their inner experience, and her relationships with them, Judy clearly differs from Aaron. As we saw, Aaron is certainly perceptive about other people, but this is hardly a leading theme in his life, taking a back seat to athletics and music. In general, the adolescent girls in our sample devote more time, in the interviews as well as in their lives, to thinking consciously about relationships and feelings.[1] In other respects, Aaron and Judy are more similar. Both are alert to and interested in how they have changed. Judy tells the interviewer of the changes in her reactions to people and of the transformations in her future plans. Thanks to her talks with her mother, she now has fewer fears of people and of "breaking the ice." In these talks her mother has "given me a little thing to think about. . . . My mother keeps on telling me you shouldn't worry about every word that comes out of your mouth is golden and beautiful and everything." Judy's visions of the future are also new. When she was younger, she considered becoming a physician, a veterinarian, or a marine biologist, but now, "As I got a little older, I realized it wasn't just the snap of the finger that got you into things." When the interviewer comments, "So now you're less clear about what you want to do," Judy corrects her, replying, "I'm not really less clear, but sort of, like it's not a specific career that I can say the name of."

JUDY'S FAMILY

Judy has definite and complex ideas about how her parents have contributed to her development. Her accounts of her parents and her younger brother provide us with detailed, subtle pictures of them, particularly her mother. Judy is the older of two children; her brother is one year younger. Early in her interview, Judy spontaneously introduces her family. Recounting her relatively smooth adjustment to her new high school, she goes on to tell the interviewer of the many family moves, beginning before grade school, moves associated with parents' careers and marital problems. It is unlikely that those early familial perturbations are, paradoxically, critical determinants of Judy's high level of development. Yet there is the strong possibility that the way those changes were *handled* with Judy, how she was informed, the openness of communication that she maintained with both parents, sparked or sustained the curiosity and complexity of thought that she now cherishes. Judy recalls her parents' reactions to her many questions when she was younger:

> They always wanted to make sure I wasn't confused about something. Sometimes they may not [answer a question]. Like if I asked a personal question that they thought I wasn't really ready to understand yet, they'd say, "You know, if you ask me that in a couple of years." But it's always like, if I ask in a couple of years, they'd tell me.

Judy points out that her parents were not simply evading her through these promises:

> Because I always had so many questions. I didn't know what was going on, and the only way I could find out was to ask

questions. So it was really a great relief to be able to talk to them about it. They had gone to couples' counseling for three years, so they're used to talking about things like that.

In these early adolescent years the most prominent person in Judy's life is her mother, "the stronger-willed sort of person." Mrs. Movine, thirty-seven years old, has completed a masters degree and works in an area of applied social sciences. Her ego development is at a high postconformist level, the "autonomous" stage. In addition to supporting her daughter's curiosity and answering her questions, Judy's mother is very affectionate: "We sometimes have these incidents where she wants to come up and just hug you. . . . It's kind of slobbering." While this warmth is targeted to Judy, Mrs. Movine is also concerned with the feelings of others, both inside and outside the family: "She always cares about what's going on with people, and she wants to see if they're having problems, she wants to help them." Those attractive qualities are not figments of a daughter's idealized view of her mother. Mrs. Movine's sentence completions corroborate and extend Judy's picture:

The thing I like about myself "is my curiosity and my determination to keep going—even though I have down times."

When a child will not join in group activities "there can be many reasons—newness, shyness, lack of self-confidence, and it would help if the group could try to be welcoming."

When she thought of her mother "she wished she could make her feel good about herself."

Being with other people "can be a real pleasure when I feel I am receiving as well as giving."

Mrs. Movine also expresses her commitment to parents' promoting independence, placing high values on self-reliance and individuality:

A girl has the right to "explore her options and be the person she wants to be."

I am "trying to be the best and fullest version of myself as I see it."

A good mother "tries to let her children be themselves."

A wife should "try to understand her husband's needs, but not let them completely override her own."

For a woman a career is "something she should be prepared to enter: If, as, and when she may need to or want to."

A woman feels good "when she can manage her own life."

A woman should always "try to be self-reliant."

Although she does not directly cite these aspects of her mother, Judy's commitment to independence and awareness of differences between herself and others may reflect her mother's valuing of autonomy and individuality.

Finally, it is likely that underlying Mrs. Movine's ability to "understand people," so fully and lovingly described by Judy in the interview, is an awareness of her own inner contradictions and conflicts, as well as those within others:

My father "represented two forces in my life—a daring to try new things and a contradictory fear of failure."

The worst thing about being a woman "is trying to cope with everyone's notions of who or what you should or shouldn't be."

There are also more problematic moments between Judy and her mother. At the time of the interview, for instance, her mother was worried about a low grade Judy had received in biology. She insisted that Judy stay at home for the next several weeks and devote all her time to her school work. Later, her mother apologized for the overreaction, explaining that it had to do with her own parents' anxiety over her academic performance. Judy's reaction to her mother's candor was twofold. Instead of becoming discouraged and withdrawing from her school difficulties, she threw herself into her course and eventually excelled. Furthermore, she recounts this experience with her mother with considerable sympathy, as well as an understanding of the historical roots of her mother's reaction. Her mother's way of managing the incident is also noteworthy. Mrs. Movine first reviewed the incident with Judy and then disclosed her own analysis of how her personal history had influenced her reaction. Thus, the revealing disclosures that her parents provide of the inner dynamics of their own lives are an important source of Judy's complex perceptions and understanding of others.

Judy portrays her father in less striking tones than her mother. He is quiet, gentle, intelligent, and "exceptionally humorous. . . . Sometimes he can be so humorous it's disgusting." Although he is the quieter of the two parents, Judy is quick to insist that she does not consider this a flaw:

. . . that [mother stands out more] doesn't mean that I think my father is really meek or something. He's not always quiet but can be . . . just like that sometimes.

Mr. Movine is thirty-six years old, has completed some graduate training, and functions at the transition between the conscientious and autonomous stages. His main interest is in writing fiction and poetry, although he is currently working as a technical writer. Judy emphasizes that this work is of minor importance to her father. In his eyes, technical writing is a distant second from his dedication to writing poetry and his "wishes to be famous." Despite her father's joking asides about these ambitions, Judy is convinced that they are deeply held. Perhaps because of her mother's conflicts over Judy's schoolwork, she approaches her father first whenever she has school problems. Nonetheless, she feels generally "more comfortable" with her mother.

Judy offers a less detailed picture of her father, probably as a result of the many interruptions in their relationship and the uneven contacts she has had with him over the course of several physical separations. In addition, she suggests in many ways that he is somewhat detached even when with her. Mr. Movine's sentence completions amplify this picture of him and suggest that his messages to Judy may at times be idiosyncratic, not so readily decipherable by her. He stresses his preoccupation with "verbalization":

The thing I like about myself is "my verbalizations—when it tracks with satisfaction and (less so) security."

What gets me in trouble is "verbalization without (much) attention to the practical details of living."

What Mr. Movine most compellingly expresses are his dawning awareness of self-determination and his regrets:

A man's job is "what he makes it, often (this an evidently recent illumination on my part)."

When I am with a woman "I am often more confident than when I am alone (Ah such inherent mechanisms!)"

I feel sorry "→ period."

My main problem is "passivity, delay, not coping, a living by indirection and idle verbalization."

When I am criticized "I'm affable, if not moved to act; people later find I (practically) disagree."

Sometimes he wished that "? he could."

If I can't get what I want "I manipulate reality a bit, and get some variant of what I want; not good."

In his sentence completions about parents, Mr. Movine expresses his sorrow over "hardly communicating," formality, and inadequacy:

If my mother calls "I'll be quite amazed! She usually expects me to call on 'formal' days. I do/don't."

When he thought of his mother "he wasn't any too happy about his relationship with her over the 36.5 years."

My father and I "hardly communicate, a pity if not a tragedy, a still powerful legacy."

A good father "is no accident. It appears to take more work than I had any idea of—and I often under-perform."

Apparent in these completions are Mr. Movine's self-criticisms, yearnings, and sadness about his experiences with his parents. Possibly this demoralized, depressed side of her father is also behind Judy's tendency to turn more often to her mother, availing herself of Mrs. Movine's "strong-willed" nature, curiosity, and ultimate optimism.

The third member of Judy's immediate family, her younger brother, is similar to her father in his quietness and "gentleness." He has been a keen ally and companion to Judy in her early years. She fondly recalls being with him when her parents were arguing in the adjoining room. When she is "emotional" and fighting with her mother, it is her brother who is quiet and more reflective. He is less visibly moved and has been available to her for many years: "We both like to talk to each other about problems." While she "explodes" in family arguments, her brother waits until the arguments are over and is then more reflective with his sister. He is very studious and principled. Judy describes "setting [my] moral standards to his, because he's so calm-tempered and can contain his reactions and stuff. I'm usually the more rowdy of the two." These remarks suggest how a sibling, somewhat like her father, but perhaps less sad and more available to her, may have contributed to her growth particularly during the early unstable years within her family.

Both of Judy's parents function at high levels of ego development. The most important contributions of her parents' own advanced development to Judy's accelerated development may be through their disclosures of their inner life, offering her—in ways that she can grasp—views of their history, perceptions, understandings, and current states of mind. We have already seen that Judy has the capacity to use these offerings. So, too, Judy describes her brother in a very positive light, a key family "friend" who enhances her parents' strengths and provides a calming influence. Those important strengths, as well as some unanticipated liabilities, emerge in the family discussions.

JUDY WITHIN HER FAMILY

As we might have expected, Judy and her parents engage in spirited discussions of the moral dilemmas. All three defend their positions, disclose the logic and feelings that lead to their differing viewpoints, and show much curiosity about one another's ideas. The level of respect, acceptance, and encouragement of the expression of each other's ideas is daunting. For instance, well into the first family discussion, after Judy presents much of her thinking about why Heinz should not steal and why one shouldn't steal for a pet, the family confronts the question of whether it's immoral to break a law. With some discomfort, Judy delineates her position about what's illegal and immoral, and it becomes clear that her perspective differs from that of her parents. Her father summarizes Judy's thinking: "Okay, against the law equals morally wrong." Judy immediately acknowledges her uncertainty, which leads to one of her father's cryptic statements, reminiscent of his sentence completions:

JUDY: I think I, I, I think I have a very naïve grasp of the law. (*laughs*) I mean I, I, tend to think that most laws are made by people.

FATHER: No. There are a lot more, many more motivations for constructing the laws.

JUDY: See. I don't know [what's behind constructing laws].

FATHER: Some of which, are, criminal. Some laws are, are criminally motivated by evil people.

MOTHER: That's right. That's what—

FATHER: (*interrupting*) And the laws are simply whitewashed crime. It's, it's frightening.

Both parents go on to lecture Judy about the bribery of jurors and "Jim Crow" laws. They then together respond to her unsureness, her "naïveté," to which she has self-consciously called attention throughout this phase of the discussion:

MOTHER: Morality is relative.

FATHER: Yes, that's the point you have to learn, Judy.

JUDY: Well, (*sigh*) I'm a fourteen-year-old kid; I feel.

FATHER: No, you're doing, you're doing great, kid. You're working very hard with the ideas.

MOTHER: When we were fourteen, we were both incredibly more naïve than you are, very idealistic, incredibly naïve. And we both had to painfully, very painfully (*laughs*) learn a few things.

JUDY: Don't let me get very headstrong, keep on telling me how terrific I am and I might start to believe it. (*laughs*)

MOTHER: Well, you are.

FATHER: Yah.

JUDY: Well, I mean . . .

MOTHER: You could use a little of that.

FATHER: Yah, you could.

In this brief episode, we see Judy's parents recognizing her discouragement about being too innocent and simple, and moving quickly to support her thoughtfulness. Along with encouraging her involvement in the discussion, they tell her how they were at her age. Such disclosure recurs repeatedly between the Movines and Judy. Early in her interview, Judy had told of her parents' openness, and of how responsive they were to her persistent curiosity, as they "always answered my questions," often by revealing aspects of their own experience, current and past.

There are several ways that Judy is exposed to her parents' perceptions and thoughts. One is through their descriptions of how they differ from one another. In this next excerpt, Mrs. Movine points out the passive and pessimistic stance that Mr. Movine takes, as she discusses his opinion that Officer Brown should not report Heinz:

MOTHER: But Dick, (*slight pause*) I think you tend . . . I . . . You and I had some of the same experiences. You know how it can happen in the worst way. In other words, you, you tend to believe that the the minute somebody gets arrested, you know, they're practically being shipped away.

FATHER: But that's not true in actual practice.

MOTHER: No, but I mean you tend to think more in those terms than I do.

FATHER: I do.

It is in the final discussion of the evening that the Movines' self-disclosure to Judy is most visible. They are discussing their ideas about what a father and son should be concerned about in their relationship with one another. Each family member is attempting to clarify his or her views. The discussion is multifaceted, touching on many issues, including sex differences. They consider what it's like to be a man or woman and how difficult it is to convey these personal experiences. The discussion suddenly shifts from this abstract issue to one about parental fears and inadequacies. And then, even more dramatically, the Movines launch into memories of the children, when much younger, and parents tumbling about, climbing on top of one another! It is in this setting, as they publicly recall these intimate experiences and relationships, that each family member reveals subtle and moving inner moments:

JUDY: I know [love and trust from parents are] essential, but I'm saying that a parent can love their child and yet do the wrong things for them. (*speaks loud and clearly*)

FATHER: I think my father feared me (*pause*) which I finally figured out over the years. He was afraid of me somehow.

MOTHER: Afraid of what you represented? (*asked softly*)

FATHER: I don't know. See, that's the problem. I'll never know. . . . He could never tell me.

JUDY: What does, I can't (*moving about*) . . . afraid of you? I, I couldn't think of what you represent. (*small laugh*)

FATHER: Well, first when I was a first-born, I was, I was a preemie, and he thought I was going to die, and he got very guilty about it. He told my mother.

JUDY: What? He thought he had bad genes or something?

FATHER: They never had children again. Yes, I believe he felt it was, ah, his fault.

Mrs. Movine reminds him of how he got so big, and Mr. Movine then says, "Maybe, he [his father] was afraid that I was so big." He sticks to his point about his father's fearing him and concludes, "At any rate, he never trusted me very much; didn't seem to like me."

A touching discussion now unfolds, sparked by Judy's wistful reflection, "Well, I guess it sort of feels like magic to be able to have Father pick you up, with these big huge arms, right? To carry you?" The conversation first turns to how the family has changed over the years, illustrating Judy's sensitivity to how family members comfort one another:

FATHER: Well, your mother sure as hell can't do it [carry Judy or her brother]. . . . But the point is that I only did it because he [brother] kept on sort of indicating he wanted it.

JUDY: It's fun, it's fun.

FATHER: He doesn't want it now.

MOTHER: I used to do tumbling with them when they were babies, but the point was . . . when they got bigger, I couldn't do it any more 'cause I wasn't physically strong enough . . . but you [father] could do it.

FATHER: They sort of transferred that to me. But it was originally mother—child.

JUDY: Well, it's good it switched off.

MOTHER: Yeah. I mean, what's wrong with that?

FATHER: Linda's trying to set the record straight as to where it came from and where it went. (*talking extremely fast*)

JUDY: We sound like we're trying to counsel each other. (*laughs*)

FATHER: (*to mother*) Are you, are you hurting?

MOTHER: No.

FATHER: I didn't think so. (*laughs*)

And from here Judy's parents go on to consider, with sensitivity and candor, parent—child relations in their generation:

MOTHER: I think, if anything, maybe I sometimes fall into the trap of being overly mystical about this stuff [father—son relations]. But I sometimes think you [father] fall into the trap of overly denying it.

FATHER: Yeah, yeah, that's agreed.

MOTHER: Yeah, because I know it was so painful between you and your father. . . . I didn't have any of that going with my parents. I mean, they sort of did everything in the reverse too. My father was the one who was saying, you know, be strong, be smart, be this, be that, you know, the opposite of the routine that fathers are typically supposed to do on their little girls.

FATHER: Yeah, I think your whole . . . situation's funny too.

MOTHER: Yeah, and my mother was the same way because she said, "I'm not one of those frilly babies and you're obviously not going to be either." You know? Look at you [Judy]. (*small laugh*) Got shoulders.

JUDY: Well, you were—

MOTHER: (*interrupting*)—like a football player, you know?

JUDY: What does that have to do with being frilly?

MOTHER: That was part of my mother's beliefs about okay female types.

JUDY: Oh, you mean the body build determined the—

MOTHER: (*interrupting*) Well, I was never going to be a cute little dolly, you know?

JUDY: Suppose you were, would your mother have treated you like that? (*small laugh*)

MOTHER: I think that if I had been, I honestly think my mother would probably have been very uncomfortable with me, in similar ways to the way Dick's father was with him.

FATHER: I think I was too large by his expectations.

MOTHER: If I had been little and cute, I think it would have made my mother nervous.

FATHER: Sort of my father's build and stuff . . .

JUDY: You mean sort of short and thin-boned or something?

FATHER: Mid—mid-sized. But I was larger, and I think, you know, I don't think he ever coped with it.

MOTHER: Yeah . . .

JUDY: 'Cause you were taller than him by the time you were what, sixteen or something?

FATHER: I think he could very seriously sense that I have a different physiological destiny than he did, and that was frightening.

MOTHER: Hmm.

JUDY: He never tried to talk to you 'cause that wasn't really the thing people did in those days?

FATHER: For an intelligent man, he could articulate almost nothing. (*sighs*) . . . It was really very sad (*low voice*) . . . you know. (*soft voice*)

MOTHER: Well, it wasn't completely under your control.

Mr. and Mrs. Movine openly and touchingly remember early experiences with their parents, and Judy participates in these exchanges with ease. Such dialogues were certainly alluded to by Judy in her earlier interview. Yet we did not know how far-reaching her parents' openness would be, nor could we have readily imagined the ease with which Judy connects with them at these times.

In our more detailed analyses of the Movines' conversations, there are many indications of Judy's strong bonds with both parents, especially her mother. While she directs many explaining, focusing, and curiosity-seeking speeches to her father, she is considerably more encouraging, accepting, and empathic toward her mother. At the same time, Judy also interrupts her mother more often. This blend of acceptance and interruption reflects the high level of engagement between Judy and her mother, the special relationship that Judy describes at length in her interview.

There are many reciprocal exchanges in the family. Mr. Movine and Judy engage in explaining and focusing exchanges with one another, while Mrs. Movine and Judy express mutual acceptance. These observations confirm what the family members have separately described about themselves and about one another. With respect to Mr. Movine, according to both Judy and himself, he is a more detached and often cryptic figure. Exclusively cognitive exchanges (explaining, focusing) are consistent with his more distant interpersonal style. And such distance may further encourage the warm, confiding (mutual accepting) bond that exists between Judy and her mother.

These speech profiles suggest possible family contributions to Judy's accelerated ego development: She has been exposed to her parents' inner conflicts, yearnings, and disappointments, as well as to the differences between them. It is likely that this experience has helped Judy perceive and verbalize the ways in which people can differ and the nature of her relationships with others.

In terms of openness to new ideas and encouragement of individual expression, the Movines are reminiscent of the Wingers. Yet there are also noteworthy differences, evident in the extensive self-disclosures by both Movine parents and the seeming absence of family conflict over Judy's differences from her parents.

It is important to recognize that neither we nor the Movines believe that blanket parental self-disclosure leads to or guarantees accelerated development in an adolescent daughter or son. In fact, Judy and her father point out the limitations and dangers of indiscriminate parental disclosures:

FATHER: I'm willing to articulate almost anything to the point where . . . make you want to turn your ears off. (*mother and Judy laugh*). However, I agreed talking off-camera here, in the other room . . . that I have reluctantly, but finally, come to realize that there were certain formal exchanges between parent and child, let's put it that way, which are necessary. You just can't; like I want my father to tell me all about himself like he never would. But it's an imposition on a child to, to dump life on them, okay? At any, certain stages, you know.

JUDY: Especially when you include your problems. (*laughs*)

A third family configuration is presented by Sarah Resilie, who was hospitalized early in her adolescent years.

SARAH RESILIE

Sarah was sixteen years old when we first met with her. In her second year at the hospital, and now living in a less structured setting, she was clearer about her mood swings and the desperate feelings that had led to overdoses and wrist slashing in the past three years. Sarah is one of only two psychiatric patients who entered the study at a high ego development level (postconformist or above). Her interview is marked, from the first moments, by clear indications of her advanced development, as she describes, with much nuance and complexity, her recent painful experiences. At the same time she conveys intense but vacillating self-deprecation, telling the interviewer how she is the "screwed-up one in my family."

Sarah traces the first signs of the depression that ultimately led to her hospital admission. When she was twelve, she began taking drugs, putting in less effort at school, overeating, and becoming upset with herself over her food and weight problems. She then enrolled at a private high school and, after briefly connecting with a new set of friends, became intensely uncomfortable around people:

> I just never knew what to say. There was this girl who always tried to hang around with us. She was such a blah and, you know, she never had anything to say. And I was always thinking, "God if I don't keep up the conversation, they're going to think I'm like that," even though I wasn't. Instead of spending time with friends, I started staying home weekends more . . . feeling bored a lot and very restless, but never wanted to do anything. . . . I stopped going to school as much, and then I went away that summer and there were times I was very depressed. . . . [After returning to school] I began to get more and more uncomfortable around people. I could see the withdrawal was in steps. . . . I had a harder time concentrating on school work. . . . I was skipping a lot of [athletic] practice. It just wasn't me. I wasn't enjoying much of anything.

By the time she was fifteen, Sarah felt like "a blob." After reading Sylvia Plath's *The Bell Jar,* she became convinced that the cure for her feelings was suicide. Several months later she overdosed with sleeping pills and tranquilizers. Briefly hospitalized at a local pediatric hospital, she began psychotherapy. Shortly after leaving the hospital she again became severely depressed and slashed her wrist, severing a vein. When she saw her blood she became frightened and called her therapist, who warned Sarah that she would require hospitalization if her self-destructive behavior continued.

Six months later, shortly before her sixteenth birthday, she returned from an overseas trip with friends and suddenly realized she was depressed: "It happened in an instant." Nothing had any meaning for her. Without any obvious reasons, her lethargy and feelings of emptiness intensified over the next weeks. She ate excessively, distracting herself from how badly she felt. But her eating strategy exacerbated her self-disgust. She envisioned the next suicide attempt as leading to major changes in her life, helping her to escape from the disturbing feelings by sending a message to others that she needed help. She had hoped to "be out of it" for a long time, especially out of home and school. While Sarah knew that her suicide attempt was "coming," she was unable to tell her parents or therapist about those impulses. She was aware of "a part of her" that wanted to die. Telling others would imply that she was not really serious.

Sarah continues to hesitate about disclosing her sad feelings to others. Before her hospital admission, she used many indirect communications—such as suicide attempts—to convey desperate and unhappy feelings about herself. While she is no longer suicidal, the mood swings remain with her:

> When I'm in an up mood, I feel very hopeful; (*nervous laugh*) and when I'm in a down mood, (*nervous laugh*) I feel very hopeless . . . and little things can set me off . . . can put me on really bad moods and (*pause*) little things, I guess, can put me in really good moods too. They change very fast. (*nervous laugh*)

Through her sentence completions, Sarah articulates some of the feelings that may underlie her "low moods":

> When I feel angry "I often contain my anger or else direct it towards myself."

> My conscience bothers me "If I'm mean to somebody without intending to be."

> My main problem is "I'm too self-critical."

Sarah reminds us of her persistent "lows":

> I am "still very far away from getting over being really depressed."

And she brings up her unease with peers:

What gets me into trouble is "dealing with kids my age."

Being with other people "my own age sometimes makes me nervous and self-conscious."

Nonetheless, at the time of the interview the people who are most important in Sarah's life are friends from school and the hospital. She describes the increasing importance of friends as she has tried to develop more independence from her family in recent years. She speaks of her conflict over separating from her parents and being with close friends: "I'd rather spend time with my friends than my family . . . but I still like to do things with my family on weekends." Her friendships are varied. With some friends she enjoys relaxing or being drunk, not "partying that much"; with others she goes to parties and has more "aggressive" times. Sarah is accepting of many different kinds of friends:

I usually can overlook [things that bother me in other people], and they put up with an awful lot of bad things (*nervous laugh*) about me too. I'm a very moody person. (*pause*) I don't see how people can stand me when I'm in one of my bad moods.

Although here she again refers to her self-hatred, other important features of Sarah appear within in this self-reflection. There is her perceived similarity to others, her tolerance of others' foibles, and her recognition that they accept hers. She tells the interviewer how important it is for a friend to listen, to be "sympathetic and everything." Andrea, a close and supportive friend, listened during the summer before Sarah's hospitalization. Sarah's friendships are all with girls; "guys" still make her uncomfortable. At the very end of her interview, when asked about topics that were left uncovered, Sarah brings up "guys," and her "not going out with very many kids because unless I like them . . . " Sarah returns to this theme through the stem "When I'm with a man," to which she responds, "I'm at ease; when I'm with a boy, I'm not."

Sarah's visions of the future are long-range and ambitious, despite her fluctuating moods. Ever since she was little, Sarah has wanted to be an architect ("not a therapist, I don't think that I could take, you know, listening to people talk about [personal] problems all day"), a wish that continues at age sixteen. In addition, she describes her interest in science and "languages" and vaguely indicates that she might "like to do something like that [science and 'languages'] someday."

SARAH'S FAMILY

Sarah is the older of two children. She describes her brother, four years younger, as "more outgoing," involved in parties, and less studious than her. They "get along" very well, except for occasional altercations, which Sarah feels he provokes. Her parents are health service and teaching professionals. At first glance her family appears to be cohesive and involved with one another through skiing, tennis, apple picking, and going to restaurants together. Yet the tension between Sarah's isolation and her wishes to be closer to them is almost palpable. Their surface togetherness is belied by her sense that "we're just not all that close." She expands upon her perceived lack of closeness within her family, as she describes how her parents tell each other their feelings, "but not really half as much" as there is to tell. The theme of closeness threads through her descriptions of each parent.

Her mother, Mrs. Resilie, is thirty-eight years old and functions at a postconformist (conscientious) ego development level. Since being in the hospital, Sarah has become aware of an increasing closeness with her mother, coupled with the wish to pull away from her:

I think I have become a little closer, especially to my mother. (*long pause*) And that's funny, because at the same time that I say we're not that close, I'd like to be a little more close. I'm also feeling that I'm ready to leave the hospital now and I'm living at Roades House.

The yearning for her mother and the idea that this yearning has not been fulfilled are also expressed in one of her sentence completions: "If my mother and I had talked more about problems when was younger, I might not have gotten as depressed as I am now." In her own sentence completions, Mrs. Resilie portrays herself as "upbeat," persevering, and devoted:

When they avoided me "I tried to forgive them."

When I get mad "I try to get it out of me as quickly as possible and then I forget about it."

My mother and I "have troubles getting along, but I still love her."

A woman should always "be kind and thoughtful to those nearest and dearest to her."

The thing I like about myself is "my positive attitude on life."

A wife "should be a good companion and friend to her husband."

I am "a happy person and have much to be contented about."

Although she expresses some regrets and concerns, they are but minor, as Mrs. Resilie clearly gives precedence to her "positive attitude to life":

My main problem "is that I did not receive an advanced education in my early twenties."

The worst thing about being a woman "is growing old."

Sometimes she wished that "she had been more patient with the children."

Possibly Sarah's perceived lack of closeness with her mother has to do with Mrs. Resilie's leanings toward devotion and her decidedly optimistic outlook. Mrs. Resilie may be reluctant, or unable, to connect sensitively with Sarah's darker side, her bleak and stormy feelings, and her degraded views of herself.

Mr. Resilie is a forty-four-year-old health professional, functioning at a very high ego level (at the transition between the conscientious and autonomous stages). Sarah experiences less conflict as well as less disappointment with him. She sees him as very "intellectual" and, in contrast to her mother, less openly expressive of his feelings, especially "upset" ones. "I've seen my dad before when he's very upset and tried to hide it by acting angry." Shaken after one of Sarah's overdoses, her father questioned her "sternly," "but I knew that he wasn't angry, he was really upset, he was just trying to hide it." Her father's greater emotional restraint figures prominently in Sarah's memories of her mother and father when she was younger. She recalls open anger between her and her mother for years: "We'd fight all the time, so it seems we got out our anger." These open displays did not occur with her father, and she comments, with some compassion: "My father's parents never raised their voice even when they were mad."

In contrast to the several one-dimensional descriptions expressed by Mrs. Resilie, Mr. Resilie presents many-sided views of people and situations. He stresses difficulties, sadness, regrets, and coping. In describing what he likes about himself, Mr. Resilie says, "I seem to be able to survive and function completely, even in the face of adversity of major proportions." These themes also appear in several other sentence completions:

I feel sorry "that I did not spot the symptoms of my daughter's depression much earlier, for I suspect treatment years before might well have saved her a lot of pain."

If I can't get what I want "I often remain unhappy and irritable for several days or even weeks; but I usually pull myself out of it."

My main problem is, "that I do not seem to communicate well the warmth of my feelings to those whom it is most important to do so."

The regret touched on about communication in the last response is reminiscent of Sarah's disappointment with the limited communication in her family. Besides her father's awareness of his difficulties conveying warm feelings, the seemingly large gap between his own and his wife's emotional styles may also contribute to Sarah's idea of the family's communication problems. Consider their responses to the sentence that begins, "A wife should." Mrs. Resilie completes it with "be a good companion and friend to her husband." In contrast, Mr. Resilie says, "be supportive of her husband emotionally, and be sensitive to his moods and problems, but should be able to expect the same in return and should not subordinate her individuality to his." Also noteworthy is Mr. Resilie's sensitivity to the effects of his actions on others, a realization he expresses implicitly in the responses already cited and more explicitly as well:

What gets me into trouble is "speaking my feelings too impulsively, without thinking of their impact on the other person, and not realizing how sharply my words can sting."

Mr. Resilie expands upon his understandings of social roles and forces:

Men are lucky because "the society that we live in has given us all sorts of social and economic mobility, based pretty much on brains and skills."

A husband has a right to "have his opinions and strong feelings on family issues heard and given serious, respectful consideration."

The worst thing about being a man is "that society imposes certain behavioral stereotypes on you that may just not fit your feelings and desires."

The unmistakable differences between Sarah's parents' perceptions and perspectives are amply illustrated in these varied responses. Overall, her mother's level of ego development is conscientious, at the start of the postconformist stages, while her father is functioning at the transition between the conscientious and autonomous stages, solidly within the postconformist range of development. How do her parents' different inner worlds and views intersect and contribute to Sarah's accelerated path of ego development?

SARAH WITHIN HER FAMILY

The moral dilemma discussions uncover ways in which these individual characteristics and special relationships appear within the family. Sarah and her parents participate in lively exchanges and challenges in the course of their discussions, showing many signs of their attentiveness to each other's ideas. Family members consistently tell one another when they are veering from the question at hand. For instance, in discussing whether Heinz should rob the store, the family begins to discuss punishment, having been led in this direction by Mr. Resilie, who has concluded that Heinz should not be punished for stealing:

FATHER: I think it was morally wrong to steal. Even in this case; on the other hand, I don't think—

SARAH: (*interrupting*) In this case?

FATHER: —that he should be punished for it.

MOTHER: Oh, I think he should be punished for it, but he should be given a very light kind of sentence.

FATHER: I think he should be brought to trial.

SARAH: I think he should be freed.

MOTHER: Yes, I think that's the next question.

FATHER: I think he should be brought to trial, I think that he should be brought to trial.

SARAH: That's not . . . the question is really . . .

Mrs. Resilie and then Sarah redirect Mr. Resilie toward consideration of the "correct" question in this early phase of the family's discussion.

The Resilies engage in complex discussions about the rationale for their specific answers and their underlying logic, describing how their thoughts unfolded. This can be seen as Sarah and her father try to resolve their difference with Mrs. Resilie over whether Heinz should steal the drug. Both believe that Heinz should steal the drug, while her mother thinks that he should not steal it:

FATHER: (*to mother*) Want to defend yourself?

MOTHER: Uh hum. I said that my answer, my feeling was that he should . . . explore other alternatives before he broke the rules of society. That it was important that he try to explore every single alternative, ah, because if we had people going around breaking rules, breaking society's rules, such as stealing, we'd have total anarchy, no matter how severe the reasons were, and I—

SARAH: (*interrupting*) Well, I felt it was implied in the story that there wasn't any other choice, that this was, you know, the one thing that would save his wife, and . . . if that was the only thing, I think he should. I think the druggist is in the wrong. Of course he's breaking the law, but he's, has a, a very, very strong motive to steal it.

MOTHER: But there's no guarantee that this would save his wife—in fact the story was specific—specifically said that that there was, that it thought it might not cure; but it wasn't a proven, wasn't a proven cure.

FATHER: Well, what they're dealing with is, you know, not a guarantee of cure, but, the right or wrong of the act.

MOTHER: Right, and I think the act is wrong, and I also said that I thought that one of the things they hadn't tried was the very people that had loaned the, Heinz, the money could, perhaps, as peer pressure be brought to bear on the druggist. That that hadn't been tried, that they ought to get together and try. I just felt that every motive should still be explored and that the story hadn't explained—

SARAH: (*interrupting*) I can't see why they, the druggist, didn't give the drug on credit. You know, he has the thousand dollars as down payment, and I think—

MOTHER: (*interrupting*) Well, I agree with you, Sarah.

FATHER: Well, but that isn't the hypothetical. I mean, what they're doing, obviously, is stacking the deck in this by putting it in Europe so there isn't any help available, and they don't tell you what time it was. They talk about radium; it might have been the 1890s, you know . . .

MOTHER: Why do you think that he should steal?

FATHER: Well, I didn't, and that's why I am so amused because I started out saying, "Now, he shouldn't steal," and then I sort of weasled my way around to the fact that if, indeed, this hypothetical was intended to ask you the question, which is a higher priority of value—the human life or breaking the rule, the law—then I've got to say that if that's the real question, then certainly the human life is the higher value, and I changed my answer (*laughing*) from no to yes, that he should steal it.

SARAH: That's what I felt it came down to; uhmm, is it okay to break the law when it's for a human life? I felt also that . . . I made a distinction between somebody who is family or close friend and a stranger, but Dr. Loren [the family interviewer] said, "Well, should he have . . . done that for a stranger?" And I said, "no," because he doesn't have the same kind of concern for a stranger's life. You know, I'm sure he feels, you'd feel, very badly if the stranger did, but I don't think he [Heinz] would . . . feel that it's his duty whereas his wife, somebody he loves and cares about . . .

In this conversation, drawn from an opening phase of the family's discussion, all three members connect with one another from their different perspectives. Both parents express a broad repertoire of enabling interactions—explaining, problem-solving, curiosity, empathy—as they speak with each other and with Sarah. Mrs. Resilie's level of participation is significant here, as we see her actively initiating and responding to Sarah and her husband. We see her involvement in these exchanges and openness to other perspectives as she eventually changes her position:

MOTHER: Well, okay if it's a question of, if it's brought down to the moral issue of human life versus stealing, I will agree with the two of you.

But such three-person interactions soon become rare. What gradually evolves is a coalition of Sarah and her father, excluding her mother in ways both subtle and transparent. The increasing exclusion of Mrs. Resilie is not a surprise, in light of the conflicts and incompatibilities among the family members. Sarah reported many overt conflicts between her and her mother. Moreover, the sentence completions of Sarah and her father pointed to many similarities between them, as each highlighted complex perceptions of themselves and others. Within the family, the first signs of the coalition between Sarah and her father appear when Sarah is arguing, against both parents, that officer Brown should not report Heinz:

MOTHER: Why did you say no, Sarah, since that was his job as a police officer to report it? We're not talking about the crime itself, whether the crime was right or wrong. We're talking about Officer Brown's duty.

SARAH: I don't like people who rat on—

MOTHER: (*interrupting*) Yes, but when he takes an oath of office—

FATHER: (*interrupting*) Oh, yeah, he's an officer of the court. Yeah, I think he has an obligation.

SARAH: There are things people aren't . . . Wait a minute. I heard that he knew about Heinz—Heinz's wife.

FATHER: Yeah, they told me that too.

MOTHER: Yeah, Yeah.

SARAH: Um, I feel, I don't care what your job is. I think that your human feelings should come first, and . . . wouldn't want to see Heinz get in trouble for doing something, even if it was, you know. It just comes back to the fact that I don't think it was morally wrong in this situation, so I don't think he should be reported.

FATHER: But we can't leave those things up to each person to judge.

SARAH: Yeah.

FATHER: I mean we have a judicial structure that determines whether something was lawful or not lawful.

SARAH: Yeah, I guess you'd, I guess I can agree with your side of this in that he should be brought to court.

MOTHER: And then let them decide.

FATHER: It's almost a harder case if he isn't a policeman.

MOTHER: Right. Right. Right.

FATHER: If he's just somebody else. But where he's a policeman . . .

MOTHER: And has sworn to—

SARAH: (*interrupting*) No, I don't think it's the policeman part at all. I feel that part of the argument doesn't sway me one way or the other. But I think the fact that it shouldn't be up to each person to decide whether . . . a crime is right or wrong, though I know that personally, um, I wouldn't report him. (*pause*) If I, suppose I saw a kid stealing a candy bar in the store, I, I would not report that kid.

MOTHER: Suppose you're an officer of the law, Honey?

SARAH: Suppose I'm policeman?

MOTHER: Uh hmm.

SARAH: It still doesn't matter.

MOTHER: You still wouldn't?

FATHER: What happens if you saw somebody killing someone else?

SARAH: I certainly would.

FATHER: What happens if the killing was justified?

SARAH: I still would. As I'm saying, I think in this . . . case—

FATHER: (*interrupting*) You're not the avenging or pardoning angel. We have a structure, a system to do that, and it seems to me each person, especially an officer of the law, takes to himself the responsibility for the judicial system and the trial process and all that—

SARAH: (*interrupting*) No. I'm saying, me, personally. I wouldn't do that. But I can see what you mean that each person should not, that the process, that the decision of whether somebody . . . should—what they did was right or wrong—it should not be in the hands of the person. It should be in the hands of the court, and in that case . . . the policeman should . . . report him. I don't think, however, being a policeman has to do with it.

FATHER: HMM.: That's interesting.

SARAH: And I think that me, personally, it would, with me personally it would depend on the crime. But I feel that, in general, (*nervous laugh*) yes, you're right; people shouldn't individually decide whether they should steal or not.

Mrs. Resilie has virtually dropped out of the discussion, leaving Sarah and her father to continue the lively argument between themselves. Sarah's many contributions are predominantly explaining and accepting speeches. And her father persistently challenges, suggests, and offers didactic speeches, most of them directed to Sarah.

The ardent exchanges between Sarah and her father become even more prominent when the family considers the problem of Joe's father wanting the money earned by his son in order to go on a suddenly planned fishing trip. She and Mr. Resilie present and discuss their many opinions about this conflict. A powerful connection between this accelerated young adolescent and her more intellectual and emotionally distant father unfolds. This father–daughter dialogue is but rarely punctuated by Mrs. Resilie:

SARAH: Well the first thing, [it] was, I mean that was a much easier thing to decide on than the other case, the case, the case of Heinz. I was just shocked that the parent could be so hypocritical as to say to their child, you know, if you want to do this. The fact that he promised him he could go to camp and then didn't let him is one thing. But what's most important is that he said to his child, if you want to do something go out and earn the money. And the kid did.

And father wants to do something and he wants to take the kid's money, the kid earned for himself, and the father, ahh, that's completely a double standard.

MOTHER: I . . . totally agree with you, and I also said that the most important thing I felt in the parent–child relationship was trust. And the father had said to the son that if he wants to go camp, he'd have to go out and earn the money. The son did so, and that the father had an obligation to keep his word, just like the son did what was expected of him, and I feel—

SARAH: (*interrupting*) Yeah, I thought the promise was an important part, and trust is . . .

MOTHER: Yes.

FATHER: Yeah, I think—

SARAH: (*interrupting*) of the father, you know, setting a complete double standard.

FATHER: I think it was too black-and-white a situation. I suggest he could conceive of a situation in which the father needed money, not to gratify his own caprices, but because, let's say, the sister needed, desperately needed some medicine and the family was poor, you know, it was a question of giving up.

MOTHER: But don't change the rules of the game.

FATHER: No, but I'm saying, and I think under those circumstances, the father could, perhaps, have a motive for coming to the son, asking him to let him out of the promise on the basis of—

SARAH: (*interrupting*) Sure.

FATHER: —the fact. But that this was such a black-and-white case of betrayal.

SARAH: Yeah.

FATHER: And I also felt it was kind of an ugly example to set of breaking a word, of . . . really betraying, going back on . . . because a parent does set certain examples, of values, a behavior pattern.

SARAH: "A parent can teach a child values" is what he's saying in a sense.

MOTHER: I think we ought to—

FATHER: (*interrupting*) And that child is gonna . . . forever be untrusting . . . not keeping his word kind of person. That's a terrible contribution to society.

SARAH: What part did you think was worse: Breaking of the promise, or the fact that the father told the son to earn the money and wouldn't go out and earn his own?

FATHER: Oh, I don't think it has to do with the money so much. I think that it would be the same thing if the father had said, "You get good grades in school and you can go to camp." Or, "You do your chores around the house and you can go to camp." Yeah, what did you [to Sarah] say?

SARAH: No, the fact that the father told his son, which, you know, something that is good for a kid to do, to go out and earn your own money, but when the father wanted to do something, he did not go out and earn money. He dared to take it from his son, who had worked for it, worked for something he wanted And . . . the kid is going to say like, "Why should I have to go and earn my own money when my father doesn't?"

FATHER: Well, that's a tough one. I wouldn't let the moral issue hang on the question of the money, because I think that the father—

SARAH: (*interrupting*) No, I think it's not the money, Daddy. I think it's that the parent is being a hypocrite. The parent is, ahh, is setting a standard for his kid which is different from his standards for himself.

FATHER: Well, not exactly, Sarah, because the parent, it seems to me, although you're not sympathetically inclined toward the parent on the facts that are given, the parent can rationalize money he spends supporting the kid, paying for the kid's needs . . . was in fact money—

SARAH: (*interrupting*) But it's not the money, Daddy.

FATHER: Well, that's what I want to make clear. It shouldn't be the money.

SARAH: It isn't the money. . . . A parent tells a kid to return something they stole to the drug store, but the parent doesn't return money to the IRS, that he cheated them money on his tax returns. I find it the same sort of thing. I think the parent is going completely against what he's trying to teach his child.

FATHER: Yeah, I think that's true. I think there's an incongruity, that's what I thought.

Later Mrs. Resilie returns to the discussion, but her contributions take a different form:

MOTHER: Wasn't there a larger question that was asked here? About family relationships and what are the most important within a family relationship?

SARAH: Yeah, we're leading up to that. It was just . . . the story.

MOTHER: What are some of the other important things?

SARAH: I mean, obviously, the trust within a family, you know, a parent keeping his promise. I can see breaking your promise only in a case where you have to . . . and I don't think that's just within a family. I, ahh, think that should represent everybody.

MOTHER: I do too. (*yawning*) I agree with that. It's very important to give your—

SARAH: (*interrupting*) I think Daddy's right, that the example, that in order to keep your word, you have to learn it through your parents keeping their word.

FATHER: Well, I think it's hard to learn to keep your word when you've been, when you've had somebody break their word to you, especially somebody, somebody you don't expect to.

SARAH: Okay. Yeah, especially somebody who, you know, I guess people, kids learn those, their morals—

FATHER: (interrupting) That kids—

SARAH: (interrupting) and their values from their parents.

FATHER: But if you're going to break your word, it seems to me there ought to be a better reason than that, and you ought to explain it.

MOTHER: Absolutely. I mean, certainly just to say I want a, I want to go on a fishing trip is not a good reason, a good example.

FATHER: We [family interviewer and Mr. Resilie], we had an interesting conversation about that, because we got into the subject of whether it's different between fathers and sons than it is between mothers and daughters.

MOTHER: I don't see any difference. Do you, Sarah?

FATHER: Not whether it should be, whether it actually is.

MOTHER: No, why? Why would it be different?

FATHER: I think it is.

MOTHER: Why?

FATHER: And I don't know why except that my own observations of those relationships that I know, close friends and family, are that there is, there is, more friction in the first fifteen years of life together between mothers and daughters than there is between fathers and sons. Now whether it reverses and later it becomes . . . and later it becomes more difficult as the father and son become "macho," dueling with each other or not, I don't know.

SARAH: I think you're right.

FATHER: I think I am.

SARAH: Though in our family it's hard to tell because Billy [her brother] has always been such a sweet kid. (*laughter between them*)

Mrs. Resilie's episodic participation is largely through focusing, challenging, and occasional accepting speeches. The disagreements and challenges are most obvious in the charged argument about whether relationships between fathers and sons differ from those between mothers and daughters. Moreover, Mrs. Resilie persistently hears Sarah proclaim that "Daddy is right" following disagreements. In these interactions Sarah and her father expose their strong connection with each other and their exclusion of Mrs. Resilie, not allowing her access to the discussion or minimizing her contributions. Mrs. Resilie reacts to these restrictions by interrupting and distracting more often than her husband. She is vying for recognition, as Sarah and her father intently discuss the moral dilemmas. On the other hand, Mr. Resilie can also be devaluing and angrily indifferent toward Sarah, reminding us of the angry, problematic aspects of this intense father–daughter relationship, alluded to earlier by Sarah.

As was true for Aaron and Judy, Sarah expresses more enabling speeches to her father, a pattern especially apparent for explaining and accepting. Sarah is consistent in her constraining speeches. She is strikingly more distracting and gratifying toward her father. Taken together, these detailed speech-by-speech observations trace Sarah's relationship with her father, as she both assists (through explaining and empathy) and duels (through her challenges and interruptions) him during these discussions.

We see similar patterns in Mr. and Mrs. Resilie's interaction. With respect to enabling, Mr. Resilie expresses higher levels of explaining and accepting to Sarah, paralleling her enabling to him. But both parents express more varied enabling speeches—problem-solving, curiosity, and empathy.

Through these case studies we identify intricate dynamics in the families of adolescents with accelerated ego development. What aspects of these patterns stand out as possible sources for this precociously high development? First, there is the strong self-disclosure, of feelings and thoughts, by both parents, often reciprocated by their child. We have already speculated about the impacts these adolescents have on their families. The parents' disclosures and spirited exchanges are undoubtedly enhanced as their son or daughter elicits, listens, and encourages them to "tell more." One could argue that this engagement by the child precedes the parental disclosure and already reflects the advanced development. But the disclosing style of the parents—sensitively attuned to the child and not overwhelming his or her inner world—cannot be seen as simply a child-effect. Second, there is the listening, the openness (permeability) of the parents, their mutuality with the adolescent. Finally, family relationships are clearly characterized by the features of assertiveness and individuality described as so characteristic of individuated relationships.[2]

Review and Prospects

Sustaining or Endangering Adolescents' Growth

In other words, the human environment must permit and safeguard a series of more or less discontinuous and yet culturally and psychologically consistent steps, each extending further along the radius of expanding life tasks.[1]

FAMILY RELATIONSHIPS AND PATHS OF DEVELOPMENT

At the heart of this book is one human environment, the family, and the question of how it can safeguard, enhance, *and* obstruct development—sometimes explosive development—during the teenage years. In pursuing this broad and perplexing question we have listened closely to family conversations—between teenagers and their parents, and between parents. In addition, we have drawn upon intensive interviews and written materials to shed further light on the ambience of the family and the vicissitudes of adolescent experience. Central to our analyses and case studies is the theme of *diversity*. There is no single path of adolescent ego development along which progress is simply promoted or retarded. A variety of paths are possible, stretching from the profoundly arrested to the accelerated. Our portraits of family members and accounts of how they speak with one another are organized around four of these developmental trajectories.

Following twelve boys and girls, and relying on our observations of many more, we described these paths of ego development as they wound through interconnected passages of independence, separation, and intimacy. To be sure, the adolescents following these paths neither embarked on nor continued along them in isolation. They began within their families. By the time we met them, they were accompanied as well by friends, relatives, teachers, religious leaders, therapists, and neighbors. A host of significant people and institutions were influencing the direction of their development, and many of those people and institutions were undoubtedly affected in turn by the adolescents.

While aware that such an array must exist for any teenagers, we nevertheless see the family as the most important presence during adolescence. The many deep identifications that adolescents have made with their parents and siblings over the years cause them to incorporate aspects of their families' cognitive and emotional styles, defenses, strengths, vulnerabilities, and cherished beliefs. At another level, children assimilate their family's myths and paradigms for understanding the world.[2] To those imprints carried forward from childhood are added the marks of current family experiences. The responses of the family, and of individual members within it, to new initiatives, new ideas, rapid growth spurts, and unpredictable mood swings have immediate effects, among them discouragement or excitement, and long-lasting impacts on continuing ego development.

By now it must be clear to the reader that it is the teenager's *family of the present* that we have most closely observed, looking at how parents define themselves and their relationships, even more assiduously listening to how parents and adolescents speak with one another while defending powerful, often divisive, differences of opinion. Yet we do not dismiss or overlook the past history of the family. Adolescents' interview descriptions and sentence completions about parents and family provided glimpses of this family of the past, based on years of childhood experience, now incorporated within their adolescent personalities.

Much of what we have learned is reflected in our case studies of individual and family worlds in Part II. These worlds—differing in experience, understandings, and emotional style—converge and clash through the *relationships* between and within generations. Some of the relationships are associated with problematic, stalled, or seriously arrested adolescent development, others with progressive or unusually accelerated development. As we examined the perceptions, feelings, and interactions of teenagers and their parents, we discovered certain relationship patterns, or cycles, that are closely connected with those very different paths of development.

We first encountered the profoundly arrested. In the families of Charlie, Ellen, and Mike we discovered restricted, compromised relationships, as parent and teenager became immersed in combative authoritarian discussions characterized by pervasive rigidity and repeated instances of disengagement. Impatience, restlessness, and tuning out marked these families. Violence was barely contained. Violent feelings were often on the brink of erupting, as they had in the past for Mike, threatening with his gun, and Ellen, overturning tables. Or, as in the case of Charlie, terrified that he *would* put his imagined retributions into actions, these feelings were kept tightly bound.

We found more subtle relationships in the families of the steady conformists, those teenagers who had a strong need to be accepted by others and expressed meager interest in challenging the existing order. Sheila's family had little patience with ambiguity. Often goaded by Lou, the Provos intensely voiced their unwavering beliefs about the importance of firm rules, together with their dogged opposition to any deviation from family values or—more concretely—from the topic of the family's discussion. This dance of conformity was only occasionally and briefly interrupted by unexpected new rhythms. Lou and his parents struggled over many matters, but in the end Lou always returned to the family fold. The dance was more subdued in Amy's family, as she and her mother quietly embraced family ideals after being mocked or threatened with rejection when experimenting with new thoughts or feelings.

The important point is that, when challenged by uncertainty and change, the members of these families consistently related in ways intended to restore the previous order: prematurely ending discussions, distracting one another, or abruptly withdrawing from ongoing conversation. These families opposed any apparent differentiation of individual members, whether adolescent or parent, and discouraged exploration, curiosity, or new moves of any kind.

In a second large group of teenagers—those who were *progressing* or unusually *accelerated* in their development—families, teenagers, and parents listened closely to one another, receptive to new perspectives and willing to change their views and perceptions through active persuasion or new conversations. Instead of shrinking from uncertainty and ambiguity, these families sought such experiences, promoting them by raising questions, voicing many doubts and challenges. Certain striking patterns of relating were especially evident. In Lois's family we heard repeated instances of protection cycles, in which, for instance, Lois could count on the support of her mother when thinking aloud or when struggling with new feelings and ideas. There were also engagement cycles in these families, as parents and teenagers remained closely attuned to unfolding ideas and questions being expressed by one other. Those writing about attachment relationships have long stressed the importance of emotional availability.[3] In these families we see the salience of a parallel cognitive availability and connection.

A third characteristic of these families was *parental disclosure:* Within important limits defined by the parents, a mother or father would share pertinent inner conflicts or recall painful incidents from his or her own childhood. Recall Judy's parents, telling her of their awkward moments with their own parents; and Judy's mother speaking of her new-found idealism in adolescence:

MOTHER: When we were fourteen, we were both incredibly more naïve than you are, very idealistic, incredibly naive. And we both had to painfully, very painfully (*laughs*) learn a few things.

This sharing was prompted by the current family discussion, not by the parent's pressing need for more intimacy, connection, or confession with a teenager. In other words, these significant disclosures were well timed and well placed; they were not fueled by a parent's self-serving agenda to form a special alliance with a teenage child in the service of luring him or her to take sides in a chronic marital struggle.

Yet these families were not free of conflict. There were times of tense disagreement and discomfort, surrounded by anger, regret, and confusion. Such experiences were generally acknowledged, tolerated, and confronted within the family, a style most dramatically illustrated by the Wellers' formal family meetings.

Aaron's questioning could be tolerated only so far by his parents, who finally let him know that their patience was almost exhausted. However, Aaron was not fully subdued. He continued to challenge their beliefs and conclusions, and was *not* met with mockery, distraction, or indifference by them. Sarah's mother was frequently excluded by her family, as Sarah and her father intently pursued a given issue. But Mrs. Resilie persistently returned to the discussion, unwilling to cope with those difficult episodes by withdrawing, distracting, or being seductive in her praise of Sarah.

These configurations of relationships reflect the varied family experiences associated with different paths of adolescent development. The immediate and often touching interactions in these families are not conveyed by identifying those abstract patterns—"engagement cycles"—and relationship themes. Indeed, our belief in the importance of appreciating family members' unique experiences, interactions, and relationships is the very reason for including four chapters devoted entirely to accounts of specific teenagers and their families. We encourage the interested reader to return to those individual and family narratives to discover the many emotional tones and meanings of those relationship patterns or to find new ones unidentified by us.

APPLICATIONS

How can these understandings of adolescents and their families help others, especially parents, assist in navigating the potentially difficult passage to adulthood with the fewest casualties? One way is through refining consciousness, about the predictable hazards of that passage. In closing this final chapter, then, we turn from theory and research observation to the practical, to consider how parents can facilitate the entry of their teenage sons and daughters into new worlds of independence and intimacy. But we must first review the by now familiar conundrum about family influences.

DIRECTIONS OF INFLUENCE: WHO CHANGES WHOM?

In youth the table of childhood dependence begins slowly to turn: no longer is it merely for the old to teach the young the meaning of life, whether individual or collective. It is the young who, by their responses and actions, tell the old whether life as represented by the old and as presented to the young has meaning; and it is the young who carry in them the power to confirm those who confirm them and, joining the issues, to re-new and to regenerate, or to reform and to rebel.[4]

Early theories of socialization depicted the child or adolescent as "outcome," passively formed by powerful family forces. In this view, the child is a blotter, absorbing the effects of parenting styles. Many now seriously challenge this model of socialization, pointing out how children can elicit immediate reactions and continuing styles of inter-acting from their parents, and can become teachers of their parents, as portrayed by Erik Erikson in the eloquent vision of the slow turning of dependence between the generations, quoted above.[5] Nonetheless, clinical observers, lay people, and the media often imply or insist that the child is in some way a *victim* of the family. The most extreme version of this belief is reflected in ideas about schizophrenogenic mothers, once considered in some way responsible for creating their disturbed children's behavior.[6]

Our observations of family interactions flag the myriad ways that teenagers influence their parents. We hear Mr. Brown, a once eager, curious father, finally back off from his persistently rejecting, verbally abusive son. We observe Lou enticing his moody father into belligerent exchanges. On the other hand, we witness Lois's deepening connection with her mother, as she draws new ideas, views, and feelings from Mrs. Weller through her new—openly shared—anguishes and questions. These observations provide an important cautionary note, reminding us that family contributions to adolescent development are not simply a matter of parents' character or personality. In watching families, we have repeatedly seen teenagers evoke intense feelings and attitudes in their parents, adding those powerful experiences to the expanding family history that flows through the teenage years.

We know, then, that adolescents exert an influence in moment-to-moment interactions with their parents, and when we speak of parenting styles, we must recall how adolescents influence those styles.[7] What we are less clear about is how profoundly families change as a result of their adolescent members. In other words, to what extent—and how—does developmental change during adolescence transform family relationships?[8] As we analyze later years of family observations, we shall be in an excellent position to discover how the family itself changes, sometimes in synchrony with the evolving teenager, and at other times in fervent opposition to the new ideas and worlds thrust upon it by a challenging teenage family member. Such opposition may, to be sure, represent the family's inability to evolve in response to the changing experiences of its adolescent member.

CRISES IN TEENAGE DEVELOPMENT: PARENTS' CONTRIBUTIONS TO COMPETENT SOLUTIONS

Summing up her excursions into many major novels and some books by psychological theorists, Patricia Spacks reminds us of the depth and complexity of adolescent–parent relationships:

> The young embody our most profound vulnerabilities and our most intimate strengths. They speak to us of our past and of our future. We can imagine them as licensed transgressors, surrogates for ourselves, or as prophets of salvation; as violators or precursors of [the] system. . . . The struggle of father and son, mother and daughter, is no critical metaphor but a fact of experience—as is the love between generations.[9]

Even though we are now more sophisticated about not holding parents responsible for all the trouble and struggles of their children, we can nonetheless speculate about the enormous significance of parental and overall family influences during the teenage years. In these last sections we consider ways that parents and families may support or hinder adolescent ventures into the confusing, frightening, and exciting worlds of independence and intimacy.

So far as independence is concerned, adolescence brings conflicting feelings, thoughts, and actions. Simultaneously, and not always so smoothly, teenagers are developing new relationships within their families and with old and new friends. Those changes were mentioned, often at length, by virtually all of the adolescents with whom we spoke each year. Until recently many theories about adolescence viewed gains in independence as requiring *detachment* from the family, the breaking of dependent bonds,[10] thus overlooking the fact that in the process of becoming more independent, teenagers forge close new connections with parents, siblings, and friends. Rather than see these sometimes profound adolescent changes as requiring a linear exchange, characterized by dependence on friends in exchange for dependence on family, we now see a more complex amalgam, involving adolescent differentiation *and* enduring family bonds, as new movements toward autonomy draw upon and transform family relationships.[11]

We return to the large question with which we began: How does family life facilitate or obstruct these cumulative momentous advances in adolescent development, advances that are often, when least expected, fragile and potentially calamitous? A basic answer about facilitating points to what can be the most difficult task for a parent: to remain devoted and engaged with the adolescent—in the vernacular, "to hang in"—even when circumstances visibly repel such engagement.[12] There is a fundamental need for continued support, recognition, and appreciation, *especially* in the midst of discouraging adversity.

Those teenagers who began at low levels of ego development and then progressed to higher levels were in families that expressed acceptance and mutuality. The point is not that mindless acceptance of an adolescent's ideas, feelings, and actions will promote his or her growth. In fact, blind encouragement will more often backfire, as the teenager correctly perceives that this essentially unengaged parent is really pretending. What is critical to convey as a parent is loyalty, understanding, and tenacity in the face of tough problems and dilemmas. This can come across in a number of forms. For instance, the parent does not "take it personally," when directly confronted, often rudely, by the teenage child experimenting with new ways of challenging adults, trying to discover how candor or authenticity differ from outrageousness. The helpful parental response is to be firm and engaged, not excessively sweet and effusive, or deeply offended. However tempting, a response that is distancing, restrictive, or reciprocally abusive—in word or deed—is at such moments surely the most damaging. Indeed, it is at precisely this juncture that one of the most significant *differences* between parent and adolescent becomes patent. We have persistently argued that adolescents may provoke many strong feelings and associated impulses in their parents, *but* it is the very ability to contain these feelings and impulses, to block their transformation into untoward words or actions and to be reasonable, that characterizes the competent and mature parent.

No less important is a mother's or father's ability to remain connected, despite the less obvious rebuffs of silence and withdrawal. It is not easy to remain on the field when the other player—one's teenage daughter or son—has quit. Teenagers can dramatically withdraw, physically and psychologically: "Later, man." When they reappear, frequently unexpected and unannounced, a compelling experience is to discover that the parent, however frustrated and forlorn, is still available, that the loving bond was not permanently ruptured by the teenager's escape from some impossible encounter with his or her parents.

Two contemporary movies illustrate these dynamics of "hanging in there." In *Dirty Dancing* a teenage daughter strays from her upper-middle-class physician father's values through her romantic relationship with a working-class dance teacher at the resort where the family is vacationing. While this leads to stormy times for her and her parents, the connection between them is never completely severed; her father stays involved, even rendering medical services to an old girlfriend of his daughter's unwelcome lover. Ultimately a moving rapprochement occurs between daughter and father.

The father–son relationship in *Dead Poets' Society* provides a stark contrast. A teenage son away at prep school suddenly discovers, through the powerful influence of a new teacher, his love of poetry and theater, and thereby deviates from his father's agenda, a carefully laid plan for him to study science and become a physician. This new direction in his son's plans, as well as the new mentor in his life, is taken as a personal affront by the father. Enraged and hurt, he removes his son from the school and takes him home, setting in motion a plan to transfer him to a military school. After a last confrontation, the son quietly withdraws from his father over the next hours, and then forever by killing himself. Although these stories certainly differ in many substantial ways, one difference is especially poignant. In the first story, a father's tenacity and awareness of his daughter's situation protect their relationship. While for a time tempestuous, their connection is never disrupted. In the second story, a father's single-minded attention to his own plans, not his son's, leads to a ruptured connection, an unmistakable and ultimately permanent break.

Another remarkable parenting response is illustrated in the portrait of Judy Movine, one of the accelerated adolescents. As we described earlier in the chapter, parents can become more revealing of themselves to their struggling teenagers. In the face of Judy's self-doubt about being able to "make it" outside her family with friends, doubts that extend to hours and days, her mother relates her own experience of vulnerability during these same teenage years. Judy's parents describe their uncertainties and worries in the midst of Judy's harsh self-criticism about her naïveté during the family discussion. Their sharing of those inner experiences was not intended as glib reassurance, nor was it the first instance of this kind of communication. Many such exchanges had taken place before and during Judy's teenage years. These acts of parental disclosure offer connections across the generations, revealing whatever insights and understandings parents may have gained during, and about, their own adolescence.

Remaining present and revealing one's own experiences are courageous and dramatic acts if they occur while a son or daughter is experiencing turbulence and discouragement. The parent's presence is offered as a unique and reliable resource. But there are less dramatic occasions when parents can facilitate their adolescents' growth. These quieter moments were the ones that we observed most closely, as parents and their teenage children struggled with one another over recognized differences in values, invoking deeply held principles of life, death, loyalty, and integrity. Listening, actively recognizing and clarifying their son's and daughter's voices were parental responses consistently linked with advanced or advancing ego development. On the other hand, in families of adolescents who were arrested in their ego development, parents tended to demonstrate impatience by turning away from their teenager's voices (especially when they were expressing a new rhythm or melody).

How do these positive engagements—from the most dramatic to the most subtle—enhance adolescent development? What is it about them that contributes so affirmatively? Here we enter especially speculative waters. Several processes may establish connections between adolescent development and parental responsiveness. The best known is identification: The teenager watches and listens to his or her parent, internalizing representations of parental thoughts, feelings, and deeds. Identification does not, of course, begin in the teenage years. The fifth grade daughter of a scientist begins to write school papers about health and disease. The son of a dedicated artist becomes increasingly involved in his new pottery class. Within the family, a daughter is keenly aware of how carefully her father and mother listen and are curious, as they build upon her new-found ideas. Taken so seriously at home, she is known among her peers as a good friend, someone who can be trusted to listen and be sympathetic.

Moving beyond identification, the chances that a teenager will embrace new perceptions or understandings are greater when the family encourages curiosity and problem-solving. Development is more likely to be advanced when parents accept their adolescent's compelling new tastes—for example, importing into the family unusual sounds, faces, and styles—some of which may be offensive. And here we encounter yet another realm of family life, *values*, the visions and assumptions shared, often silently, within the family. Although we have repeatedly alluded to family values, our focus has been upon interpersonal processes that enable or constrain the complex growth of adolescents. Such processes do not occur in a vacuum. They are closely connected with the family's values and beliefs. For instance, underlying careful listening and responsiveness are values favoring flexibility, openness, and change.

Yet another family characteristic enhancing change and growth is tolerance of feelings. Families have various ways of handling emotions, especially those that are potentially disruptive, such as anger, aggression, and envy. Some families abhor the expression or even the experience of those feelings; there may be a pervasive repulsion of feelings by a dominant member. In such a climate it is hardly safe for the adolescent to challenge a parent angrily or to risk introducing even ripples of testiness by challenging her mother or father. New perceptions and ideas are prematurely choked, never to be explored—playfully aired or more seriously tested—by the teenager with his or her parents.

Other families specialize in conflict and disruption, perhaps because of severe marital strains[13] or as a way of masking more dependent or loving feelings. In such an atmosphere of chaos and tension, there is little chance for quiet reflection or thoughtful listening to the adolescent or parents. Only rarely were the ideas of Lou Provo, a steady conformist, or either of his parents heard at length. At another extreme are those families who invite and take delight in a range of feelings, from the most loving to the angriest. Within those settings few constraints are placed on surprises; challenges are not fraught with danger. To put it more positively, new directions in thought and feeling are encouraged, and individual change is valued.

TRANSFORMING RELATIONSHIPS

Related to the handling of feelings by the adolescent and his or her family is a second major theme in teenage development: the formation of new close relationships with parents and friends. While most of the adolescents we interviewed commented in one way or another about changes in their relationships with family and friends, we did not analyze these issues at length or examine their association with the paths of ego development. As many have recently observed,[14] renegotiated family intimacy is less fully conceptualized and studied than independence and autonomy, perhaps because the prevailing view is that adolescence involves increasing independence. To be sure, if teenagers are seeking and experiencing new kinds of independence, it follows that relationships with families and friends must be changing; there may, for instance, be more distance, new expectations, and new tensions. But are relationship changes limited to those that are reactive to shifting autonomy? Or are some basic changes reactive to emergent wishes for new connections and intimacy?

New research on adolescents, especially girls, has strongly focused on the transformations of relationships during this major growth period.[15] While our evidence does not point to the *unique* importance of relationships to female adolescents, the significance of evolving relationships during this period of development is hard to overestimate. Several theorists argue that concerns with caring, connecting with others, and developing close relationships with family members and peers gain in prominence during adolescence. Moreover, these new relationships are not established at the cost of preceding ones but actually build upon them. How do family bonds facilitate these transformations within and outside the family? In families where accepting and empathic interactions predominate, teenagers may "carry over" these qualities to their relationships outside the family. Listening, focusing, and expressing curiosity can also be conducive to new and sustained relationships. But they can undermine the growing interest in care and connectedness if they become overly intellectual, inhibiting the experience and expression of strong feelings.

Parents who are threatened by evolving close relationships outside the family may attempt to thwart the new connections. In their campaign to keep their children attached to them, they overtly intrude, devalue, withdraw, or behave seductively with their teenagers. Such binding strategies may work in the short run, but—deeply flawed—they ultimately fail, precipitating a sharp break in the parent–adolescent relationship.[16]

HOW FAMILY LIFE ENHANCES
AND OBSTRUCTS ADOLESCENT GROWTH

In this chapter, and throughout our varied accounts of the paths of ego development, we have entertained many observations and speculations about the influences that flow between adolescents and other family members. Four themes stand out as especially important, and lead to four conclusions about how families can nurture or interfere with the new growth of their adolescent members.

1. *Enduring engagement.* Repeatedly, we have commented on and observed the importance of parents' and other family members' "hanging in," especially when they are most tempted to leave. Enduring and even making authentic attempts to engage with an abusive and rejecting son or daughter may be one of the most meaningful acts a parent can perform during these adolescent years.

2. *Parental disclosure.* This point refers to the parent's special role as a teacher. Disclosing, at the right moments, aspects of their inner lives, offering—in ways that their son or daughter can grasp—views of their own history, perceptions, understandings and current states of mind can enhance their adolescent's development by revealing other ways of approaching and grasping experience. So, too, these special communications can offer poignant confirmation to the adolescent of their unique relationship with the parent who is so willing to share this less accessible knowledge.

3. *Tolerance of novelty, ambiguity and uncertainty.* The chances of a teenager experimenting with new ideas and embracing new perceptions are greatly increased when he or she is in a family where curiosity and open-mindedness are valued and uncertainty is tolerated. Many of our observations highlight the significance of this family quality, a characteristic that was especially striking in our observations of discussions in the families of accelerated adolescents.

4. *Tolerance of unwanted and unexpected emotions.* Being willing and able to weather storms of disruptive and at times deeply offensive

feelings, such as intense anger and rejection, is an important general family strength, one especially called upon during the adolescence of one of its members. Transient rejections, surprising and "inappropriate" mood swings erupt in these years. This strength is powerfully illustrated in *Dirty Dancing,* which we discussed earlier in the chapter, and is closely related of course to the idea of "hanging in there."

THE LARGER CONTEXT

These reflections about how family relationships may enhance or interfere with adolescent development are based on our observations of white middle-class teenagers who live with two parents. But what about minority group adolescents, those living in single-parent homes, and those from economically less privileged families? There is no reason to assume that relationships are necessarily more troubled or radically different in such families.[17] Yet once we set aside the stereotypes of strain and trouble in these other settings, we must also acknowledge the inadequacy of our understanding of how social and economic forces affect the family and developmentally important family relationships.[18] The connections between family processes and individual development in other family contexts remain to be explored. It would be scientifically questionable, and arrogant, for us to claim that our results can be generalized to families from such different social backgrounds. A pressing research frontier, then, is the study of how socially diverse families influence and respond to the development of their adolescent children. Only through such cross-cultural efforts, within our own society and across societies, will we be able to gain a broader and deeper understanding of the ties between adolescent development and family processes. We can then go on to consider how this knowledge should influence policies and intervention programs designed to enhance and protect teenage development.

Recruiting Procedures
and Sample Characteristics

RECRUITING

Two samples were recruited, the first from a local high school; the second from the children's unit of a private psychiatric hospital.

Dr. Hauser and Dr. Powers visited all freshman classes in the high school, telling the students about their plans for a new project to study teenagers and their families through the course of high school. The students were also told that they would be paid ten dollars each year for their participation, and that their families would receive thirty dollars each year. All interested students then took an informed consent form to their parents for signatures. Two hundred and fifty students, from a total class size of more than five hundred, returned the signed forms.

In the hospital, the sample was drawn from consecutive early adolescent admissions. All fourteen- to sixteen-year-olds who were nonpsychotic and also showed no evidence of organic impairment (e.g. attention disorders, learning disorders), were approached over a period of two years by Dr. Noam, who explained the prospective nature of the project, the inclusion of families, and compensation for participating. Dr. Noam also spoke with the patients' families prior to their joining the project. Seventy adolescents and their families from a pool of 80 eligible patients volunteered to participate. Since both one- and two-parent families were eligible (and volunteered) from the psychiatric group, the high school group was then matched with the psychiatric one in terms of number of parents in the family. In other words, because 40 percent of the psychiatric group were from one-parent families, the same proportion of one-parent families was drawn from the high school volunteers. Additional characteristics used to match the two samples included gender and age.

SAMPLE CHARACTERISTICS

In order to provide more detail about the precise nature of these samples, we provide two sets of summaries in this section. A first table describes the overall group of adolescents and families who were studied in year one, in terms of psychiatric status, family features, and parental and adolescent characteristics (Table A1). This kind of detail is then separately given for the high school and psychiatric samples (Tables A2 and A3).

Finally, we present family and individual features of all the ego development trajectories (Tables A4 and A5). Many aspects of these descriptions are included in the text narrative. However, this even more complete description is presented here, to benefit readers who are especially interested in considering all eight trajectories (regression and moratorium are also included in Table A5) with respect to this greater detail (e.g. parental ego development, birth order).

Table A1 Characteristics of Year One Sample

Adolescents	
Age	14.43 (.87)[a]
Gender	
Boys	73
Girls	73
Psychiatric status	
High school	70
Patients	76
Average ego development stage[b]	
Boys	2.96 (1.67)[a]
Girls	3.48 (1.69)[a]
Parents	
Age	
Mothers	41.99 (5.54)[a]
Fathers	44.89 (6.43)[a]
Ego development (average stage)[c]	
Mother	5.56 (1.17)[a]
Father	5.45 (1.19)[a]
Family	
Social class[c]	
Upper middle	49
Middle; lower middle	78
Working; lower	18
Family structure	
Two-parent	92
One-parent	54
Number of siblings	2.15 (1.18)[a]
Birth order	2.34 (1.38)[a]
Firstborn	47

[a] Average and (standard deviation).
[b] Where 1 = impulsive; 2 = self-protective; 3 = self-protective/conformist; 4 = conformist; 5 = conformist/conscientious (self-aware); 6 = conscientious; 7 = conscientious/autonomous; 8 = autonomous; 9 = integrated.
[c] One family could not be classifed because of insufficient information.

Table A2   Characteristics of Year One High School Sample

Adolescents	
Age	14.57 (0.55)[a]
Gender	
Boys	34
Girls	42
Average ego development stage[b]	
Boys	3.88 (1.43)[a]
Girls	4.50 (1.27)[a]
Parents	
Age	
Mothers	42.41 (5.04)[a]
Fathers	45.60 (5.36)[a]
Ego development (average stage)[b]	
Mother	5.70 (1.02)[a]
Father	5.84 (0.86)[a]
Family	
Social class[c]	
Upper middle	43
Middle; lower middle	31
Working; lower	1
Family structure	
Two-parent	51
One-parent	25
Number of siblings	2.07 (1.20)[a]
Birth order	2.34 (1.38)[a]
Firstborn	23

[a] Average and (standard deviation).
[b] Where 1 = impulsive; 2 = self-protective; 3 = self-protective/conformist; 4 = conformist; 5 = conformist/conscientious (self-aware); 6 = conscientious; 7 = conscientious/autonomous; 8 = autonomous; 9 = integrated.
[c] One family could not be classifed because of insufficient information.

Table A3 Characteristics of Year One Psychiatric Sample

Adolescents	
Age	14.29 (1.11)[a]
Gender	
Boys	39
Girls	31
Average ego development stage[b]	
Boys	2.15 (1.44)[a]
Girls	2.10 (1.11)[a]
Parents	
Age	
Mothers	42.41 (5.04)[a]
Fathers	44.16 (7.32)[a]
Ego development (average stage)[b]	
Mother	5.41 (1.32)[a]
Father	5.07 (1.34)[a]
Family	
Social class	
Upper middle	6
Middle, lower middle	47
Working; lower	17
Family structure	
Two-parent	41
One-parent	29
Number of siblings	2.25 (1.17)[a]
Birth order	2.37 (1.47)[a]
Firstborn	23

[a] Average and (standard deviation).
[b] Where 1 = impulsive; 2 = self-protective; 3 = self-protective/conformist; 4 = conformist; 5 = conformist/conscientious (self-aware); 6 = conscientious; 7 = conscientious/autonomous; 8 = autonomous; 9 = integrated.

Table A4 Characteristics of Sample Used in Ego Development Trajectory (Path) Analyses

Adolescents	
Average age	14.42
Gender	
Boys	64
Girls	69
Psychiatric status	
High school	70
Patients	63
Parents	
Age	
Mothers	42.24 (5.55)[a]
Fathers	45.17 (6.37)[a]
Ego development (average stage)[b]	
Mother	5.55 (1.10)[a]
Father	5.45 (1.14)[a]
Family	
Social class	
Upper middle	46
Middle; lower middle	70
Working; lower	17
Family structure	
Two-parent	85
One-parent	48
Number of siblings	2.16 (1.16)[a]
Birth order	2.38 (1.39)[a]
Firstborn	43

[a] Average and (standard deviation).
[b] Where 1 = impulsive; 2 = self-protective; 3 = self-protective/conformist; 4 = conformist; 5 = conformist/conscientious (self-aware); 6 = conscientious; 7 = conscientious/autonomous; 8 = autonomous; 9 = integrated.

Table A5 Characteristics of Adolescents Following the Ego
Development Trajectories

PROFOUND ARRESTS	
Number of adolescents	41
Age	14.13 (1.11)[a]
Gender	
Boys	25
Girls	16
Psychiatric status	
High school	7
Psychiatric	34
Parents	
Age	
Mothers	42.07 (6.50)[a]
Fathers	44.54 (8.10)[a]
Ego development (average stage)[b]	
Mothers	5.13 (0.98)[a]
Fathers	4.96 (1.30)[a]
Families	
Social class	
Upper middle	1
Middle; lower middle	32
Working; lower	8
Family structure	
Two-parent	22
One-parent	19
Number of siblings	2.32 (1.40)[a]
Birth order	2.55 (1.63)[a]
Firstborn	14
STEADY CONFORMISTS	
Number of adolescents	24
Age	14.63 (0.50)[a]
Gender	
Boys	12
Girls	12
Psychiatric status	
High school	22
Psychiatric	5
Parents	
Age	
Mothers	42.42 (4.51)[a]
Fathers	46.09 (6.45)[a]
Ego development (average stage)[b]	
Mothers	5.55 (0.91)[a]
Fathers	5.75 (0.68)[a]

Table A5 *(continued)*

Families	
Social class	
Upper middle	11
Middle; lower middle	12
Working; lower	1
Family structure	
Two-parent	17
One-parent	7
Number of siblings	2.13 (1.11)[a]
Birth order	2.29 (1.37)[a]
Firstborn	8
PROGRESSIONS:	
1. Early progression	
Number of adolescents	34
Age	14.53 (0.96)[a]
Gender	
Boys	15
Girls	19
Psychiatric status	
High school	17
Psychiatric	17
Parents	
Age	
Mothers	42.50 (5.23)[a]
Fathers	45.99 (5.64)[a]
Ego development (average stage)[b]	
Mothers	5.84 (0.95)[a]
Fathers	5.28 (1.32)[a]
Families	
Social class	
Upper middle	12
Middle; lower middle	16
Working; lower	6
Family structure	
Two-parent	21
One-parent	13
Number of siblings	2.15 (0.96)[a]
Birth order	2.44 (1.40)[a]
Firstborn	10
2. Advanced Progression	
Number of adolescents	6
Age	14.33 (0.52)[a]

Table A5 *(continued)*

Gender	
Boys	2
Girls	4
Psychiatric status	
High school	6
Psychiatric	0
Parents	
Age	
Mothers	43.12 (6.81)[a]
Fathers	44.39 (3.88)[a]
Ego development (average stage)[b]	
Mothers	6.40 (0.89)[a]
Fathers	6.20 (1.10)[a]
Families	
Social class	
Upper middle	5
Middle; lower middle	1
Working; lower	0
Family structure	
Two-parent	2
One-parent	4
Number of siblings	1.5 (1.05)[a]
Birth order	2.00 (1.27)[a]
Firstborn	3
3. *Dramatic Progressions*	
Number of adolescents	3
Age	15.33 (0.57)[a]
Gender	
Boys	1
Girls	2
Psychiatric status	
High school	0
Psychiatric	3
Parents	
Age	
Mothers	40.93 (7.05)[a]
Fathers	44.28 (3.84)[a]
Ego development (average stage)[b]	
Mothers	5.00 (1.00)[a]
Fathers	5.67 (0.58)[a]
Families	
Social class	
Upper middle	1

Table A5 *(continued)*

Middle; lower middle	2
Working; lower	0
Family structure	
Two-parent	3
One-parent	0
Number of siblings	1.67 (1.16)[a]
Birth order	3.00 (1.73)[a]
Firstborn	1
ACCELERATED	
Number of adolescents	7
Age	14.33 (0.52)[a]
Gender	
Boys	2
Girls	5
Psychiatric status	
High school	6
Psychiatric	1
Parents	
Age	
Mothers	42.09 (3.23)[a]
Fathers	44.87 (4.37)[a]
Ego development (average stage)[b]	
Mothers	6.40 (1.14)[a]
Fathers	5.60 (1.14)[a]
Families	
Social class	
Upper middle	6
Middle; lower middle	1
Working; lower	0
Family structure	
Two-parent	7
One-parent	0
Number of siblings	2.5 (1.38)[a]
Birth order	2.67 (1.37)[a]
Firstborn	2
REGRESSION	
Number of adolescents	9
Age	14.56 (0.88)[a]
Gender	
Boys	3
Girls	6
Psychiatric status	

Table A5 *(continued)*

High school	5
Psychiatric	4
Parents	
Age	
Mothers	43.20 (7.28)[a]
Fathers	45.52 (6.38)[a]
Ego development (average stage)[b]	
Mothers	5.13 (1.73)[a]
Fathers	6.00 (1.16)[a]
Families	
Social class	
Upper middle	7
Middle; lower middle	2
Working; lower	0
Family structure	
Two-parent	4
One-parent	5
Number of siblings	1.78 (1.09)[a]
Birth order	1.86 (0.60)[a]
Firstborn	2
MORATORIUM	
Number of adolescents	10
Age	14.50 (0.71)[a]
Gender	
Boys	4
Girls	6
Psychiatric status	
High school	7
Psychiatric	3
Parents	
Age	
Mothers	40.69 (4.39)[a]
Fathers	43.56 (4.31)[a]
Ego development (average stage)[b]	
Mothers	5.89 (1.27)[a]
Fathers	5.75 (0.71)[a]
Families	
Social class	
Upper middle	4
Middle; lower middle	4
Working; lower	2
Family structure	
Two-parent	8

Table A5 *(continued)*

One-parent	2
Number of siblings	2.3 (0.82)[a]
Birth order	1.90 (0.74)[a]
Firstborn	3

[a] Average and (standard deviation).
[b] Where 1 = impulsive; 2 = self-protective; 3 = self-protective/conformist; 4 = conformist; 5 = conformist/conscientious (self-aware); 6 = conscientious; 7 = conscientious/autonomous; 8 = autonomous; 9 = integrated.

B

Assessments Obtained Annually from All Adolescents and Their Parents

ANNUAL ADOLESCENT OBSERVATIONS

1. Ego development (Washington University Sentence Completion Test, Loevinger and Wessler, 1970).
2. Self-esteem (Coopersmith self-esteem inventory, Coopersmith, 1967).
3. Self-image integration and continuity (Self-image Q-sort, Hauser, 1970; Hauser *et al.*, 1983).
4. Ego defenses and other adaptive processes (ratings of annual clinical interviews with defense and adaptive strength scales, Beardslee *et al.*, 1986, 1990; Jacobson *et al.* 1986; Hauser, 1986).
5. Moral development (Kohlberg moral dilemmas, Colby *et al.*, 1987).

ANNUAL PARENTAL OBSERVATIONS

1. Ego development (Washington University Sentence Completion Test, Loevinger and Wessler, 1970).
2. Moral development (Kohlberg moral dilemmas, Colby *et al.*, 1987).

FAMILIES (ADOLESCENTS AND THEIR PARENTS)

1. Constraining and enabling interactions (through application of constraining and enabling scales to the recorded/transcribed

revealed differences family discussions, Hauser *et al.*, 1984, 1989).

2. Constraining and enabling sequences (sequential analyses of constraining and enabling ratings, Hauser *et al.*, 1987, in press).

3. Developmental environment interactions (through application of developmental interactions scoring system, Powers *et al.*, 1983).

Moral Dilemmas Used
for Family Discussions

Each year two different moral dilemmas (from Colby and Kohlberg, 1987) were presented individually to all parents and adolescents, who were then brought together to discuss their differences of opinion (described more fully in Chapter 4). The two dilemmas used in the first-year discussions, presented in the narratives of the twelve families in Chapters 6 through 9, were about Heinz and Joe. The entire story that was read to each family member, and the probes that immediately followed, are reproduced below.

HEINZ

In Europe, a woman was near death from a special form of cancer. There was one drug that doctors thought might save her. It was a form of radium that a druggist in the same town had recently discovered. The drug was expensive to make, but the druggist was charging ten times what it cost him to make it. He paid $200 for the radium and charged $2,000 for a small dose of the drug. The sick woman's husband, Heinz, went to everyone he knew to borrow the money, but could only get together about $1,000, which is half of what it cost. He told the druggist that his wife was dying and asked him to sell it cheaper or let him pay later. But the druggist said, "No, I discovered the drug and I'm going to make money from it." So Heinz gets desperate and considers breaking into the man's store to steal the drug for his wife.

After each of the following probes, which lead to "yes" or "no" answers, the interviewer inquires about the *reasons* for the answer: How come? Why does he make that decision? etc.

1. Should Heinz steal the drug?
2. If Heinz doesn't love his wife, should he steal for her?
3. Suppose the person dying is not his wife but a stranger. Should Heinz steal the drug for the stranger?
4. Suppose it's a pet animal he loves. Should Heinz steal to save the pet animal?
5. Is it important to do everything one can to save another's life?
6. It is against the law for Heinz to steal. Does that make it morally wrong?
7. Should people try to do everything they can to obey the law?

Heinz did break into the store. He stole the drug and gave it to his wife. In the newpapers the next day, there was an account of the robbery. Mr. Brown, a police officer who knew Heinz, read the account. He remembered seeing Heinz running away from the store and realized that it was Heinz who stole the drug. Mr. Brown wonders whether he should report that Heinz was the robber.

1. Should Officer Brown report Heinz for stealing?

Officer Brown finds and arrests Heinz. Heinz is brought to court, and a jury is selected. The jury's job is to find whether a person is innocent or guilty of committing a crime. The jury finds Heinz guilty. It is up to the judge to determine the sentence.

1. Should the judge give Heinz some sentence, or should he suspend the sentence and let Heinz go free?
2. Thinking in terms of society, should people who break the law be punished?
3. Heinz was doing what his conscience told him when he stole the drug. Should a lawbreaker be punished if he is acting out of conscience?

JOE

Joe is a fourteen-year-old boy who wanted to go to camp very much. His father promised him he could go if he saved up the money for himself. So Joe worked hard at his newspaper route and saved up the $40 it cost to go to camp, and a little more besides. But just before camp was going to start, his father changed his mind. Some of his friends decided to go on a special fishing trip, and Joe's father was short of the money it would cost. So he told Joe to give him the money from the paper route. Joe didn't want to give up going to camp. So he thinks of refusing to give his father the money.

1. Should Joe refuse to give his father the money?
2. Is the fact that Joe earned the money himself the most important thing in the situation?
3. The father promised Joe he could go to camp if he earned the money. Is the fact that the father made a promise the most important thing in the situation?
4. Is it important to keep a promise?
5. Is it important to keep a promise to someone you don't know well, and probably won't see again?
6. What do you think is the most important thing a son should be concerned with in his relationship to his father? [For female adolescents, this question was always followed with: What do you think is the most important thing a daughter should be concerned with in her relationship to her father?]
7. What do you think is the most important thing a father should be concerned about in relationship to his son? [Like question 6, this question was also rephrased for female adolescents in relation to their fathers.]

Constraining and Enabling Coding System: Abbreviated Instructions for Applying the Codes and Five Coding Sections from the Family Coding Manual*

INTRODUCTION TO CONSTRAINING AND ENABLING SCORING SYSTEM

The scoring system considers three aspects of family interaction: *Constraining, Enabling,* and *Discourse Change.* A brief introduction to each dimension is given here for the purpose of initially acquainting the new coder with the overall scoring system. Detailed descriptions and scoring rules for each dimension and its corresponding categories and codes are given in respective sections of the manual.

1. Elements of Constraining and Enabling are assessed for each speech. Constraining or Enabling dimensions consist of categories classified as Cognitive and Affective. These categories are further divided into a number of codes in the following way:

CONSTRAINING

Cognitive Category

1. Distracting
2. Withholding
3. Judgmental

Affective Category

1. Indifference
2. Gratifying/affective excess
3. Devaluing

*Readers interested in using this coding system on other family interaction materials, or related data (such as psychotherapy) may obtain the entire looseleaf bound *Constraining and Enabling Coding System Manual* from Dr. Stuart T. Hauser, Harvard Medical School, Department of Psychiatry, 74 Fenwood Road, Boston, Massachusetts, for $10.00 to cover costs of printing and mailing.

ENABLING

Cognitive Category

1. Explaining
2. Focusing/empathy
3. Problem-solving
4. Curiosity

Affective Category

1. Accepting
2. Active understanding

DISCOURSE CHANGE

2. *Discourse Change* reflects shifts in direction or tone (e.g. regressive or progressive patterns) and shifts in topic (topic changes) that an individual speaker expresses during the course of the family discussion. Discourse change is assessed across successive pairs of an individual family member's speeches. One of six mutually exclusive codes is assigned which describes the overall tone of a family member's pair of speeches and reflects whether or not the content has changed substantially across successive speeches. These codes are shown below:

TOPIC

No Change

1. Regression
2. Progression
3. Foreclosure

Topic Change

1. Topic change regression
2. Topic change progression
3. Topic change equivalent

GENERAL CODING PRINCIPLES

1. The unit of analysis for assessing *Constraining* and *Enabling* is a single numbered speech in a transcript. A speech is defined as a lengthy statement, phrase, fragment or utterance initiated by a family member (a turn-taking).

2. The unit of analysis for determining *Discourse Change* is a *pair* of successive speeches uttered by an individual family member. This dimension is more fully explained below.

3. A coder should avoid being impressionistic or reading too much into a speech. Trial scoring has revealed that vague and subjective assessment leads to unreliability among coders. The most effective coding policy is to refer continually to the manual's descriptions and

examples of scoring categories, codes, and intensity levels. A coder should be able to cite concrete evidence in a speech for each code applied to that speech.

4. The scorer should be aware that both *Constraining* and *Enabling* elements may coexist in the same speech. However, before assigning codes from both dimensions, the scorer should be certain that the speech serves to both constrain and facilitate the other's expression or understanding.

CODING PROCEDURE GUIDELINES

OVERVIEW

To begin, read through the transcript to gain an overview and an understanding of the context of the conversation. Then follow these recommended steps:

1. Begin to number the speeches on the transcript. (Complete numbering rules are elaborated in the full CECS manual, available as described above).

2. Read and consider each speech one at a time, and determine the appropriate codes. (Complete descriptions of all the codes are included in later sections of the manual.) It is helpful to begin with an impression or feeling regarding which codes may be applicable. The scorer should then check his or her impression with the actual descriptions of the codes.

  a. Once a scorer has determined the code(s) that apply to a speech, it is necessary to rate each code for level of intensity: (1) *low level* applies to speeches characterized by a minimal to moderate degree of a particular code; (2) *high level* applies to speeches characterized by the extensive presence of a particular code. The scorer should consult with the descriptions and examples of *intensity levels* before assigning intensity level to a speech.

  b. In general, the best way to "check" one's choice of codes is to see whether there is a concrete correspondence between the code assigned to a particular speech and the manual's descriptions and examples of that code. Apply a code only if the qualities of the speech actually fit with the description of the code.

3. The scorer will occasionally find speeches that are marked "unclear" due to transcription problems (i.e., inaudibility of speech on the tape) and not due to a speaker's lack of clarity. In some cases clear

fragments of the speech may provide enough information to infer what was said. The scorer should attempt to code these unclear speeches as accurately as possible, relying on the context of the conversation. If an entire speech is "unclear," the scorer should *listen to the actual tape* of the transcript and see if he/she can hear what the speaker is saying. If the scorer can hear the speech or part of the speech, he/she should write it down on the transcript and then code the speech accordingly. In cases where the speech is inaudible, the rating for uncodable should be recorded.

CODING RULES

COGNITIVE AND ENABLING DIMENSIONS

Each numbered speech is coded and then assigned a high or low level intensity rating. No more than one code from a single category (the categories are: *Cognitive Constraining, Cognitive Enabling, Affective Constraining,* and *Affective Enabling*) can be scored for any particular speech. When more than one code within a category applies to a single speech, the following scoring rules are invoked:

1. *Intensity rule.* In cases where elements of two or more codes within a single category are present, the code that is present in *greater intensity* is socred for that speech. The lower intensity code is dropped. For example, if a speech contains *low level Distracting* elements and *high level Judgmental* elements, the speech is given the high level *Judgmental* score, and the *Distracting* score is not used.

2. *Specificity rule.* If two or more codes from a single category are present on an *equal* level, then the code that is defined as the *most specific* according to the hierarchy of differentiated codes is scored. The more global score is dropped. The hierarchy is arranged in ascending order (from least to most specific) below:

Code Differentiation Hierarchy (from at least to most specific)

CONSTRAINING

Cognitive	*Affective*
Distracting	Indifference
↓	↓
Withholding	Gratifying/affective excess
↓	↓
Judgemental	Devaluing

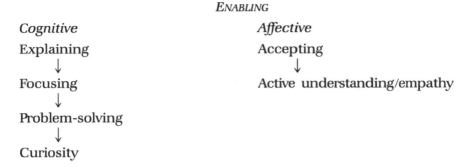

For example, within the same category, *Active understanding/empathy* is considered more specific than *Accepting*. Therefore, if a speech has equal levels of both *Accepting* and *Active understanding/empathy*, the speech will be scored for *Active understanding/empathy*.

DISCOURSE CHANGE DIMENSION

Shifts across pairs of individual family members' speeches are scored by selecting one of the six codes that constitute the *Discourse Change Dimension*. They are: *Regression, Progression, Foreclosure, Topic change regression, Topic change progression,* and *Topic change equivalent*. The code which the scorer deems appropriate is then assigned a high or low level intensity rating. The six codes that make up this dimension are considered mutually exclusive; only one may be scored for a pair of speeches. The first speech in the speech pair is called the *first position speech*, while the second speech is called the *second position speech*. (See "Numbering Rules" for instructions regarding position speeches.) All speeches that are not paired as position speeches are called *nonposition speeches*.

TWO CONSTRAINING CODES

1. DISTRACTING

A *Distracting* speech interferes with the preceding statement. This may occur through dramatic subject change, interruptions, or confusion of another's ideas. Distractions may be irrelevant, tangential, or unclear interjections. Speeches may distract by oversimplifying or glossing over distinctions or complexities in another person's statement. Regardless of intent, *Distracting* speeches may interfere with another person's self-awareness of self-possession. The other's train of thought or concentration is unsettled or, in extreme instances, undermined.

It is important to distinguish *Distracting* from related categories such as *Indifference*, characterized by a failure of acknowledgement, and *Devaluing*, characterized by overt negative content.

Most interruptions are coded as *Distracting*. However, there are three exceptions to this rule: (1) interruptions that indicate *Accepting*, such as "yeah," "okay," "umhum"; (2) interruptions that indicate *Active Understanding/Empathy*, such as "I see," "I know what you mean," "that's what I thought"; and (3) interruptions that are embedded in another's speech but begin after the initial speaker has completed a sentence and do not inhibit the initial speaker's efforts. For example, in the following interchange, mother would *not* receive a distracting code. (In this, and all following examples, F, M, and A refer to father, mother, and adolescent):

F: I thought so.
M: *(interrupting)* I guess . . .
F: What about the policeman?

1. *Low level* means minimal to some evidence of *Distracting* elements. Speech may be disruptive but is still related to topic. Brief interjections into another's speech (such as "well . . . ," "no . . . ," or "I . . . ") are coded *low level Distracting*, unless they occur after the initial speaker has completed his or her thought (as described above).

2. *High level* means moderate to extensive evidence of *Distracting* elements. Speeches that temporarily interrupt or break into another person's speech, and are clearly tangential, confused, or unrelated to the discussion should be coded *high level Distracting*.

LOW LEVEL DISTRACTING EXAMPLES

The following examples contain similar elements of *Distracting*:

F: Well, see, you say that she—
*A: *(interrupting)* Yeah, but—

or

F: The question is what should we do with the drug. Mom said—
*A: *(interrupting)* Yeah, but—
F: —yes and so did you.
A: Yeah, but—
F: And I said no.

Both of A's asterisked speeches are unsuccessful attempts to interrupt or distract F. Since these speeches do not fully prevent F from making his point, they merit *low level* ratings. The unmarked adolescent speech is not an example of *Distracting* because A speaks after F finishes his sentence. All three adolescent speeches are scored *low level Explaining* and *low level Accepting* as well, since they are statements of position and acknowledgement.

A: I think Heinz should steal the drug, because his wife is—

*M: *(interrupting)* But stealing is illegal and he could go to jail and be there when she dies.

A: But that's not the point. His wife is *dying* and he might be able to save her.

This example is rated as *Distracting* because M interrupts A, temporarily unsettling her train of thought. A *low level* rating is sufficient since M remains topic-oriented, allowing A to resume explanation of her thoughts. This speech is an example of the many instances in which long interruptions should not automatically be considered *high level Distracting;* the content of the speech merits only a *low level* score. Note that M's speech is also an example of *low level Focusing,* since she attempts to show A the implications of her position.

HIGH LEVEL DISTRACTING EXAMPLES

F begins to explain his position, stating, "Well, I took a rather different position." A interrupts him, saying:

*A: That's because you're a lawyer.

A's statement is considered *high level Distracting* because she diverts attention away from the substance of F's speech, disrupting his momentum through her interruption. There is also a *Devaluing* quality to her speech, for she undercuts or minimizes the impact of F's explanation. This is achieved through insinuating that F's views are mere reflections of his professional role, rather than the products of rational and valid reasoning. A *low level Devaluing* code captures this implicit rejection of F's position.

In another example, A interrupts M in the following manner:

M: It's not morally wrong, no because it's—you know.

*A: *(interrupting)* It's not the same one. The interviewer didn't leave no card.

M: You could not say it's morally wrong. It's only morally wrong if you feel it's morally wrong. *(A starts playing with microphone)*

A's speech is confusing and tangential to the ongoing topic of conversation. A *high level Distracting* rating captures the irrelevant and disruptive elements of A's speech. A rating of *low level Problem–Solving* is also warranted, since A refers to the interviewer and the task.

 In the middle of M's discussion about keeping promises, A bursts in:

*A: Couldn't we not discuss this—Why don't we call the lady? We just earned our thirty bucks? *(laughs)*

In addition to interrupting M's speech, A inteferes with resolution of the task by requesting a premature end to the discussion. A rating of *high level Distracting* is warranted since A's speech is disruptive and irrelevant to the ongoing conversation. A's speech is additionally coded for *low level Indifference/Unyielding Conviction* for he does not respond, in any meaningful way, to M's statement.

2. JUDGMENTAL

 The key message conveyed in a *Judgmental* speech is "You're wrong." The speech evaluates and passes negative judgment on another's thoughts, feelings, character, wishes, or ambitions. *Judgmental* speeches may classify issues as "good" or "bad," or impose absolute methods of discussing or reasoning (e.g. "You must see it this way."). Speeches that indicate that another's position is morally or intellectually wrong are considered *Judgmental*. Similarly, statements that express some kind of rigid belief that another's (i.e. other family member or story character) ideas, opinions, or beliefs are objectively "incorrect" are rated with this code.

 The scorer should be careful not to automatically rate what might be considered "giveaway" terms like "certainly", and "absolutely" as *Judgmental*. These terms may occur in emphatic or definitive statements, such as strong agreement; in these contexts, speeches are not considered *Judgmental*. It is very important to apply this scale only when *speeches clearly contain judgments regarding another person's opinions or feelings*. Forcefully stated arguments or continued insistence of one's own opinion does not necessarily qualify as *Judgmental*. Such speeches must be clearly evaluative (right/wrong; good/bad) of the other individuals' ideas. This is different from a speaker holding firm to a belief, not listening, which would be scored as *Indifference*.

Finally, the scorer should be aware that *Judgmental* speeches often occur as interruptions. Since interruptions are generally considered *Distracting*, the scorer should be careful to determine whether a speech may be more appropriately scored on the *Judgmental* scale. These scales cannot be scored simultaneously since they are both in the *Cognitive Constraining* category. When there are equal levels of *Distracting* and *Judgmental* in a speech, the specificity rule should be invoked, and the speech should be coded as *Judgmental*.

1. *Low level* means minimal to some evidence of rigid moral beliefs and absolute negative opinions regarding the other speaker's statements.

2. *High level* means moderate to extensive evidence of *Judgmental* elements. These speeches are condemnatory and implicitly or explicitly evaluate whether another speech is "good or bad," "right or wrong." Speech may appear to impose a specific way of reasoning or discussing on the other person.

LOW LEVEL JUDGMENTAL EXAMPLES

After a lengthy statement by A (the conclusion of which is shown here), M responds:

A: . . . So, that's why he should not steal.
*M: That may not be quite morally correct.

M's speech is considered *Judgmental* because she suggests to A that his position may be objectively incorrect. Due to the nonconfrontational quality of M's statement, a *low level* score is appropriate. Note that M's speech is also rated as *low level Explaining* since it is a statement of her views.

On the subject of whether or not one can make assumptions in answering the moral dilemmas, A and F have the following discussion:

A: But they don't give you any assumptions, so you can't make any assumptions so what else can you say?
F: Well, if they don't give you any assumptions then you make assumptions.
*A: No, you can't make you own assumptions, because they're asking you for a general answer.

A's second speech is coded as *Judgmental* because she appears unwilling to consider F's point of view. Instead, she reiterates her position, attempting to impose on F a rigid way of approaching the dilemma. Her statement warrants a *low level* code since she claims to be adhering to the "rules" of the task. The dogmatic quality of her speech is tempered by this element of *Problem-Solving;* a rating of *low level Problem-Solving* is also warranted.

HIGH LEVEL JUDGMENTAL EXAMPLES

When F begins to explore possible solutions to the Officer Brown dilemma, A interrupts him, saying:

*A: It has to be yes or no, that's all.

In this example, A tries to impose on F a supposedly "right" way to resolve the dilemma. The rigid quality of A's statement, particularly evident in the phrase "that's all," indicates that a rating of *high level Judgmental* is appropriate. Since A refers directly to the task, his speech is also scored as *low level Problem-Solving.*

* "Absolutely no."
* "You're wrong."
* "Heinz was absolutely wrong to ever do that." (Previous speaker has just said that Heinz should have done it.)

The above statements are rigid, uncompromising, and critical. The judgmental tenor of these speeches is not tempered by any attempt to facilitate communication. A *high level Judgmental* code is appropriate for speeches of this type. Note that the first and second statements are *not* additionally coded as *low level Explaining* since they are dogmatic expressions with little explanatory value. The third does indicate some effort on the part of the speaker to state a position, and thus warrants a *low level Explaining* code.

During a discussion of whether or not the officer should report Heinz, M says to A:

*M: You are answering the question in the wrong way. You must first look at whether the officer really knew Heinz or not.

M's speech negatively evaluates A's resolution of the dilemma. She attempts to impose on A an absolute way of answering the question, stating explicitly that her way is the right and only way. A rating of *high level Judgmental* is warranted. M's statement is also considered *low level Problem-Solving* since she refers directly to the task.

TWO ENABLING CODES

1. FOCUSING

Focusing speeches are oriented to facilitate or clarify the other's understanding of his or her own ideas or perspective. For example, the speaker may attempt to sharpen the previous speaker's point of view by clarifying the meaning of the statement. *Focusing* may also include dramatizations or paraphrases of a previous speaker's position. A speaker may focus another person by introducing the implications or consequences of another's point of view. This is often achieved through the use of hypothetical cases. *An important point to remember is that Focusing can be applied only if the speaker is clarifying another's already stated perspective.*

Discriminating between explaining and focusing speeches requires that the coder evaluate whether the speech is designed to illustrate another's point, or enhance one's own position. Speeches that primarily present the speaker's opinions or position are scored as *Explaining.* Often a speaker will attempt to clear up a misconception held by another in regard to the speaker's point of view. Such a speech would be considered *Focusing* only to the extent that the speaker clarifies the other's perspective; if the thrust of the speech is to elaborate upon the speaker's own ideas, the speech is coded for *Explaining* (see also *Intensity* Rule).

It is sometimes difficult to distinguish between the *Focusing* and *Problem-Solving* codes. *Problem-Solving* refers to attempts to orient another person to the task by discussing the terms of the task or underlying processes involved in decision-making. *Focusing* speeches attempt to orient another person's thinking about his/her position, or subtly guide the other to pick up the original thread or discussion without mention of the terms or process of the task.

The *Focusing* code should also be differentiated from the *Active Understanding/Empathy* rating. The intent of a *Focusing* speech is to clarify another person's understanding of his or her own ideas. In contrast, a speech merits a rating of *Active Understanding/Empathy* when the speaker demonstrates genuine understanding of someone else's ideas. A speech is coded for both *Active Understanding/Empathy* and *Focusing* when a speaker indicates that she or he has "tuned in" to another person's position, while clearly attempting to facilitate the other's understanding of his or her own views. This occurs when a speaker uses hypothetical cases or paraphrases in conjunction with such words as "I see," "That's how I looked at it," or "We both see that."

1. *Low level* means minimal to some evidence of *Focusing* within the speech; general attempts to clarify the other's speech or to encourage further discussion, but without specific reference to the implications or elaborations of the other's speech.

2. *High level* means moderate to extensive evidence of *Focusing*. Speech contains explicit attempts to clarify particular points, dramatize the other's point through rephrasing, possibly introducing hypothetical cases or introducing implications of the other person's position.

LOW LEVEL FOCUSING EXAMPLES

On the subject of whether or not Officer Brown should report Heinz, M and A have the following exchange:

  A: If he's— if— I don't know. If he knows what was going on, then I don't think he should say anything. But still, it's his job.

*M: So basically, you feel—

  A: *(interrupting)* And then, I still think it is unfair.

M attempts to clarify A's understanding of his position by paraphrasing or summarizing A's contradictory statement. A rating of *Focusing* captures M's attempt to rephrase A's stated position. A's interruption of M's speech prevents us from knowing how successful her attempt at *Focusing* would have been. In cases like this, a *low level* code is warranted.

During a discussion of whether or not Heinz should steal the drug for his wife, the following interchange occurs:

  M: But you think the chances are not good enough to make it worth . . .

*A: *(interrupting)* Yeah, besides when he gets himself in trouble.

This speech contains elements of both *Accepting* and *Focusing*. *Accepting* is indicated by the word "Yeah"; *Focusing* is seen in the way A completes M's thought through drawing out the implications of her remark. Note that A's speech is also an example of *low level Distracting* since she interrupts M.

The following remarks are generally considered *Focusing*. The level should be determined by the context of the speech.

  *"In other words"
  *"So basically, you think"

*"Let's say"
*"So what you're saying"

HIGH LEVEL FOCUSING EXAMPLES

During a discussion of whether or not Heinz was wrong to steal the drug for his wife, the following exchange occurs:

A: I mean, I don't think it's wrong, the stealing part. I just, it's the prolonging the life business.

*M: In other words, the stealing part isn't wrong, but prolonging the life part is?

A: Yeah.

M's thoughtful and accurate paraphrasing of A's speech demonstrates a considerable effort to clarify A's perspective. Clearly M is interested in learning more about A's point of view, but the intent of her question is to deepen A's understanding of his own ideas. The elements of *Curiosity* in this speech are superseded by the *high level* of *Focusing*.

M's ability to accurately paraphrase A's position indicates that she has grasped his perspective. A's affirmation of M's statement is further validation that M is attuned to A's point of view. A rating of *low level Active Understanding/Empathy* is also warranted. The scorer should note that if A had disagreed with M's interpretation, a rating of *Active Understanding/Empathy* would not be applicable.

In response to A's statement that it is wrong to artificially prolong life, F remarks:

*F: Say you've got an appendicitis, you've got an appendicitis, and your side was hurting like hell, is it wrong for the doctor to prolong your life?

F sets up a hypothetical situation to encourage A to consider the implications of her position. His speech ends with a question, but his intent is to create a concrete situation where A can re-evaluate her perspective. A *high level Focusing* score is warranted. The scorer should note that there are elements of *Curiosity* in this speech, but the main intent of F's statement is not to elicit information. Rather, the goal of this speech is to clarify A's ideas.

M responds to A's difficulty in articulating his position, stating:

*M: I think you wanted to defend your statement as to why you think it was all right because . . . "

A *high level Focusing* rating captures M's attempt to paraphrase and succinctly state why A took a certain position. M addresses A's uncertainty, clarifying *his* understanding rather than her own. There is evidence of *low level Problem-Solving* as well, since M guides A toward the task at hand. However, since *Focusing* is the predominant element, the speech is rated with the *Focusing* code.

A: Well, just take the dog. Would you steal something for, say Alex is dying? Would you steal something from the Vet?

F: Alex is a cat.

A: Well, they said an animal.

*M: It depends upon how important that animal is to you. Alex isn't important to me, but he's important to you.

M's speech is considered *Focusing* because she encourages A to pick up the original thread of the discussion by responding to A's original question. M uses *Focusing* in a subtle but effective manner; a *high level* rating is warranted.

2. ACCEPTING

Speech shows accepting of the other's position through acknowledgment, agreement, support of the other's ideas, or encouragement of the other to continue on with his/her speech.

The scorer should be careful not to automatically score typical "accepting" words like "yeah," "right," or "sure" as indications of this scale. These words may be used in an unaccepting or pseudoaccepting manner in the form of sarcasm, skepticism, or mechanical or inappropriate agreement (examples are given in the *Devaluing* and *Gratifying/Affective Excess* sections of the coding manual).

1. *Low level* means minimal to some suggestion of *Accepting*. In general, this level indicates mere agreement or acknowledgment which may be in the form of one-word or brief comments. Brief agreement followed by a qualification of what the other has said (e.g. correction, criticism, questioning) is also noted here. Speeches which "echo" what another has said, or express indirect support for another's ideas (often in the context of a speech not directed toward the person with the initial idea) merit *low level* scores.

2. *High level* means moderate to extensive evidence of *Accepting;* speech expresses more than agreement by exhibiting solid support for what the other has said without any type of qualification.

LOW LEVEL ACCEPTING EXAMPLES

M: But a lot would depend on what he knows about—
*A: *(interrupting)* Yeah.
M: —the situation. I don't think there's an absolute should.

A says "Yeah" to indicate that he supports M's position. A rating of *low level Accepting* captures both the brevity of A's speech, and A's agreement with M. A's speech is not considered *low level Distracting* even though it is embedded within M's statement. In general, embedded speeches which indicate *Accepting*, such as "I know," "That's right," or "I agree," are not rated as *Distracting*. This is because these speeches are brief, enabling, and nondisruptive to the initial speaker.

A: No, they said that Officer Brown wasn't on duty when he saw Heinz running from the store.
*M: Oh.

M's speech, although brief, acknowledges A's statement and is therefore rated for *low level Accepting*.

A: They said in the story that it was wrong for him to charge that much.
*F: Yeah, but they said it was legal for him to charge that much.

A rating of *low level Accepting* captures F's brief acknowledgment of A's position. Since F attempts to qualify A's perspective by referring to the terms of the task, a *low level Problem-Solving* score is also warranted.

The following commonly used expressions of agreement or acknowledgment are rated with the *Accepting* code. They should not be double-coded as *Explaining* when they are not statements of position. A rating of *Active Understanding/Empathy* is similarly inappropriate, since there is no evidence in these speeches of true perspective taking.

* "Yeah, I know."
* "That's very true."
* "I guess so."
* "That's fine."
* "That's good."
* "Yes."
* "Right."

When the above speeches are embedded within another person's statement, a *low level Accepting* rating is appropriate. When speeches of this type are "free-standing" rather than interjections, a *high level Accepting* code is warranted.

Simple convention over years of coders has dictated that the words, "okay," "yeah," or "all right" occurring alone, receive *low level* rather than *high level Accepting*. This is true regardless of whether or not they are interruptions.

HIGH LEVEL ACCEPTING EXAMPLES

A: Yeah, but they didn't say anything about the court system in the story.

*M: Right, I agree with you.

M conveys unqualified support for A in her brief but clear response. A rating of *high level Accepting* is warranted.

M: Because the story's different now.

*A: Yeah, it's different now.

A's whole-hearted endorsement of M's position warrants a *high level Accepting* rating. The scorer should note that A's word choice differs slightly from the words M uses in her statement. If A had simply expressed an exact repetition of M's speech, a *low level* score would be appropriate.

F: We would all agree that whoever the captain ordered to do it would in fact do it.

*A: He would do it.

A's statement reflects an unmitigated endorsement of his father's position and thus receives a code of *high level Accepting*.

ONE DISCOURSE CHANGE CODE

The codes that this dimension comprises measure shifts between individual family member's pairs of speeches. Unlike the Constraining and Enabling Codes, which are assessed for each individual speech, those for Discourse Change evaluate shifts in the flow of conversation across the family discussion. This is accomplished by noting changes between pairs of an individual family member's speeches. Shifts in the direction or tone of the discussion (progression, regression, etc.) and in the topic of conversation ("topic change" codes) reflect some of the ways in which family members' may be influenced by one another in the process of family discussion.

PROGRESSION

The shift from the first to second speech indicates greater complexity, new distinctions, new terms, or greater clarity. A family member may also express *Progression* by maintaining the forward flow of conversation through an elaboration, continuation, or conclusion of a train of thought begun earlier. At times the individual may be continuing a thought that had been interrupted, either by other family members or by a phrase initiated by the individual himself. At other times the family member may be beginning an entirely new speech, which furthers the conversational flow.

The scorer should be careful to note that the addition of one word to a speech does not automatically indicate *Progression;* it *may* be an example of *Foreclosure* (redundancy across the pair of speeches). On the other hand, increased brevity or simplicity is not necessarily evidence for *Regression;* shortened or simpler speeches that indicate greater forcefulness or clarity of thought are rated as *Progression.* Scorers should also note that *Progression* can occur even within pairs of *Constraining* speeches. Thus, although both speeches may have *Constraining* elements, they may also demonstrate a relative increase in complexity, clarity or contribution to discussion. (See *low level* examples)

1. *Low level* means minimal to some indications of *Progression;* slight increase in complexity, clarity, or conviction. A second speech that reveals some degree of continuation, elaboration or extension of ideas presented in first speech also merits a *low level* rating.

2. *High level* means moderate to extensive evidence of *Progression.* Second speech presents a clear step forward in terms of clarity, complexity, completion of thought, or self-assurance relative to the person's preceding speech.

LOW LEVEL PROGRESSION EXAMPLES

While discussing whether or not Joe's father should let him go to camp, M asks A to repeat his point, and the following exchange occurs:

M: Well I didn't hear what you said.

*A: Maybe they'll play you the tape. *(laughs)*

M: Maybe they will.

F: 'Cause the father promised?

**A: Uh-huh. That was a good enough reason.

In this adolescent speech pair, A moves from a *Withholding* statement to a speech which offers greater clarification of his position. A rating of *low level Progression* captures both the brevity of A's second speech and the change in mode from *Constraining* to *Enabling*.

On the subject of whether or not Officer Brown should report Heinz, M and A have the following exchange:

*M: Well— if— the only reason why I say "No he shouldn't"— if the Officer Brown knew that the court system was gonna hang him because he didn't have the money to hire a good lawyer.

A: Then he shouldn't report him. *(listlessly)*

**M: Then he shouldn't report him, or he should just turn his back on him.

In her second speech, M elaborates upon her position. A rating of *low level Progression* captures her effort to "keep the ball rolling."

When exploring M's view that Joe should give his father the money that he'd earned for his own camping trip, the following exchange occurs:

A: 'Cause the father promised?

*M: Uh-huh. That was a good enough reason.

F: Suppose the kid didn't earn the money. Suppose somebody gave it to him.

**M: It says the kid earned the money though.

In her second speech, M continues her thought by clarifying the terms of the task. A rating of *Progression* captures her continuing contribution to the discussion. The similarity in mode and complexity between these speeches renders a *low level* score appropriate.

HIGH LEVEL PROGRESSION EXAMPLES

As F clarifies his position regarding the Officer Brown question, the following exchange occurs:

*F: I don't know. I didn't, you know.

M: Uh-huh.

**F: I think that he should have a sentence, but I don't think it should be as long or as severe as if it was somebody just stealing something.

F's first speech is confused and incoherent, while his second statement shows a substantial increase in clarity and complexity. His articulation of a well-developed position contrasts with the hesitancy of his first speech. A *high level Progression* rating captures this shift toward greater self-assurance, clarity, and complexity.

On the subject of whether or not Heinz should steal the drug, A states:

*A: I, I said doing, yah, that doing—

M: *(interrupting)* That's in effect what I said, that he should be boycotted or—

**A: That doing *(unclear)* assuming he had done that, he should steal the drug. He would be saving his wife's life.

In this speech pair, A moves from an incomplete speech (in which he was interrupted by M) to a fully developed statement. A's second speech is unclear due to transcription difficulty, but it may be inferred from the context of the conversation that he delivers this speech in a clear and coherent manner. The contrast between speeches is significant enough to warrant a rating of *high level Progression*.

Notes

CHAPTER 1

Introduction—The Challenge and Paradox of Adolescence

1. Csikszentmihalyi and Larson (1984), p. xiii.

2. See Louise Kaplan's *Farewell to Childhood* (1984), an especially well-written summary of this time of life, especially with respect to narcissistic and psychosexual aspects of adolescence.

3. See L. Steinberg (1981, 1988), Hill (1987), Hill *et al.* (1985a), and Brooks-Gunn, Petersen and Eichorn (1985).

4. A clear reflection of the extent of interest in adolescence is the continued focus of scholars and laymen on the topic of "identity" (Hauser and Follansbee, 1984). Theoretical writings about identity development, particularly Erik Erikson's (1958, 1968), emphasize the diverse processes that influence adolescent development and are in turn touched by the lives of adolescents: historical events, cultural patterns, social roles, and social institutions (e.g. the family).

5. Several recent reviews of the socialization literature discuss the significance of power as a dimension in the family, e.g. Rollins and Thomas (1979) and Maccoby and Martin (1983).

6. Highly relevant works here include the contributions of Baumrind (1968, 1971, 1989) and Rollins and Thomas (1979). In adolescence the significance of extrafamilial influences, such as friends, other social institutions (school), and "popular" culture is also clearly visible. Those influences are at times congruent with, but often strongly divergent from, parental values and views (Montemayor, 1982; Bowerman and Kinch, 1959; Berndt, 1979). The family's impacts do not simply diminish with the emergence of these other influences. Rather, as Montemayor (1982) has recently argued, the adolescent now contends with varying combinations of involvements with significant friends as well as family members. On a more technical level, the work that we and other groups, such as Cooper and Grotevant (Cooper *et al.*, 1983; Grotevant and Cooper, 1986) are now carrying out

benefits from the impressive sophistication recently achieved within social interaction research. Cairns (1982) points out: "Significant break-throughs have been achieved within the past decade in the development of methodologies for the study of social interactions. . . . Progress has been made in virtually all aspects of methodology; in formulation, in design, in techniques for data collection, and in statistical interaction" (p. 1).

7. See Blos (1962); Petersen (1988); Petersen and Spiga (1982); Brooks-Gunn and Petersen (1983).

8. See Steinberg (1977), Steinberg and Hill (1978) and Hill (1987).

9. See Erikson (1958; 1968); Henggeler (1982); and Murphey et al., (1963).

10. Weiner (1970); Blos (1962; 1979).

11. Block (1971); Offer (1969); Blos (1962).

12. Lewis et al. (1976); Goldstein (1985); Goldstein and Strachan (1987); Grote-vant and Cooper (1985, 1986); Bell and Bell (1982).

CHAPTER 2
Ego Development

1. The intellectual and clinical roots of this construct, together with more extended discussion of its meanings, can be found in Jane Loevinger's book, Ego Development (1976), addressing the construct and measure, and in more recent discussions by Loevinger (1984), as well as in critical reviews by Holt (1980), Hauser (1976), Loevinger (1979), and Noam (1984).

2. Our use of this construct is based on the model and measure developed over the past twenty five years by Loevinger and her collaborators. See Loevinger and Wessler (1970); Loevinger et al. (1970); Loevinger (1976, 1979); Hauser (1976); and Holt (1980).

3. More extended discussion of this idea about the relevance of ego develop-ment can be found in several of our previous contributions (e.g. Hauser et al., 1984, 1986; Noam et al., 1984; Powers et al., 1989) and in a review by Loevinger (1979). We shall return to this point throughout the book, illustrating it in the various case study chapters.

4. More detail about these important initial studies of the instrument (The Washington University Sentence Completion Test) are reviewed by Hauser (1976), Loevinger (1979), and Loevinger and Wessler (1970).

5. Among the contributors to the growing number of systematic clinical studies using this measure of ego development are Barglow et al. (1983); Browning (1986); Dill and Noam (1990); Dubrow et al. (1987); Frank and Quinlan (1976); Jacobson et al. (1984); Kirshner (1988); Labouvie-Vieff et al. (1987); Noam et al. (1984); Noam, 1988; Noam et al., 1989; Rosznafsky (1981); and Wilbur et al. (1982).

6. Browning (1986) and Roszanfsky (1981) and Noam (1988, 1989, 1990) provide fuller discussions about the clinical relevance of the ego development construct. Noam (1988) has introduced a developmental psycho-pathology model incorporating this construct.

7. In two related articles Swensen (1980; Swenson *et al.*, 1981) discusses ego development stages and relationships. More recently, Noam *et al.* (1990) have considered this question through a new interview method.

8. We have made a distinction between phases of development, marked by age and related developmental tasks and stages, defined by an underlying organization of meanings about self and other, as well as these tasks to be coped with in adolescence (Noam, 1985).

9. There is an even earlier ego development stage, consisting of presocial and symbiotic phases. In the presocial phase, the infant is described as oblivious to everything but gratification of his or her immediate needs. At that point animate and inanimate parts of the environment are not distinguished. In the symbiotic phase, however, the child has a strong attachment to the mother (or mother surrogate), distinguishing this figure from the rest of the environment. But he or she does not yet differentiate himself from his or her mother. This first stage comes to an end at approximately the time that use of language is acquired. Since all of our measures of ego development are based on written responses to a special ego development protocol, adolescents at this first stage are not included in our case studies, and our conceptualization of passages through adolescence starts at a later developmental stage (impulsive).

10. These examples of ego development responses, and all the following ones in this chapter, are direct quotes from Loevinger and colleagues' ego development manual (1970). On the other hand, all *other examples* of ego development responses, given primarily in the case study chapters, are direct quotes from the adolescents and parents in our study.

11. Noted by Loevinger and Wessler (1970).

12. Various studies report more persons at this stage than at any other. These contributions include: Haan, Stroud, and Holstein (1973); Harakel (1971); Lambert (1972); and Redmore and Waldman (1975).

13. Hoppe and Loevinger (1977).

14. Loevinger (1966), p. 200.

15. Loevinger and Wessler (1970), p. 9.

16. While it is consistent with their discussions of ego development, the interpretation of the steady conformist path representing a form of arrest is our own, not directly suggested by Loevinger and colleagues.

17. There are other possible paths of ego development; specifically those in which adolescents clearly decline in their stages (regression) and those that vary from one year to the next (moratorium). These are not consid-

ered in greater detail in this book because of the relatively small number of subjects who followed these more unusual but clinically meaningful trajectories.

18. Discussed by Gould (1978); Levinson (1978); Smelser and Erikson (1981); Hauser and Greene (forthcoming); Hauser and Kates (1982), and Noam and Dill (in press).

19. More quantitative analyses supporting these observations can be found in two recent papers from our group (Hauser *et al.*, 1984, 1987).

CHAPTER 3
The Family Setting

1. Numerous papers and volumes have covered theoretical and empirical aspects of family contributions to development. Major reviews include Hill (1987); Lerner and Spanier (1978); Lewis and Feiring (1978); Maccoby and Martin (1983); Rutter (1980); and Westley and Epstein (1969).

2. Examples of this can be found in Barber and Rollins (1987); Hill (1987); and Powers, Hauser, and Kilner (1989).

3. Many of these studies are reviewed and discussed in our recent article, "Adolescent Mental Health" (Powers, Hauser, and Kilner, 1989).

4. This perspective on family relations and adolescent development is indebted to the work of Grotevant and Cooper (1985, 1986), Cooper and Grotevant (1987) and Cooper (1988), as well as other analysts of close relationships (e.g. Huston and Robins, 1982; Kelley *et al.*, 1983), and is also rooted in the conceptualizations of family systems–oriented clinicians, such as Minuchin (1974).

5. These notions regarding connectedness, and the related ones of individuation and individuality are derived from the many thoughtful contributions of Grotevant and Cooper, cited in note 4.

6. More detailed discussion of this area can be found in several reviews by Rutter (1979, 1983, 1987).

7. The entire theoretical framework used by Stierlin in this clinical analysis is presented in his book *Separating Parents and Adolescents* (1974).

8. The coding scheme we use to measure these interactions is described in greater technical detail, including reliability and validity properties, in two articles (Hauser, Powers *et al.*, 1984, and Hauser, Jacobson *et al.*, 1986).

9. Distracting falls in the domain of attentional focus difficulties discussed by Lyman Wynne and his colleagues in their studies of communication deviance (Wynne and Singer, 1963; Wynne, Singer, Bartko, and Toohey, 1977; Wynne, Singer, and Toohey, 1976).

10. Doane and her associates (Doane *et al.*, 1981) describe associations between observed familial negative (guilt-laden) affective style in adolescence and subsequent adult schizophrenic spectrum disorders. Her work, in turn, is based on the extensive expressed emotion (EE) literature

addressing the family atmosphere experienced by psychiatric patients. Studies based on the expressed emotion construct have addressed associations between "the extent to which relatives of psychiatric patients express critical, hostile, or emotionally overinvolved attitudes toward their disturbed family member during an interview conducted with a researcher or clinician in the patient's absence" (Hooley and Teasdale, 1989; p. 229). While constraining interactions are theoretically related to those "attitudes" shown in the expressed emotion studies, our focus on variations in adolescent development clearly differs, as does our approach (directly observing interactions rather than interview relatives apart from the patient). Nonetheless, given the seeming overlap in the CECS and EE frameworks, future efforts exploring links between these methods and constructs should be worthwhile. Recent relevant reviews include Hooley (1985), Hooley and Teasdale (1989), Konigsberg and Handley (1986), and Leff and Vaughn (1985).

11. In the expressed emotion literature *criticism* is considered a central component of this family response style that is often associated with relapses from schizophrenic and depressive illness (Hooley, 1985; Hooley and Teasdale, 1989).

12. When we think about family interactions that promote, catalyze, or reflect accelerations and progressions in adolescent ego development, an alternative theoretical model is also possible, namely that antecedent family members' behaviors will bear no relation to the adolescent's psychosocial development, since this development is either genetically driven or powerfully shaped by extrafamilial forces, such as friendships. If this view were correct, we would expect to find no links between our (or anyone else's) measures of antecedent family processes and subsequent adolescent ego development, though there may be *some* consistent associations between this development and how family members *respond* to it. Our argument, for which we present supporting evidence in this book, is that family interactions shape adolescent ego development *and* are responsive to aspects of this development.

13. Sometimes a speech appears to be focusing, yet on closer inspection proves to be an attempt to clarify the speaker's own uncertainties or confusions, a rhetorical question, or a reiteration of the speaker's own prior point. This pseudofocusing, reminiscent of pseudomutuality, may actually serve to constrain rather than enable to other person.

14. See Loevinger (1966, 1976). Additional empirical support for this idea can be found in Lieber's (1977) study of families of disturbed, but nonpsychotic, adolescents. Lieber found that focusing strongly discriminated among families of adolescents who had been independently classified in terms of risk for later schizophrenic-spectrum disorders. Parents of low-risk adolescents expressed significantly more positive focusing behaviors than did parents of adolescents in any of the other risk groups.

15. See such theoretical and clinical contributions as those of Lieber (1977), Masterson (1972), Shapiro (1968), and Stierlin (1974).

16. See Loewald (1980) and Schafer (1960) for a fuller discussion of internalizations.

17. See Wynne, Ryckoff, Day, and Hirsch (1958).

18. See Hauser (1978).

19. See Bell and Bell (1983). In addition, Baldwin and his associates (1982) reported that active, warm parent–child interactions were associated with children's school adjustment, particularly cognitive functioning and involvement in school work. While the children in Baldwin's study were only seven to ten years old, these directly observed family patterns suggest the possibility that accepting family transactions underlie possible behavioral manifestations of optimal ego development (e.g., cognitive performance, school motivation).

20. When Alexander (1973a, 1973b) analyzed the families of normal and delinquent adolescents, he observed that adolescents in the normal families were consistently more supportive to their parents than were their delinquent counterparts.

21. See Maccoby (1968), Maccoby and Martin (1983), Rollins and Thomas (1979), and Westley and Epstein (1969).

22. See Rollins and Thomas (1979).

23. See Hauser *et al.* (1984). In addition, a study recently completed in this project suggests that the ways that parents speak with one another in family discussions are linked with the ego development of their son or daughter (Rogell, 1990).

24. See Loewald (1980), Erikson (1968), Schaefer (1963), Bandura and Walters (1963).

CHAPTER 4
Assessing Ego Development and Mapping Interactions

1. A vast literature considers features of such severely disturbed adolescents. Among the major contributors are Peter Blos (1962, 1979), Erik Erikson (1958, 1965, 1968), Anna Freud (1946, 1958), Michael Goldstein (1978), and Helm Stierlin (1974). Much of this work, and the contributions of other clinicians and clinical researchers, is brought together in reviews by Weiner (1970, 1980) and Graham and Rutter (1985).

2. We knew from previous work (Hauser, 1978) that we would have little chance of finding such a range of ego development types by using a more traditional method of randomly sampling a larger population (e.g. an entire high school). In an earlier study of one hundred middle-class high school girls we found that fewer than 10 percent were at the lowest (preconformist) stages (Hauser 1978). Jack Block (1971) refers to our

strategy in addressing the problem of "defining the universe of subjects for a longitudinal study." He notes that random selection from a definable universe may not be "necessarily the most efficient strategy for developing understanding. Randomness, unaided, cannot be depended upon to represent sufficiently often certain types of individuals who, although not numerically frequent, are nevertheless of great conceptual significance" (p. 23).

3. Based on social class scores using the Hollingshead (1957) index.

4. This measure was developed by Jane Loevinger and associates (Loevinger *et al.*, 1970) and is described in greater detail in this original book; in review papers by Hauser (1976), Holt (1980), and Loevinger (1979); and in other recent contributions by Loevinger (1984, 1985; Loevinger *et al.*, 1985). Further background of the measure is reviewed in Chapter 2.

5. The interviewers were William Beardslee, M.D.; Alan Jacobson, M.D.; Ornea Medeas, M.D.; Gil Noam, Dipl. Psych., Ed.D.; Sally Powers, Ed.D.; Eileen Schwartz, Ed.D.; Judith Wolch, M.S.W.; and Stuart Hauser, M.D., Ph.D.

6. See Hauser (1976), Hauser and Follansbee (1984), and Loevinger (1976, 1979, 1985).

7. The test itself can be found in Loevinger and Wessler (1970). The scoring manual for all thirty-six stems, which can be self-taught, is provided in Loevinger *et al.* (1970).

8. See Hauser (1976), and Loevinger and Wessler (1970).

9. More inclusive reviews can be found in the volumes edited by L'Abate (1985) and Jacob (1987). Specifically, the chapters by Swensen (1985) and Grossman and Pollock (1985) are most relevant to conceptual and empirical aspects of our study.

10. See reviews of this work in Hauser *et al.* (1984), Jacob (1987), L'Abate (1985), and Maccoby and Martin (1983). Such self-report studies need not be restricted to "socialization." One set of investigations, for instance, is based on teenagers' reports of relationships with peers and parents, with teenagers reporting "familial aggravations" that were occurring when signaled by an electronic pacer (Csikszentmihalyi and Larson, 1984).

11. See Moos (1974), Moos and Moos (1976, 1984).

12. See Olson and Portner (1983), Olson, Sprenkle and Russell (1979), and Olson, Russell, and Sprenkle (1983).

13. See McCubbin *et al.* (1980), McCubbin and Patterson (1982), and McCubbin and Figley (1983a, 1983b). The instruments of Olson and McCubbin are both used in a study of more than a thousand families (Olson *et al.*, 1983). In addition, two later review chapters discuss Olson's family systems approach and McCubbin's family coping contributions (Reiss and Klein, 1987; Skinner, 1987).

14. Fisher and colleagues have written a highly relevant discussion of these issues (Fisher *et al.*, 1985).

15. See Beardslee *et al.* (1986, 1990), Jacobson *et al.* (1986), Josselson (1980), Offer (1969), Offer and Offer (1975), and Vaillant (1977).

16. See Shapiro (1968) and Zinner and Shapiro (1975).

17. See Minuchin (1974), Minuchin and Fishman (1981), Minuchin *et al.* (1978), and Steinglass (1987) for an overview of this realm of family therapy.

18. These contributions represent a continued stream of theoretical and clinical reports about this perspective, one strongly based on psychoanalytic considerations (Berkowitz *et al.*, 1974; E. Shapiro, 1982; R. Shapiro, 1968; and Zinner and Shapiro, 1975).

19. These descriptions represent a blend of historical recollection, current observation, and interpretation. Similar work has been done by Stierlin (1974), based in large part on observations of families of "runaway" adolescents. Material gained from these studies is rich and suggestive. Such observations and clinical inferences can generate new hypotheses and measurement techniques, which can then be applied to the study of normal as well as disturbed families. Indeed, as already noted in Chapter three, Stierlin's work provides important theoretical underpinnings for the conceptual scaffolding that we use to observe families. Rather than dismiss these clinical methods as "opposed" to direct systematic observational procedures, a more fruitful strategy is to exploit their harvest, building new constructs and conceptual systems from their insights.

20. See Murphey *et al.* (1963) and Coehlo *et al.* (1963).

21. Approaches that use "field studies" include Jules Henry's *Pathways to Madness* (1965), *The Family Shadow* by Reynolds and Farberow (1983), and *Being Adolescent* by Csikszentmihalyi and Larson (1984). The interested reader can pursue the topic of observational methods through Bakeman and Gottman's (1987) recent excellent review chapter.

22. Colby and Kohlberg (1987).

23. See Strodtbeck (1958) for description of this family task. Although we used the same basic technique for generating the family interaction data, our approach differed through its use of the moral dilemmas as the discussion topics.

24. On rare occasions a family did not have a difference for a given coalition, e.g. mother and father versus adolescent. In those cases the interviewer proceeded to choose the next coalition in sequence (e.g. after father and adolescent vs. mother, the family was asked to resolve the coalition of mother and adolescent versus father).

25. Among the theorists of this developmental era, Erik Erikson has written most forcefully, and eloquently, about the importance of fidelity and moral issues during adolescence (Erikson, 1958, 1965, 1968). Other relevant contributions include Kohlberg and Gilligan (1971).

26. We considered, and piloted, other experimental tasks, such as "plan a vacation," or "plan a menu," as well as a procedure where parents and adolescent are asked to discuss matters they had disagreed about, as they recalled these differences (unrevealed-differences procedure). However, these alternative experimental techniques were not as engaging to all family members, and also appeared to lead to discussions that could be more strongly controlled by dominant parental roles regarding such matters as menus, vacations, and the allocation of resources (e.g. money), or rules against disagreeing with one of the parents.

27. More extensive systematic analyses of this interesting question involving parent ego development and the family system are covered in two recent contributions: Hauser, Houlihan et al. (in press) and Rogell (1990).

CHAPTER 5

Paths Through Adolescence

1. Although six paths are discussed in detail in this book, a total of eight paths could be discerned. The other two are regression and moratorium. Since these unusual paths are of much theoretical and clinical interest, we note them here and have described them briefly in chapter two, as well as in table 5. However, relatively few adolescents represented them. That is why they are not discussed in greater depth in the text, and not because they are judged to lack importance. It should be noted that the accelerated group, also comprised of relatively few adolescents, *is* discussed at length in the text, in light of its special theoretical connections with family relationships.

2. See note 1 with respect to other possible paths.

3. See Hauser, Houlihan et al. (in press).

4. Among these strategies were logical analysis, empathy, suppression, and tolerance of ambiguity, discussed in Hauser, Borman et al., forthcoming.

5. Possibly these teenagers were functioning at higher levels of development before their hospitalization. Their dramatic progression would then represent a return to previous functioning. Even so, we still must wonder what individual or family factors contributed to their return to optimal functioning.

6. See Patricia Minuchin's (1985) thoughtful discussion of circular and non-linear influences in families and development.

CHAPTER 6

Profoundly Arrested Ego Development

1. Recall a similar dynamic suggested in Chapter 5 for the entire group of these adolescents, as noted in the high levels of focusing and curiosity expressed by their parents.

CHAPTER 7
Steady Conforming Ego Development

1. Just as Lou's conflicts with his parents cannot be reduced to representing his phase of development, parent dimensions, or their special individual conflicts with one another, we are not arguing that the family commitment to consensus is the only determinant of these interactions. The point we emphasize here, and throughout this book, is the importance of including family themes or belief systems as *components* of our explanations of family interactions and individual development.

2. Special alliances and coalitions in disturbed families have been addressed by Minuchin (1974; Minuchin and Fishman, 1981) and other family therapists (See Steinglass, 1987).

CHAPTER 8
Progressions in Ego Development

1. Lois is an exception to our previous observation that, in family discussions, adolescents direct most of their interruptions at their fathers. See Hauser, Book *et al.* (1987).

2. This is an example of progressive discourse change, discussed in Chapter 3 and defined in more detail in Appendix D.

3. Jill, a fifteen-year-old who followed the dramatic progression path, also stressed the significance of friends. In her first year she referred to their steadying influence. She had several close friends. One was especially important, knowing of her "two sides," often persuading her to prevent her "bitchy" side from dominating her and persuading her instead to be "nice," more accommodating, to her parents. Jill was terrified of her parents, particularly the prospect that they might not be able to tolerate her tentative, often awkward expressions of her own will.

4. Like Larry, Jill intermittently surprised her interviewer with flashes of self-awareness and self-understanding. She spoke knowingly of her manipulativeness toward her mother and its relation to her father's long absences from home: "I don't know when he's gonna be home and when he's not gonna be home. *(voice softens)* And, or when to manipulate my mother. *(nervous laugh)* I don't know when not to. *(nervous giggle)* I mean, once in a while—it's okay. But the rate I had done it—was bad. It's just that I wanted the attention of my mother because my father wasn't there to give me his attention. So I wanted my mother to give me the attention of both of them."

CHAPTER 9
Accelerated Ego Development

1. The subject of gender differences along these lines is currently attracting much professional and popular interest. Although our analyses have not

been organized along these lines, we consider it an important realm, worthy of more intensive study in general and within our data in particular. The interested reader can find relevant discussions and analyses in Apter (1990); Chodorow (1978) Gilligan (1987), Hauser, Book *et al.* (1987), Maccoby (1990) and Noam (1985).

2. The theoretical and empirical work of Grotevant and Cooper repeatedly underlines the importance of the relationship features. See Cooper (1988), Cooper *et al.* (1983), and Grotevant and Cooper (1985, 1986).

CHAPTER 10
Sustaining or Endangering Adolescents' Growth

1. Erikson (1958), p. 150.

2. The work of David Reiss (1984; Reiss and Klein 1987) most extensively deals with this topic, considerably beyond the scope of this book.

3. See, for instance, discussions by Emde (1988), Sameroff and Emde (1990), Sroufe (1979).

4. See Erikson (1965), p. 24.

5. The most explicit early challenge was presented by Richard Bell (1968), later summarized in Bell and Harper (1977), with continuing discussion in the review by Maccoby and Martin (1983). Also relevant is Patterson's (1980) monograph.

6. See the most recent reviews of this literature by Michael Goldstein (1988), and Goldstein and Strachan (1987)

7. In addition to the numerous examples presented in chapters 5 through 9, see Steinberg (1981, 1987, 1988).

8. See Hill (1987), Steinberg and Hill (1978), and summaries of work in this realm by Powers *et al.* (1989).

9. Spacks (1981), p. 296.

10. Autonomy and independence are being used synonymously here. S. Frank's usage (Frank *et al.*, 1988) is closest to our own. On the other hand, a different usage is suggested in the recent paper by Ryan and Lynch (1989). The evolution of autonomy and independence is neither linear nor continuous for most adolescents. In fact, these terms have distinct meanings, meanings that point to the range of processes encompassed by these significant aspects of adolescent experience. Autonomy refers to self-governance and self-regulations, while independence involves self-reliance, the ability to care for oneself. Most observers agree upon the importance of these processes during the adolescent years. Autonomy and independence can be seen as components of the six paths of ego development. The severe arrests show minimal self-governance, self-regulation, and self-reliance. Steady conformists certainly have interests and capabilities in these areas, but they remain the same; they do not

appear to want to change. On the other hand, the progressive and accelerated adolescents treasure change and seek new experiences with independence; where possible, they "go for it" within their families, with their friends, and with other adults.

11. See discussions by Gilligan (1987), Ryan and Lynch (1989), Hill (1987), Noam (1985) and Powers *et al.* (1989).

12. An idea suggested by John Mack, personal communication.

13. See Gottman (1983).

14. See Gilligan (1987) and Powers *et al.* (1989).

15. See Gilligan (1987), Cooper and Ayers-Lopez (1985), and Apter (1990).

16. This is the area Stierlin (1974) actively considered in his original considerations of binding in families of runaway adolescents.

17. See Steinberg, L. (1990).

18. See recent review by Spencer and Dornbush (1990) pointing out the likely important influences of ethnicity and social class on adolescent development and family relationships. However, theories of family relations and the research literature in this area is not well developed regarding specific mechanisms of influence or even specific direct influences. While not directly focused on family interactions, also relevant here are the contributions of Dornbush *et al.* (1987) and Baldwin and Baldwin (1989) regarding authoritative parents styles in varied ethnic and socioeconomic groups. In the forthcoming volume *At The Threshhold.: The Developing Adolescent*, several chapters attempt to cover this still underresearched and undertheorized area, e.g. chapters by Hauser and Bowlds (1990), Spencer and Dornbush (1990), and Steinberg (1990).

References

Alexander, J. F. 1973a. Defensive and supportive communication in normal and deviant families. *Journal of Consulting and Clinical Psychology*, 40:223–31.

———. 1973b. Defensive and supportive communications in family systems. *Journal of Marriage and the Family*, 35: 613–17.

Apter, T. 1990. *Altered Loves: Mothers and Daughters During Adolescence*. N.Y.: St. Martin's Press.

Bakeman, R., and J. M. Gottman. 1987. Applying observational Methods: A systematic View. In J. Osofsky (Ed.) *Handbook of Infant Psychology*. Second Edition. New York: Wiley.

Baldwin, C., and A. Baldwin. 1989. The role of family interaction in the prediction of adolescent competence. Symposium presented at Society for Research in Child Development biennial meetings, Kansas City, Mo.

Baldwin, A.; R. Cole; and C. Baldwin (eds.). 1982. Parental pathology, family interaction, and the competence of the child in school. *Monographs of the Society for Research in Child Development*, 42 (1): 197.

Bandura, A. 1964. The stormy decade: Fact or fiction? *Psychology in the Schools*, 1: 224–31.

Bandura, A., and R. H. Walters. *Social Learning and Personality Development*. New York: Holt, Rinehart & Winston.

Barber, B., and B. Rollins (eds.). 1987. Special Issue on Parent-Adolescent Relationships. *Family Perspective*, 21.

Barglow, P.; D. V. Edidin; A. S. Budlong-Springer; D. Berndt; R. Phillips; and E. Dubrow. Diabetic control in children and adolescents: Psychosocial factors and therapeutic efficacy. *Journal of Youth and Adolescence*, 12: 77–94.

Baumrind, D. 1968. Authoritarian versus authoritative parental control. *Adolescence*, 3: 255–72.

———. 1971. Current patterns of parental authority. *Developmental Psychology Monographs*, 4, (1), part 2.

————. 1989. Rearing competent children. In W. Damon (ed.), *New Directions for Child Development: Child Development Today and Tomorrow.* San Francisco: Jossey-Bass.

Beardslee, W. R.; A. M. Jacobson; S. T. Hauser; G. V. Noam; S. I. Powers; J. Houlihan; and E. Rider. 1986. An approach to evaluating adolescent adaptive processes: Validity of an interview-based measure. *Journal of Youth and Adolescence, 15:* 355–75.

Beardslee, W. R.; S. I. Powers; S. T. Hauser; J. Houlihan; A. M. Jacobson; G. V. Noam, E. Macias; and J. Hopfenbeck. 1990. Adaptation in adolescence: The influence of time and severe psychiatric disorder. *Journal of the Academy of Child and Adolescent Psychiatry, 29:* 429–39.

Bell, D. G., and L. G. Bell. 1983. Parental validation and support in the development of adolescent daughters. In H. D. Grotevant and C. R. Cooper (eds.), *Adolescent Development in the Family.* San Francisco: Jossey-Bass.

Bell, L. G., and D. G. Bell. 1982. Family climate and the role of the female adolescent: Determinants of functioning. *Family Relations, 31:* 519–27.

Bell, R. Q. 1968. A reinterpretation of the direction of effects in studies of socialization. *Psychological Review, 4:* 81–95.

Bell, R. Q., and L. V. Harper. 1977. *Child Effects on Adults.* Hillsdale, N.J.: Lawrence Erlbaum Associates.

Berndt, T. 1979. Developmental changes in conformity to peers and parents. *Developmental psychology, 15:* 608–16.

Berkowitz, D. A.; R. L. Shapiro; J. Zinner; and E. R. Shapiro. 1974. Concurrent family treatment of narcissistic personalities in adolescence. *International Journal of Psychoanalytic Psychotherapy, 3:* 371–96.

Bowerman, C. D., and J. W. Kinch. 1959. Changes in family and peer orientation of children between the fourth and tenth grades. *Social Forces, 37:* 206–11.

Block, J. 1971. *Lives Through Time.* Berkeley, Calif.: Bancroft Books.

Blos, P. 1962. *On Adolescence: A Psychoanalytic Interpretation.* New York: Free Press.

————. 1979. The Adolescent Passage. New York: International Universities Press.

Brooks-Gunn, J., and A. C. Petersen, eds. 1983. *Girls at Puberty: Biological and Psychosocial Perspectives.* New York: Plenum.

Brooks-Gunn, J., and M. P. Warren. 1985. Effects of delayed menarche in different contexts: Dance and nondance students. *Journal of Youth and Adolescence, 14:* 285–300.

————. 1987. Biological contributions to affective expression in young adolescent girls. Presented at the Biennial Meetings of the Society for Research in Child Development, Baltimore.

————. 1988. The psychological significance of secondary sexual characteristics in 9- to 11-year-old girls. *Child Development, 59:* 161–69.

Brooks-Gunn, J.; A. C. Petersen; D. Eichorn (eds.). 1985. Time of maturation and psychosocial functioning in adolescence. [Special Issue]. *Journal of Youth and Adolescence, 14,* 149–264.

Browning, D. L. 1986. Psychiatric ward behavior and length of stay in adolescent and young adult inpatients: A developmental approach to prediction. *Journal of Consulting and Clinical Psychology, 54:* 227–30.

———. 1987. Ego development, authoritarianism, and social status: An investigation of the incremental validity of Loevinger's Sentence Completion Test (short form). *Journal of Personality and Social Psychology, 53:* 113–18.

Burbank, V. 1988. *Aboriginal Adolescence: Maidenhood in an Australian Community.* New Brunswick, N.J.: Rutgers University Press.

Cairns, R. (ed.) 1982. *The Analysis of Social Interactions: Methods, Issues and Illustrations.* Hillsdale, N.J.: Earlbaum.

Chodorow, N. 1978. *The Reproduction of Mothering: Psychoanalysis and the Sociology of Gender.* Berkeley: University of California Press.

Coelho, G. V.; D. A. Hamburg, and E. B. Murphey. 1963. Coping strategies in a new learning environment. *Archives of General Psychiatry, 9:* 433–43.

Colby, A. and L. Kohlberg. 1987. *The Measurement of Moral Judgement* (Vols. 1 and 2) New York: Cambridge University Press.

Cooper, C. S. 1988. Commentary: The role of conflict in adolescent–parent relationships. In M. Gunnar and C. Collins (eds.), *Development During the Transition to Adolescence.* Hillsdale, N.J.: Erlbaum.

Cooper, C. R., and S. Ayers-Lopez. 1985. Family and peer systems in early adolescence: New models of the role of relationships in development. *Journal of Early Adolescence, 5:* 9–21.

Cooper, C., and H. D. Grotevant. 1987. Gender issues in the interface of family experience and adolescents' friendships and dating identity. *Journal of Youth and Adolescence, 16:* 247–64.

Cooper, C.; H. D. Grotevant; and S. M. Condon. 1983. Individuality and connectedness in the family as a context for adolescent identity and role-taking skills. In H. D. Grotevant and C. R. Cooper (eds.), *Adolescent Development in the Family.* New Directions for Child Development. San Francisco: Jossey-Bass.

Csikszentmihalyi, M., and R. Larson. 1984. *Being Adolescent.* New York: Basic Books.

Dill, D. and G. Noam. 1990. Ego development and treatment requests. *Psychiatry, 53:* 85–91.

Doane, J.; K. West; M. Goldstein; E. Rodnick; and J. Jones. 1981. Parental communication deviance and affective style. *Archives of General Psychiatry, 38:* 679–85.

Dornbush, S.; P. Ritter; P. Liederman; D. Roberts; and M. Fraleigh. 1987. The relation of parenting style to adolescent school performance. *Child Development, 58:* 1244–57.

Douvan, E., and J. Adelson. 1966. *The Adolescent Experience.* New York: Wiley.

Dubrow, E. F.; L. R. Huesmann; and L. Eron. 1987. Childhood correlates of adult ego development. *Child Development, 58:* 859–69.

Emde, R. N. 1988. Development terminable and interminable II: Recent psychoanalytic theory and therapeutic considerations. *International Journal of Psychoanalysis, 69:* 283–96.

Erikson, E. H. 1958. Identity and the life cycle. *Psychological Issues, 1:* 1–171.

———. 1965. *The Challenge of Youth.* Garden City, N.Y.: Doubleday.

———. 1968. *Identity: Youth and Crisis.* New York: Norton.

Eveleth, P. B. 1986. Timing of menarche: Secular trend and population differences. In J. B. Lancaster and B. A. Hamburg (eds.), *School-Age Pregnancy and Parenthood: Biosocial Dimensions.* Hawthorne, N.Y.: Aldine de Gruyter. Pp. 39–52.

Fisher, L.; R. Kohes; D. Ranson; S. Phillips; and P. Rudd. 1985. Alternative strategies for creating "relational" data. *Family Process, 24:* 213–24.

Frank, S. J., and D. M. Quinlan. 1976. Ego development and female delinquency: A cognitive-developmental approach. *Journal of Abnormal Psychology, 85:* 505–10.

Frank, S. J.; M. S. Laman; and C. B. Avery. 1988. Young adults' perceptions of their relationships with their parents: Individual differences in connectedness, competence, and emotional autonomy. *Developmental Psychology, 24:* 729–37.

Freud, A. 1946. *The Ego and the Mechanisms of Defense.* Trans. Cecil Baines. New York: International Universities Press.

———. 1958. Adolescence. In *Psychoanalytic Study of the Child.* Vol. 13. New York: International Universities Press.

Gilligan, C. 1982. *In a Different Voice: Psychological Theories and Women's Development.* Cambridge, Mass.: Harvard University Press.

Gilligan, C. 1987. Adolescent development reconsidered. In Irwin (1987).

Goldstein, M. J. 1978. The study of families of disturbed adolescents at risk for schizophrenia and related conditions. In E. J. Anthony, C. Koupernik, and C. Chiland (eds.), *The Child in His Family: Vulnerable Children.* (Vol. 4). New York: Wiley.

———. 1985. Family factors that antedate the onset of schizophrenia and related disorders: The results of a fifteen-year prospective longitudinal study. *Acta Psychiatrica Scandinavia, 71:* 7–18.

Goldstein, M. J. 1988. Family and psychopathology. *Annual Review of Psychology, 39:* 283–299.

Goldstein, M. J., and E. H. Rodnick. 1975. The family's contribution to the etiology of schizophrenia. *Psychological Bulletin, 14:* 48–63.

Goldstein, M. J., and A. M. Strachan. 1987. The family and schizophrenia. In Jacob (1987).

Goldstein, M. J.; L. L. Judd; E. H. Rodnick; A. A. Alkire; and E. Gould. 1968. A method for the study of social influence and coping patterns in the families of disturbed adolescents. *Journal of Nervous and Mental Diseases, 147:* 233–251.

Gottman, J. M. 1983. How children become friends. *Monographs of the Society for Research in Child Development,* vol. 48, no. 3, serial 201.

Gould, R. 1978. *Transformations.* New York: Simon and Schuster.

Graham, P., and M. Rutter. 1985. Adolescent Disorders. In M. Rutter and L. Hersov (eds.), *Child and Adolescent Psychiatry:* Modern Approaches. 2nd ed. Oxford: Blackwell.

Grossman, F., and W. Pollock. 1985. Parent–child interaction. In L'Abate (1985).

Grotevant, H. D., and C. R. Cooper. 1985. Patterns of interaction in family relationships and the development of identity exploration in adolescence. *Child Development, 56:* 415–28.

———. 1986. Individuation in family relationships. *Human Development, 29:* 82–100.

Haan, N. 1977. *Coping and Defending.* New York: Academic Press.

Haan, N.; J. Stroud; and J. Holstein. 1973. Moral and ego stages in relation to ego processes: A study of "hippies." *Journal of Personality, 41:* 596–612.

Harakel, C. M. 1971. Ego maturity and interpersonal style: A multivariate study of Loevinger's theory. Doctoral dissertation, Catholic University. *Dissertation Abstracts International, 32,* 1190B. University microfilms no. 71–19: 421.

Hauser, S. T. 1971. *Black and White Identity Formation.* New York: Wiley.

Hauser, S. T. 1976. Loevinger's model and measure of ego development: A critical review. *Psychological Bulletin, 83:* 928–55.

———. 1978. Adolescent ego development and interpersonal style. *Journal of Youth and Adolescence, 7:* 333–52.

Hauser, S. T., and M. K. Bowlds. 1990. Coping and Adaptation. In S. Feldman and G. Elliot (eds.), *At The Threshold: The Developing Adolescent.* Cambridge: Harvard University Press.

Hauser, S. T., and D. Follansbee. 1984. Developing identity: Ego growth and change during adolescence. In H. Fitzgerald, B. Lester, and M. Yogman (eds.), *Theory and Research in Behavioral Pediatrics.* New York: Plenum.

Hauser, S. T., and W. Greene. Forthcoming. Passages from late adolescence to early adulthood. To appear in G. Pollack and S. Greenspan (eds.), *The Course of Life.* New York: International Universities Press.

Hauser, S. T., and W. Kates. 1982. Understanding adults. *Psychoanalysis and Contemporary Thought, 5:* 117–46.

Hauser, S. T.; E. H. Borman; M. K. Bowlds; S. I. Powers; A. M. Jacobson; G. G. Noam; and K. Knoebber. Forthcoming. Understanding coping with adolescence: Ego development trajectories and coping styles. In A. L. Greene, E. M. Cummings, and K. Karraker (eds.), *Life-span Developmental Psychology: Perspectives on Stress and Coping*. Hillsdale, N.J.: Lawrence Erlbaum Associates.

Hauser, S. T.; B. K. Book; J. Houlihan; S. I. Powers; B. Weiss-Perry; D. Follansbee; A. M. Jacobson; and G. G. Noam. 1987. Sex differences within the family: Studies of adolescent and parent family interactions. *Journal of Youth and Adolescence, 16:* 199–220.

Hauser, S. T.; J. Houlihan; S. I. Powers; A. M. Jacobson; G. Noam; B. Weiss-Perry; and D. Follansbee. 1987. Interaction sequences in families of psychiatrically hospitalized and non-patient adolescents, *Psychiatry, 50:* 308–19.

Hauser, S. T.; J. Houlihan; S. I. Powers; A. M. Jacobson; G. G. Noam; B. Weiss-Perry; D. Follansbee; and B. K. Book. In press. Adolescent ego development within the family: Family styles and family sequences. *International Journal of Behavioral Development.*

Hauser, S. T.; A. M. Jacobson; J. Milley; D. Wertlieb; R. D. Hersowitz; J. I. Wolfsdorf; and P. Lavori. Forthcoming. Ego trajectories and adjustment to diabetes: Longitudinal studies of diabetic and acutely ill patients. L. Feagens, W. Ray, and E. Susman (eds.), *Emotion and Cognition in Child and Adolescent Health and Development*. Hillsdale, N.J.: Lawrence Erlbaum Associates.

Hauser, S. T.; A. M. Jacobson; D. Wertlieb; B. Weiss-Perry; D. Follansbee; J. I. Wolfsdorf; R. D. Herskowitz; J. Houlihan; and D. C. Rajapark. 1986. Children with recently diagnosed diabetes: Interactions within their families, *Health Psychology, 5:* 272–96.

Hauser, S. T.; S. I. Powers; A. M. Jacobson; J. Schwartz; and G. G. Noam. 1982. Family interactions and ego development in diabetic adolescents. *Pediatric and Adolescent Endocrinology, 10:* 69–76.

Hauser, S. T.; S. I. Powers; G. G. Noam; A. M. Jacobson; B. Weiss; and D. Follansbee. 1984. Familial contexts of adolescent ego development. *Child Development, 55:* 195–213.

Hauser, S. T.; S. I. Powers; G. G. Noam; and M. K. Bowlds. 1987. Family interiors of adolescent ego development. *Family Perspective, 21:* 263–84.

Henggeler, S. W. 1982. *Delinquency and Adolescent Psychopathology*. Boston: John Wright.

Henry, J. 1965. *Pathways to Madness*. New York: Random House.

Hill, J. P. 1987. Research on adolescents and their families: Past and prospect. In C. E. Irwin (ed.), Adolescent Social Behavior and Health. *New Directions for Child Development*, no. 37, San Francisco: Jossey-Bass. pp. 13–31.

———. 1980. The family. In M. Johnson (ed.), *Toward Adolescence: The Middle School Years. The Seventy-Ninth Yearbook of the National Society for the Study of Education.* Chicago: University of Chicago Press.

Hill, J. P., and G. N. Holmbeck. 1986. Attachment and autonomy during adolescence. In G. W. Whitehurst (ed.), *Annals of Child Development*. Vol. 3. Greenwich, Conn.: JAI Press.

Hill, J. P.; G. N. Holmbeck; L. Marlow; T. M. Green; and M. E. Lynch. 1985a. Menarcheal status and parent–child relations in families of seventh-grade girls. *Journal of Youth and Adolescence, 14:* 301–16.

———. 1985b. Pubertal status and parent–child relations in families of seventh-grade boys. *Journal of Early Adolescence, 5:* 31–44.

Hollingshead, A. B. 1957. *Two-Factor Index of Social Position.* Mimeographed. Yale University.

Holmbeck, G., and J. Hill. 1988. The role of family conflict in adaptation to menarche: Sequential analysis of family interaction. Submitted for publication.

Holt, R. R. 1980. Loevinger's measure of ego development: Reliability and national norms for male and female short forms. *Journal of Personality and Social Psychology, 39:* 909–20.

Hooley, J. M. 1985. Expressed emotion: A review of the critical literature. *Clinical Psychology Review, 5:* 119–39.

Hooley, J. M., and J. D. Teasdale. 1989. Predictors of relapse in unipolar depressives: Expressed emotion, marital distress, and perceived criticism. *Journal of Abnormal Psychology, 98:* 229–35.

Hoppe, C. F., and J. Loevinger. 1977. Ego development and conformity: A construct validity study of the Washington University Sentence Completion Test. *Journal of Personality Assessment, 41:* 497–504.

Huston, T. L., and E. Robins. 1982. Conceptual and methodological issues in studying close relationships. *Journal of Marriage and the Family, 43:* 901–25.

Inhoff-Germain, G.; G. Arnold; E. Nottleman; E. Susman; G. Cutler; and G. Chrousos. 1988. Relations between hormone levels and observational measures of aggressive behavior of adolescents in family interactions. *Developmental Psychology, 24,* 129–49.

Irwin, C. E. 1987. Editor's notes. In C. E. Irwin (ed.), *Adolescent Social Behavior and Health.* New Directions for Child Development, no. 37. San Francisco: Jossey-Bass.

Isaacs, K. S. 1956. *Relatability, a Proposed Construct and an Approach to Its Validation.* Unpublished doctoral dissertation, University of Chicago.

Jacob, T. (ed.). 1987. *Family Interaction and Psychopathology: Theories, Methods, and Findings.* New York: Plenum.

Jacobson, A. M.; W. Beardslee; S. T. Hauser; G. Noam; and S. Powers. 1986. Evaluating ego defense mechanisms using clinical interviews: An empirical study of adolescent diabetic and psychiatric patients. *Journal of Adolescence, 9:* 303–19.

Jacobson, A. M.; S. T. Hauser; S. Powers; and G. Noam. 1982. Ego Development in diabetic adolescents. *Pediatric and Adolescent Endocrinology, 10,* 1–8.

Jacobson, A. M.; S. T. Hauser; S. I. Powers; and G. G. Noam. 1984. The influences of chronic illness and ego development level and self-esteem in diabetic adolescents. *Journal of Youth and Adolescence, 13:* 489–507.

Josselson, R. 1980. Ego development in adolescence. In J. Adelson (ed.), *Handbook of Adolescent Psychology.* New York: Wiley.

Kaplan, L. 1984. *Farewell to Childhood.* New York: Simon & Schuster.

Kelley, H. H.; E. Berscheid; A. Christensen; J. A. Harvey; T. L. Huston; G. Levinger; E. McClintock; L. A. Peplav; and A. C. Petersen. 1983. *Close Relationships.* San Francisco: Freeman.

Kenny, M. E. 1987. The extent and function of parental attachment among first-year college students. *Journal of Youth and Adolescence, 16:* 17–29.

Kirshner, L. A. 1988. Implications of Loevinger's theory of ego development for time-limited psychotherapy. *Psychotherapy, 25,* 220–227.

Koenigsberg, H. W., and R. Handley. 1986. Expressed emotion: From predictive index to clinical construct. *American Journal of Psychiatry, 143:* 1361–73.

Kohlberg, L., and C. Gilligan. 1971. The adolescent as a philosopher: The discovery of the self in a post-conventional world. *Daedalus, 100:* 1051–1086.

L'Abate, L. (ed.). 1985. *The Handbook of Family Psychology and Therapy.* Vols. 1 and 2. Homewood, Ill.: Dorsey Press.

Labouvie-Vieff, G.; J. Hakim-Larson; and C. J. Hobart. 1987. Age, ego level, and the life-span development of coping and defense processes. *Psychology and Aging, 2,* 286–293.

Lambert, H. V. 1972. A comparison of Jane Loevinger's theory of ego development and Lawrence Kohlberg's theory of moral development. Doctoral dissertation, University of Chicago.

Leff, J., and C. E. Vaughn. 1985. *Expressed Emotion in Families.* New York: Guilford.

Lerner, R. M., and G. B. Spanier (eds.). 1978. *Child Influences on Marital and Family Interaction.* New York: Academic Press.

Levinson, D. J., with C. Darrow, E. Klein, M. Levinson, and B. McKee. *The Seasons of a Man's Life.*

Lewis, M., and C. Feiring. 1978. The child's social world. In R. Lerner and G. Spanier (eds.), *Child Influence on Marital and Family Interaction.* New York: Academic Press.

Lewis, J. M., W. R. Beavers, J. T. Gossett, and V. A. Phillip. 1976. *No Single Thread.* New York: Bruner/Mazel.

Lewis, J.; E. Rodnick; and M. Goldstein. 1981. Intrafamilial interactive behavior, parental communication deviance, and risk for schizophrenia. *Journal of Abnormal Psychology, 90:* 448–57.

Lidz, T.; A. R. Cornelison; S. Fleck; and D. Terry. 1957. The interfamilial environment of schizophrenic patients: II. Marital schism and marital skew. *American Journal of Psychiatry, 114:* 241–48.

Lieber, D. 1977. Parental focus of attention in a videotape feedback task as a function of a hypothesized risk for offspring schizophrenia. *Family Process, 16:* 467–75.

Loevinger, J. 1966. The meaning and measurement of ego development. *American Psychologist, 21:* 195–206.

———. 1969. Theories of ego development. In L. Breger (ed.), *Clinical-Cognitive Psychology: Models and Integrations.* Englewood Cliffs, N.J.: Prentice-Hall.

———. 1976. *Ego Development: Conceptions and Theories.* San Francisco: Jossey-Bass.

———. 1979. Construct validity of the ego development test. *Applied Psychological Measurement, 3:* 281–311.

———. 1984. On the self and predicting behavior. In R. A. Zucker, J. Aronoff, and A. I. Rabin (eds.), *Personality and the Prediction of Behavior.* Orlando: Academic Press.

———. 1985. Revisions of the sentence completion test for ego development. *Journal of Personality and Social Psychology, 48:* 420–27.

Loevinger, J., and R. Wessler. 1970. *Measuring Ego Development.* Vol. I. San Francisco: Jossey-Bass.

Loevinger, J.; R. Wessler; and C. Redmore. 1970. *Measuring Ego Development.* Vol. II. San Francisco: Jossey-Bass.

Loevinger, J.; L. Cohn; C. Redmore; L. Bonneville; D. Streich; and M. Sargent. 1985. Ego development in college. *Journal of Personality and Social Psychology, 48:* 947–62.

Loewald, H. 1980. Internalization, mourning, and the superego. In H. Loewald (ed.), *Papers on Psychoanalysis.* New Haven: Yale University Press.

Maccoby, E. E. 1968. The development of moral values and behavior in childhood. In J. A. Clausen (ed.), *Socialization and Society.* Boston: Little, Brown.

———. 1990. Gender and relationships: A developmental account. *American Psychologist, 45:* 513–20.

Maccoby, E. E., and J. A. Martin. 1983. Socialization in the context of the family: Parent–child interaction. In M. Hetherington (ed.), *Handbook of Child Psychology.* Volume 4. New York: Wiley.

Masterson, J. F. 1972. *Treatment of the Borderline Adolescent.* New York: Wiley.

McAdams, D.; K. Ruetzel; and J. Foley. 1986. Complexity and generativity at mid-life: Relations among social motives, ego development, and adults' plans for the future. *Journal of Personality and Social Psychology, 50:* 800–807.

McCubbin, H. I., and C. R. Figley. 1983a. *Stress and the Family,* Vol. I: *Coping with Normative Transitions.* Beverley Hills, Calif.: Sage.

————. 1983b. *Stress and the Family,* Vol. II: *Coping with Catastrophe.* Beverley Hills, Calif.: Sage.

McCubbin, H. I., and J. M. Patterson. 1982. Family adaptation to crises. In H. I. McCubbin, A. E. Cauble, and J. M. Patterson (eds.), *Family Stress, Coping and Social Support.* Springfield, Ill.: Charles C. Thomas.

McCubbin, H. I.; C. B. Joy; A. E. Cauble; J. K. Comeau; J. M. Patterson; and R. H. Needle. 1980. Family stress and coping: A decade review. *Journal of Marriage and the Family,* 42: 855–71.

Minuchin, P. 1985. Families and individual development: Provocations from the field. *Child Development,* 56: 289–302.

Minuchin, S. 1974. *Families and Family Therapy.* Cambridge: Harvard University Press.

Minuchin, S., and L. Baker. 1975. A conceptual model of psychosomatic illness in children: Family organization and family therapy. *Archives of General Psychiatry,* 32: 1031–38.

Minuchin, S., and H. C. Fishman. 1981. *Family Therapy Techniques.* Cambridge: Harvard University Press.

Minuchin, S.; B. Rosman; and L. Baker. 1978. *Psychosomatic Families.* Cambridge: Harvard University Press.

Montemayor, R. 1982. The relationship between parent-adolescent conflict and the amount of time adolescents spend alone and with parents and peers. *Child Development,* 53: 1512–19.

Montemayor, R. 1983. Parents and adolescents in conflict: All families some of the time and some families most of the time. *Journal of Early Adolescence,* 3: 83–103.

Moos, R. 1974. *The Family Environment Scale.* Palo Alto, Calif.: Consulting Psychologists Press.

Moos, R., and B. Moos. 1976. A typology of family social environments. *Family Process,* 15: 357–72.

————. 1984. The process of recovery from alcoholism: 3. Comparing functioning in families of alcoholics and matched control families. *Journal of Studies on Alcohol,* 45: 111–18.

Murphey, L.; E. Silber; G. Coelho; D. Hamburg; and I. Greenberg. 1963. Development of autonomy and parent–child interaction in late adolescents. *American Journal of Orthopsychiatry,* 33: 643–52.

Noam, G. G. 1984. Self, morality, and biography: Studies in Clinical–developmental Psychology. Doctoral dissertation, Harvard University.

————. 1985. Stage, phase and style: The developmental dynamics of the self. In: M. Berkowitz and F. Oser (eds.), *Moral Education.* Hillsdale, N.J.: Erlbaum.

————. 1988. A constructivist approach to developmental psychopathology. In E. D. Nannis and P. A. Cowan (eds.), *Developmental Psychopathology and*

Its Treatment. New Directions in Child Development, no. 4. San Francisco: Jossey-Bass.

Noam, G. G., and D. Dill. In press. Adult development and symptomatology. *Psychiatry.*

Noam, G. G.; S. T. Hauser; S. T. Santostefano; W. Garrison; A. Jacobson; S. Powers; and M. Mead. 1984. Ego development and psychopathology: A study of hospitalized adolescents. *Child Development, 55:* 184–94.

Noam, G. G.; L. Kohlberg; and J. Snarey. 1983. Steps toward a model of the self. In B. Lee and G. Noam (eds.), *Developmental Approaches to the Self.* New York: Plenum.

Noam, G. G., S. I. Powers; R. Kilkenny; and J. Beedy. 1990. The interpersonal self in life-span-developmental perspective. In P. Baltes, D. Featherman, and R. Lerner (eds.), *Life-span Development and Behavior.* Orlando: Academic Press.

Noam, G. G.; C. Recklitis; and K. Paget. 1989. Ego development, psychopathology and adaptation: A longitudinal study. *Acta Peadopsychiatrica, 52:* 254–65.

Offer, D. 1969. *The Psychological World of the Teenager: A Study of Normal Adolescent Boys.* New York: Basic Books.

Offer, D., and J. Offer. 1975. *From Teenage to Young Manhood: A Psychological Study.* New York: Basic Books.

Offer, D.; E. Ostrov; and I. Howard. 1981. *The Adolescent: A Psychological Self-portrait.* New York: Basic Books.

Offer, D., and M. Sabshin. 1984. *Normality and the Life Cycle.* New York: Basic Books.

Olson, D. H.; H. I. McCubbin; H. L. Barnes; A. S. Larsen; M. J. Muxen; and M. A. Wilson. 1983. *Families: What Makes Them Work.* Beverly Hills: Sage.

Olson, D. H., and J. Portner. 1983. Family adaptability and cohesion evaluation scales. In E. E. Filsinger (ed.), *Marriage and Family Assessment.* Beverly Hills, Calif.: Sage.

Olson, D. H.; C. S. Russell; and D. H. Sprenkle. 1983. Circumplex model of marital and family systems: 4. Theoretical update. *Family Process, 22:* 69–83.

Olson, D. H.; D. H. Sprenkle; and C. S. Russell. 1979. Circumplex model of marital and family systems: 1. Cohesion and adaptability dimensions, family types, and clinical applications. *Family Process, 18:* 3–28.

Patterson, G. R. 1980. Mothers: The unacknowledged victims. *Monographs of the Society for Research in Child Development,* no. 186.

Petersen, A. C. 1988. Adolescent development. *Annual Review of Psychology, 39:* 583–607.

Petersen, A. C., and R. Spiga. 1982. Adolescence and stress. In L. Goldberger and S. Breznitz (eds.), *Handbook of Stress: Theoretical and Clinical Aspects.* New York: Free Press. Pp. 515–28.

Petersen, A. C.; M. Tobin-Richards; and A. Boxer. 1983. Puberty: Its measurement and its meaning. *Journal of Early Adolescence, 3:* 47–62.

Peterson, G. B.; R. Hey; and L. R. Peterson. 1979. Intersection of family development and moral stage frameworks: Implications for theory and research. *Journal of Marriage and the Family, 41:* 229–35.

—————. 1988. Moral judgment development within the family. *Journal of Moral Education, 17:* 209–19.

Powers, S. I. Forthcoming. Family systems through the lifespan. In K. Kreppner and R. M. Lerner (eds.), *Family Systems and Lifespan Development.* Hillsdale, N.J.: Erlbaum.

Powers, S. I.; S. T. Hauser; and A. M. Jacobson. 1985. Parent and adolescent longitudinal trajectories of ego development. Paper presented at the meetings of the Society for Research in Child Development, April.

Powers, S. I.; S. T. Hauser; and L. Kilner. 1989. Adolescent mental health. *American Psychologist, 44:* 200–208.

Powers, S. I.; S. T. Hauser; J. Schwartz; G. G. Noam; and A. M. Jacobson. 1983. Adolescent ego development and family interactions: A structural-developmental perspective. In H. D. Grotevant and C. R. Cooper (eds.), *Adolescent Development in the Family.* New Directions for Child Development, no. 22. San Francisco: Jossey-Bass.

Redmore, C. D., and K. Waldman. 1975. Reliability of a sentence completion measure of ego development. *Journal of Personality Assessment, 39,* 236–43.

Reiss, D. 1984. *The Family's Construction of Reality.* Cambridge: Harvard University Press.

Reiss, D., and D. Klein. 1987. Paradigms and pathogenesis: A family-centered approach to problems of etiology and treatment of psychiatric disorders. In Jacob (1987).

Reynolds D. K., and N. L. Farberow. 1981. *The Family Shadow: Sources of Suicide and Schizophrenia.* Berkeley: University of California Press.

Rogell, D. 1990. Ego development and communication patterns in the marital dyad. Undergraduate thesis, Harvard University.

Rollins, B. C., and D. L. Thomas. 1979. Parental support, power, and control techniques in the socialization of children. In W. R. Burr, F. I. Nye, and I. L. Reiss (eds.), *Contemporary Theories About the Family: Research Based Theories.* New York: Free Press.

Rosznafsky, J. 1981. The relationship of ego development to Q-sort personality ratings. *Journal of Personality and Social Psychology, 41:* 99–120.

Rutter, M. 1979. Protective factors in children's responses to stress and disadvantage. In M. W. Kent and J. E. Rolf (eds.), *Primary Prevention of Psycho-*

pathology, Vol. 3: *Social Competence in Children.* Hanover: University Press of New England. Pp. 49–74.

———. 1980. *Changing Youth in a Changing Society.* Cambridge: Harvard University Press.

———. 1983. Stress, coping, and development: Some issues and some questions. In N. Garmezy and M. Rutter (eds.), *Stress, Coping and Development in Children.* New York: McGraw-Hill. Pp. 1–41.

———. 1987. Psychosocial resilience and protective mechanisms. *American Journal of Orthopsychiatry, 57:* 316–31.

Rutter, M.; P. Graham; O. Chadwick; and W. Yule. 1976. Adolescent turmoil: fact or fiction? *Journal of Child Psychology and Psychiatry, 17:* 35–56.

Ryan, R., and J. H. Lynch. 1989. Emotional autonomy versus detachment: Revisiting the vicissitudes of adolescence and young adulthood. *Child Development, 60:* 340–56.

Sameroff, A. J., and R. N. Emde. 1990. *Relationship Disturbances in Early Childhood: A Developmental Approach.* New York: Basic Books.

Schafer, R. 1960. *Aspects of Internalization.* New York: International Universities Press.

Shapiro, E. R. 1982. The holding environment and family therapy with acting out adolescents. *International Journal of Psychoanalytic Psychotherapy, 9:* 209–26.

Shapiro, R. L. 1968. Adolescent autonomy and the family. In G. Caplan and S. Lebovici (eds.), *Adolescence: Psychosocial Perspectives.* New York: Basic Books.

Simmons, R. G. 1987. Social transition and adolescent development. In C. E. Irwin (ed.), *Adolescent Social Behavior and Health.* New Directions for Child Development, no. 37. San Francisco: Jossey-Bass.

Skinner, H. A. 1987. Self-report instruments for family assessment. In Jacob (1987).

Smelser, N., and E. H. Erikson. 1981. *Themes of Work and Love in Adulthood.* Cambridge: Harvard University Press.

Smetana, J. G. 1985. Family rules, conventions, and adolescent–parent conflict. Paper presented at the Biennial Meetings of the Society for Research in Child Development, Toronto.

———. 1987. Parent factors in family relations in adolescence. Presented at Biennial Meetings of the Society for Research in Child Development, Baltimore.

———. 1988a. Adolescents' and parents' conceptions of parental authority. *Child Development, 59:* 321–35.

———. 1988b. Concepts of self and social conventions: Adolescents' and parents' reasoning about hypothetical and actual family conflicts. In M. R. Gunnar and W. A. Collins (eds.), *21st Minnesota Symposium on Child Psychology.* Hillsdale, N.J.: Erlbaum.

Spacks, P. M. 1981. *The Adolescent Idea*. New York: Basic Books.

Spencer, M., and S. Dornbush. 1990. In S. Feldman and G. Eliot (eds.), *At the Threshhold: The Developing Adolescent*. Cambridge: Harvard University Press.

Sroufe, L. A. 1979. Socioemotional Development. In J. Osofsky (ed.), *Handbook of Infant Development*. New York: Wiley.

Steinberg, L. 1981. Transformations in family relations at puberty. *Developmental Psychology, 17*:833–40.

———. 1987. The impact of puberty on family relations: Effects of pubertal status and pubertal timing. *Developmental Psychology, 23:* 451–60.

———. 1988. Reciprocal relations between parent-child distance and pubertal maturation. *Developmental Psychology, 24:* 122–28.

———. 1990. Interdependency in the family: Autonomy, conflict, and harmony. In S. Feldman and G. Eliot (eds.), *At the Threshhold: The Developing Adolescent*. Cambridge: Harvard University Press.

Steinberg, L., and J. Hill. 1978. Patterns of family interaction as a function of age, the onset of puberty, and formal thought. *Developmental Psychology, 14:* 683–84.

Steinberg, L., and S. Silverberg. 1986. The vicissitudes of autonomy in adolescence. *Child Development, 57:* 841–51.

Steinglass, P. 1987. A systems view of family interaction and psychopathology. In Jacob (1987). N.Y.: Plenum.

Stierlin, H. 1974. *Separating Parents and Adolescents*. New York: Quadrangle.

Strodtbeck, F. L. 1958. Husband–wife interaction and revealed differences. *American Sociological Review, 16:* 468–73.

Sullivan, C.; M. Q. Grant; & J. D. Grant. 1957. The Development of Interpersonal Maturity: Applications to Delinquency. *Psychiatry, 20:* 373–85.

Swensen, C. H. 1980. Ego development as general model for counseling and psychotherapy. *Personnel and Guidance Journal, 6:* 382–88.

———. 1985. Personality development in the family. In L. L'Abate (1985).

Swensen, C. H., et al. 1981. Stages of the family life cycle: Ego development. *Journal of Marriage and the Family, 43:* 841–53.

Vaillant, G. 1977. *Adaptation to Life*. Boston: Little, Brown.

Vaillant, G. E., and L. McCollough. 1987. The Washington University Sentence Completion Test compared with other measures of adult ego development. *American Journal of Psychiatry, 144:* 1189–94.

Verdonik, F., and L. Sherrod. 1984. *An Inventory of Longitudinal Research on Childhood and Adolescence*. New York: Social Science Research Council.

Weiner, I. B. 1970. *Psychological Disturbance in Adolescence*. New York: Wiley.

————. 1980. Psychopathology in adolescence. In J. Adelson (ed.) *Handbook of Adolescent Psychology.* New York: Wiley.

Westley, W., and N. Epstein. 1969. *Silent Majority.* San Francisco: Jossey-Bass.

Whiting, J. W. M.; V. K. Burbank; and M. S. Ratner. 1986. The duration of maidenhood across cultures. In J. B. Lancaster and B. A. Hamburg (eds.), *School-Age Pregnancy and Parenthood: Biosocial Dimensions.* Hawthorne, N.Y.: Aldine de Gruyter. Pp. 39–52.

Wilbur, C. H.; B. Rounsaville; A. Sugarman; J. Casey; and H. Kleber. 1982. Ego development in opiate addicts: An application of Loevinger's stage model. *Journal of Nervous and Mental Disease, 170:* 202–8.

Wynne, L. C., and M. T. Singer. 1963. Thought disorder and family relations of schizophrenics: 2. A classification of forms of thinking. *Archives of General Psychiatry, 9:* 199–206.

Wynne, L. C.; I. Ryckoff; J. Day; and S. Hirsch. 1958. Pseudomutuality in the family relations of schizophrenics. *Psychiatry, 21:* 205–20.

Wynne, L. C.; J. Jones; and M. Al-Khayyal. 1982. Family communication patterns: Observations in families "at risk" for psychopathology. In F. Walsh (ed.), *Normal Family Processes.* New York: Guilford.

Wynne, L. C.; M. T. Singer; J. Bartko; and M. Toohey. 1977. Schizophrenics and their families: Recent research on parental communication. In J. M. Tanner (ed.), *Developments in Psychiatric Research.* London: Hodden & Stoughton.

Zinner, J., and R. L. Shapiro. 1975. Splitting in families of borderline patients. In J. Mack (ed.), *Borderline States in Psychiatry.* New York: Grune & Stratton.

Index